Henry Jenkins Howland

The Worcester almanac, directory, and business advertiser,

for 1861

Henry Jenkins Howland

The Worcester almanac, directory, and business advertiser, for 1861

ISBN/EAN: 9783337712181

Printed in Europe, USA, Canada, Australia, Japan

Cover: Foto ©Suzi / pixelio.de

More available books at **www.hansebooks.com**

THE

WORCESTER ALMANAC,

DIRECTORY,

AND

BUSINESS ADVERTISER,

FOR

1861.

BY HENRY J. HOWLAND.

☞ See Page 10.

WORCESTER:
PRINTED AND PUBLISHED BY HENRY J. HOWLAND,
BUTMAN ROW, 212 MAIN STREET.

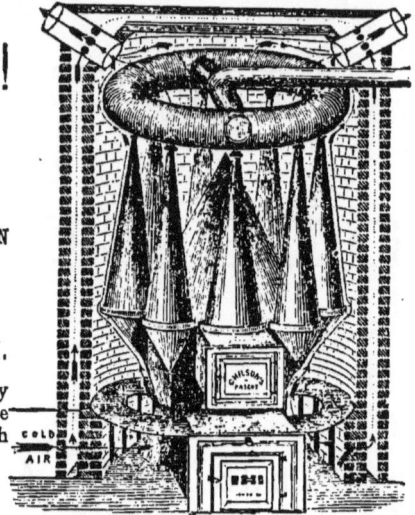
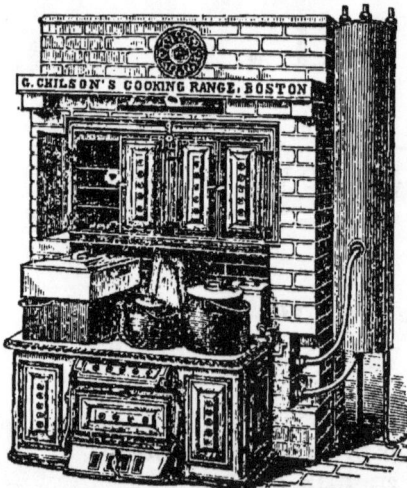

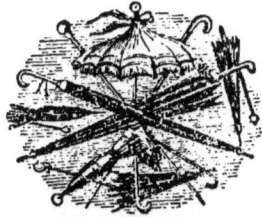

CITY OFFICERS.

The City Government for 1861 was organized on Monday, Jan. 7. and the following officers have been selected for the current year:

President of Common Council—James E. Estabrook.

Clerk of Common Council—John A. Dana.

City Clerk—Samuel Smith.

City Treasurer—Geo W. Wheeler.

City Solicitor—E B. Stoddard.

City Auditor—Gill Valentine.

City Physician—P. Hubon.

City Messenger—David Gleason.

Highway Commissioner—Henry Prentice.

City Marshal—Levi Barker.

Captain of the Watch and Constable—James McFarland.

Constables—Ebenezer Flagg, W. W. Pratt, O. B. Chase, J. B. Dexter, jr., Jeremiah Kane, Horace L. Jenks, at New Worcester.

Special Constables—John Grover, at Western Depot; C. A. Lincoln, at Junction Depot; Z. E. Berry, at Mechanics Hall; Calvin W. Pierce, at Mission Chapel; and Chas. G. Parker, at Boston and Worcester Depot.

Watchmen—Geo. F. Newton, Silas Clapp, Hollis Ball, C. W. Wentworth, John O'Driscoll, H. W. Denny. John G. Coes.

Sextons and Undertakers—Geo. Sessions, Thomas Magennis, Geo. G. Hildreth.

Measurers of Wood, Bark and Charcoal—H G. Upham at Lincoln Square; Chas. H. Whiting and A. W. Woodbury, at Washington Square; Frederick Cutting at New Worcester; David

Gleason at the City Hall; Sibley Putnam on Green street; James H. Mattoon at Quinsigamond, and Pitt Holmes at South Worcester.

Fence Viewers—Benj. Flagg, Jonas Hartshorn, and Jonathan Lyon jr.

Public Weighers—H. G. Upham, David Gleason, Fred Cutting, C. H. Whiting and A. W. Woodbury.

ECLIPSES FOR 1861.

In this year there will be three eclipses of the Sun and one of the Moon.

I. An Annular Eclipse of the Sun, Jan. 20th, visible to Australia and the Southern Ocean.

II. An Annular Eclipse of the Sun, July 7th, visible to the south-eastern portion of Asia and Australia.

III. A Partial Eclipse of the Moon, Dec. 17th, visible as follows:

Beginning,   1h. 2m. morning.
Greatest Eclipse,   3h. 24m.
End,   6h. 6m.

Magnitude of Eclipse=0.185(Moon's diameter=1)

IV. A Total Eclipse of the Sun, Dec. 31st. The Sun will rise partially eclipsed to all that portion of the United States east of a line drawn extended through the two cities of Detroit, Mich., and Austin, Texas. The eclipse will last two hours at Worcester.

Venus will be morning star until May 11th, and evening star the rest of the year. Jupiter will be morning star until Feb. 11th, then evening star until August 31st, and morning star again the rest of the year.

Index to Advertisements, or Business Directory.

Agricultural Implements—J. D. Lovell, 105
 Nouse, Mason & Co. 15
Attorneys—Dewey and Williams, 125
 E. B. Stoddard, 15°
 W. A. Williams, 107
Asphaltic Roofing and Paint—S. N. Haskell, 118
Ammunition—J. Hapgood, 23
Auctioneers—E. B. Lamson & Co. 121
Barber—Gilbert Walker, 15°
Barometers—J. M. Merrick & Co. 112
Baskets &c.—J. P. Weixler, 16
Belting—Earl Warner, 110
 A. N. Clark & Co. 21
Birds and cages—P. Young 7
Blake & Johnston's Adjustable Hemmer, 106
Blank Books—Wm. Allen, cover
 J. Keith & Co 107
 E. Mellen Jr. cover
Book & Job Printing—H. J. Howland, 10, 47
Book Binding—Wm. Allen, cover
 J. S. Wesby, cover
Book Store—Wm. Allen, cover
 E. Mellen Jr. cover
Box Factory—Harrington & Gardner, 17
Boots and shoes—L. Thayer, 111
 Simeon Clapp & Co., 110
 S. R. Heywood, 107
 T. S. Penniman, 14°
 repaired by Geo. R. Weaver, 108
  by A. Fairbanks, 11
Boot Trees &c.—E. L. Shumway, 15°
Boys Clothing—A. Walbridge, 117
Brass Foundry—W. A. Wheeler, 119
Broker, Real Estate—E. E. Abbott, 113
Boot & shoe cutters—A. M. Howe, 121
Brushes—E. Thayer. 116
Buffalo Robes—See hats and Caps
Burning Fluid & Camphene—H. Ayres, cover
Cabinet Shop—Wm. C. Blos, 120
 A. H. Davis, 108
 G. Bratz, 121
Carriages.—A. Tolman & Co. 105
Card Engraving—N. S. Dearborn, 21
Carpet Store—Barnard, Sumner & Co's, 4
Castings, Iron, Brass &c.—W. A. Wheeler, 119
Chocolate &c.—John Preston, 24
Chiropodists—Drs Kenison, 25
Clocks &c.—J. W. Healy, 108
 L. L. Mason, 112
Clothing—A. Walbridge, 117
Civil Engineer—C. W. Folsom, 25
Coffin Ware Room—Geo. Sessions, 116
Cocoa Butter, Cocoa, &c.—J. Preston, 24
Coal—F. Strong, cover
 E. F. Rogers, 3
 T. W. Wellington, 3
Collector—Lewis Thayer, 111
Counting Room Furniture—A. H. Davis, 108
Clothes Frames, Revolving—H. Holden, 111
Commissioner to take Depositions, &c.—E. B. Stoddard, 15°
Commission Merchants—Draper & Clark, 118
 J. J. Coburn, 118
Conveyancer—G. Valentine, 118
Cooking Stoves—See Stoves
Corn Oil—N. P. Hanson & Co. 20
Cornices, Sheet Iron—F. P. Oliver, 15
Counsellors—E. B. Stoddard, 15°
 Dewey & Williams, 125
 W. A. Williams, 107

Crockery &c.—J. L. Hood. 11
 E. B Lamson & Co. 121
Dentists—O. F. Harris, 3
 C. H. Jencks, cover
 J. Childs, 118
Designing—See Engraving
Dickerman's Steam Heating Apparatus—J. H. Norton, 28
Dorchester Fire Ins. Co. 17
Dodge's American Liniment, 13
Dry Goods—Barnard, Sumner & Co. 4
Dye House—H. B. Adams. 11
Eave Troughs, &c.—C. Newton, 105
Electrician, Medical—Mrs. Holt, 111
Engine Hose—E. Warner, 110
Engraving—Taylor & Adams, 20
 N. S. Dearborn. 21
 Kilburn & Mallory, 26
 Prentiss, 15°
Fancy Boxes—C. Richmond, 111
Fancy Goods &c.—E. Merrill, 109
 J. P. Weixler, 16
 P. Young, 7
 Isaac Fish, 127
 John Keith & Co. 107
Fairbanks' Scales—Fairbanks & Brown, 27
Female College, 18
Female Physician—M. W. Gerelds, 116
 Mrs. Holt, 111
File manufacturer—T. Collinson, 16
Fire Insurance—See Insurance, Fire.
Flour &c.—Draper & Clark, 118
 Geo. S. Hoppin & Co. 14°
Forging—Allen & Darling, 16
Frames—R. Weyer, 14
 J. Harker 15°
Furniture—Wm. C. Blos, 120
 G. Bratz, 121
 J. L. Hood, 11
 E. B. Lamson & Co. 121
 Taber & Chollar, 16
 E. W. Vaill. 14
Furnishing Goods, &c.—F. A. Eldred, 107
 E. & A. D. Smith, 116
Furnaces &c.—See Stoves
 G. Chilson, 6
Furs—See Hats and Caps
Galvanized Iron Cornices &c.—F. P. Oliver, 12
Gardner's Rheumatic & Neuralgia Compound, 4
Gear Cutters—S. C & S. Winslow, 121
Gilt Frames—R. Weyer, 14
 J. Harker, 15°
Glass stained &c. &c.—J. M. Cook, 23
Grain &c.—Draper & Clark, 118
 G. S. Hoppin & Co. 14°
 H. Holden, 111
Guns & Pistols—J. Hapgood, 23
Hair Dresser — Gilbert Walker, 15°
Hardware—H. W. Miller, 127
Hats, Caps, &c. — F. E. Abbott, 113
 Geo. Blood, 118
 F. A. Clapp, 107
 F. A. Eldred, 107
 J. H. Knights, 108
 E. Merrill. 109
 W. M. Shute & Son, 22
 E. & A. D. Smith, 116
Hanson's Corn Oil, 20
Hall's Cough Balsam, 13
Hemmers — Blake & Johnston's, 106
Homeopathic Medicines — C. H. Jencks, cover

Horses and Carriages for sale or to let, 112
Home Comfort Stoves, 13
House Furnishing Goods — O. N. Heath, 115
Insurance, Fire — W. S. Denny, cover
   Dorchester Ins. Co. 17
   Worcester Mutual Co. 115
Insurance, Life— N. E. Mutual Co. 125
   Mass. Mutual Co W. S. Goodwin, cover
Iron Foundry — W. A. Wheeler, 119
Iron and Wire Works — H. S. Washburn, 2
Japan Blacking — Bray & Hayes. 122
Jewelry, &c. — C. C. Coleman, 114
   Isaac Fish, 127
Jobbing in Wood — D. F. Andrews, 113
   W. C. Bios, 120
   G. Bratz. 121
   Geo. H. Tufts, 162
Jobbing in Iron — Battelle & Co. 113
   W. A. Wheeler, 119
   S. C. & S. Winslow, 121
Kerosene Lamps and Oil — H. Ayres, cover
   J. L Hood, 11
Keys — J. Wheelock, 114
   C. A. Cummings, 109
Kitchen Goods — O. N. Heath, 115
   J. H. Bigelow, 119
Knives. Machine — L. Hardy & Co. 110
Ladies Collegiate Institute, 18
Lamps, &c. — H. Ayres, cover
Landscape Gardeners.—Copeland & Folsom, 25
Leather — N. Lazell. 14
Leather Belting — Earl Warner, 110
   A. N. Clark & Co. 21
Locksmith. &c.— C A. Cummings, 109
Livery Stables — Dodge & Ammidon, 112
   J. A. & L. F. Bancroft, 117
Machinery—S. Pratt, 109
Manufacturers' Supplies - S. Pratt, 109
Marland's Fire Proof Safes—Calendar Pages
Mass. Mut. Life Ins. Co.—W. S. Goodwin, Cover
Meat Masher—Whittemore Brothers, 119
Medical Office—Hill & Thompson, 120
Midwife—Mrs. Goodwin, 107
   Mrs. Gerelds, 116
Mouldings—R. Weyer, 14
   J. Harker, 150
Music Store—J. A. Dorman & Co. 106
Nails—J. J. Coburn, 118
Napthaline Oil—Davis & Co. 123
Old Iron, &c.—J. J. Coburn, 118
Optician—J. Rosenbush, 11
Ornamental Glass—J. M. Cook, 23
Painter & Glazier—T. W. Johnson, 106
   C. W. Bulah. 109
Paper Boxes—C. Richmond, 111
Paper Hanging—C. W. Bulah, 109
   Harrington & Gardner, 17
Parasols—Joseph Lyons. 25
Pattern Maker—J. W. Healy, 108
   D. F. Andrews, 113
   G. H. Tufts, 162
Pearl Soap—J. W. Spring, 120
Peruvian Syrup—Jewett & Co. Cover
Piano Fortes—J. A. Dorman & Co. 106
   Wm. Bourne. 26
Physicians—Hill & Thomson, 120
Plows &c.—Nourse, Mason & Co. 15
   J. D. Lovell. 105
Plumbers—H. W. Miller, 127
   H. Mathews. 125
"Power Loom"—wire cloth, Childs & Howe, 120
Poland's medical preparations, 122
Preston's Patent Cocoa Butter, 24

Preston's Bromade for the Hair, 24
Printing of all kinds—Henry J. Howland, 10, 47
Pump Manufactory---Geo. T. Sutton, 108
   E. D. Jordan, 125
Ranges—See Stoves.
Real Estate--L. Thayer, 111
   E. E. Abbott, 113
Redding's Russia Salve, 124
Rheumatic Compound---C. F. Gardner's, 4
Saws---Henshaw & Co. 26
Scales---Fairbanks', 27
Seeds---J. D. Lovell, 105
Sewing Machines---Wheeler & Wilson's, 127
   Battelle & Co., 113
Shears --for binders &c.---Kean & Co., 17
Shear Blades &c.--L. Hardy & Co., 107
Shirts---A. Wolbridge, 117
   Howe & Walker, 20
   Locke, 23
Skates---S. C. & S. Winslow, 121
Soap, Spring's Pearl, 120
Spectacles---C. C. Coleman, 114
   J. Rosenbush, 11
Stained and Cut Glass &c.,--J. M. Cook, 23
Steam Heating Apparatus---J. H. Norton. 28
Stationery--J Keith & Co. 107
   J. Fish, 127
Safes— Bigelow & Hardy, calendar pages
Stables, Livery and Sale --- Dodge & Amidon, 112
   J. A. & L. F. Bancroft, 117
Sterling Gas Regulator, 140
Stoves, &c. — J. W. Jordan, 126
   Wm. Lucas. 14
   H. W. Miller, 127
   Francis P. Oliver, 12, 130
   F. F. Phelps, 117
   S. Clark, 16
   G. Chilson, 6
Surveyor, &c. --- G. Valentine, 118
   E. W. Folsom, 25
Tea, Coffee, &c. --- G. Homes & Co. 112
Tin, Copper and Sheet Iron Work --- S. Clark, 16
See Stoves.
Tobacco, &c., &c. ---D. J. Carruth, 23
Toys, &c. --- See Fancy Goods
Trip Hammer Forging --- Allen & Darling, 16
Trunks, &c. --- F. E. Abbott, 113
   F. A. Eldred, 107
   E. Merrill, 109
   John Wheelock, 114
Undertaker --- Geo. Sessions, 116
Upholsterers --- See Furniture
   Copp & Pear, 25
   Wm. Brown, 110
Varnish --- Stimson, Valentine & Co. cover
Vibrating Shears --- Kean & Co. 17
Watches and Clocks --- C. C. Coleman, 114
   Isaac Fish, 127
   L. L. Mason, 112
Webster's Unabridged Dictionary---pict.edition,28
Wheeler & Wilson s Sewing Machines, 127
Wig Maker --- Gilbert Walker, 150
Willow Ware, &c. --- J. P. Weixler, 16
Window Shades---Copp & Pear, 25
Wire Workers—J. H. Bigelow, 119
   Childs & Howe, 120
Wire Works--- H. S. Washburn, 2
Worcester Academy, 19
Worcester Press and Drill Company, 16 0
Wood Engravers --- Kilburn & Mallory, 26
   Taylor & Adams, 20
   A. Prentiss, 15
Wood Yard --- J. A. & L. F. Bancroft, 117

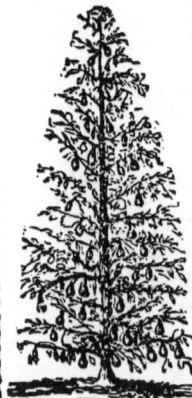

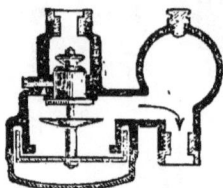

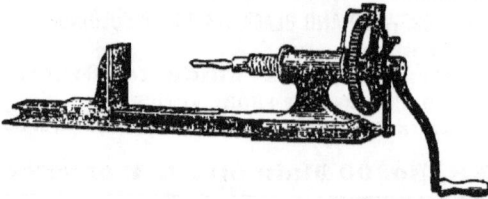

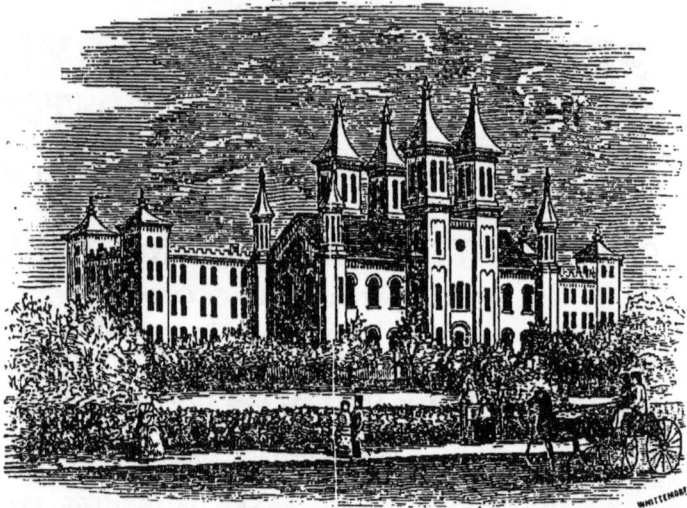

WORCESTER ACADEMY.

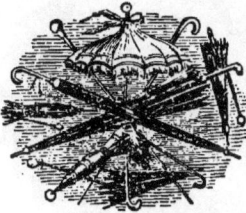

JANUARY, 1861.

H.W. Bost'n	Moon's place		Memoranda
..ases.		1	
h, 11 m. ev.		2	
h, 43 m. ev.			
11 h, 16 m. ev.		3	
ı. 21 m. ev.		4	
H M		5	
		6	
2 24	bowels	7	
3 10	bowels		
3 58	reins	8	
4 51	reins	9	
5 51	secrets	10	
6 56	secrets	11	
8 4	thighs	12	
9 9	thighs	13	
10 8	knees		
11 1	knees	14	
11 48	knees	15	
0 9	legs	16	
0 50	legs	17	
1 29	feet	18	
2 7	feet		
2 44	head	19	
3 21	head	20	
4 0	head	21	
4 46	neck	22	
5 39	neck	23	
6 35	arms		
7 37	arms	24	
8 40	arms	25	
9 39	breast	26	
10 34	breast	27	
11 25	heart		
	heart	28	
0 32	bowels	29	
1 16	bowels	30	
2 1	reins		
2 47	reins	31	

Moon's Phases.

Last Quarter, 2d d. 5 h. 16 m. mo.
New Moon, 9th d. 3 h. 20 m. ev.
First Quarter, 17th d. 7 h. 35 m. ev.
Full Moon, 24th d. 11 h. 59 m. ev.

D. M.	D. W.	Sun rises	Sun sets.	Moon sets.	H.W. Bost'n	Moon's place.	
		H M	H M	H M	H M		1
1	Fr	7 14	5 15	morn	3 35	secrets	2
2	Sa	7 13	5 16	0 55	4 29	secrets	3
3	G	7 12	5 17	2 8	5 33	thighs	4
4	M	7 11	5 19	3 16	6 43	thighs	5
5	Tu	7 9	5 20	4 16	7 52	thighs	6
6	W	7 8	5 21	5 6	8 56	knees	7
7	Th	7 7	5 23	5 47	9 52	knees	8
8	Fr	7 6	5 24	6 20	10 42	legs	9
9	Sa	7 5	5 25	sets	11 23	legs	10
10	G	7 3	5 26	6 37	———	feet	11
11	M	7 2	5 28	7 37	0 18	feet	12
12	Tu	7 0	5 29	8 37	0 53	feet	13
13	W	6 59	5 30	9 38	1 29	head	14
14	Th	6 58	5 32	10 39	2 5	head	15
15	Fr	6 57	5 33	11 41	2 42	neck	16
16	Sa	6 55	5 34	morn	3 21	neck	17
17	G	6 54	5 35	0 43	4 7	neck	18
18	M	6 52	5 37	1 44	5 0	arms	19
19	Tu	6 51	5 38	2 42	6 2	arms	20
20	W	6 49	5 39	3 36	7 8	breast	21
21	Th	6 48	5 40	4 23	8 14	breast	22
22	Fr	6 46	5 42	5 3	9 15	heart	23
23	Sa	6 45	5 43	5 38	10 10	heart	24
24	G	6 43	5 44	6 9	11 1	heart	25
25	M	6 42	5 45	rises	11 44	bowels	26
26	Tu	6 40	5 47	8 3	0 6	bowels	27
27	W	6 39	5 48	9 22	0 51	reins	28
28	Th	6 37	5 49	10 40	1 37	reins	

MEMORANDA.

H. W. Bost'n	Moon's place		
	.ases.	1	
	h. 32 m. ev.	2	
	ι. 53 m. mo.	3	
	0 h. 48 m. ev.	4	
	. 31 m. mo.	5	

H. W. Bost'n	Moon's place		
H M			
2 25	secrets	6	
3 18	secrets	7	
4 17	thighs	8	
5 23	thighs	9	
6 32	knees	10	
7 38	knees	11	
8 38	legs	12	
9 29	legs	13	
10 13	legs	14	
10 52	feet	15	
11 28	feet	16	
——	head	17	
0 19	head	18	
0 54	head	19	
1 31	neck	20	
2 10	neck	21	
2 53	arms	22	
3 39	arms	23	
4 35	arms	24	
5 36	breast	25	
6 41	breast	26	
7 46	heart	27	
8 47	heart	28	
9 41	bowels	29	
10 32	bowels	30	
11 19	reins	31	
——	reins	28	
0 27	secrets	29	
1 16	secrets	30	
2 9	thighs		
3 5	thighs	31	

ortant Testimony.

IRE AT LACONIA, N. H.,

[ovember 21st, 1860.

ιconia, under date of Nov. 30th, wrote an account of the fire ı & Co., of Boston, Safe Manufacturers, of which the follow-

ιe fire, there were in all, 14 Safes. 9 were left in the build-
. 5 were rolled out into the street. Of Wm. Adams & Co.'s
ι, Adams, Hammond & Co.,) manufacture, 4 were partially,
ıP INSIDE.

l & Co.'s, (and their predecessors, Edwards, Holman & Co.,)
ιartially, 1 was wholly burned up inside.

manufacture, 2 were partially burned inside.

Moon's Phases.

Last Quarter, 2d d. 1 h. 40 m. mo.
New Moon, 10th d. 2 h. 11 m. mo.
First Quarter, 18th d. 2 h. 1 m. mo.
Full Moon, 24th d. 5 h. 39 m. ev.

D. M.	D. W.	Sun rises	Sun sets.	Moon sets.	H.W. Bost'n	Moon's place.	
		H M	H M	H M	H M		1
1	M	5 42	6 26	0 58	4 5	knees	2
2	Tu	5 41	6 27	1 46	5 7	knees	3
3	W	5 39	6 28	2 24	6 11	legs	4
4	Th	5 37	6 29	2 55	7 11	legs	5
5	Fr	5 35	6 30	3 20	8 5	legs	6
6	Sa	5 34	6 32	3 43	8 53	feet	7
7	G	5 32	6 33	4 4	9 36	feet	8
8	M	5 30	6 34	4 25	10 16	head	9
9	Tu	5 29	6 35	4 45	10 54	head	10
10	W	5 27	6 36	sets	11 30	head	11
11	Th	5 25	6 37	8 24	———	neck	12
12	Fr	5 24	6 38	9 27	0 24	neck	13
13	Sa	5 22	6 39	10 26	1 4	arms	14
14	G	5 21	6 40	11 20	1 46	arms	15
15	M	5 19	6 42	morn	2 32	arms	16
16	Tu	5 17	6 43	0 9	3 20	breast	17
17	W	5 16	6 44	0 52	4 13	breast	18
18	Th	5 14	6 45	1 29	5 11	heart	19
19	Fr	5 13	6 46	2 1	6 12	heart	20
20	Sa	5 11	6 47	2 30	7 14	bowels	21
21	G	5 10	6 48	2 57	8 13	bowels	22
22	M	5 8	6 49	3 24	9 9	reins	23
23	Tu	5 7	6 50	3 52	10 2	reins	24
24	W	5 5	6 52	4 24	10 54	secrets	25
25	Th	5 4	6 53	rises	11 44	secrets	26
26	Fr	5 2	6 54	9 38	0 9	thighs	27
27	Sa	5 1	6 55	10 44	1 2	thighs	28
28	G	4 59	6 56	11 38	1 58	knees	29
29	M	4 58	6 57	morn	2 52	knees	30
30	Tu	4 56	6 58	0 21	3 46	knees	

Moon rises.	H.W. Bost'n	Moon's place.
Phases.		
t d. 2 h. 48 m. ev.		
. 6 h. 23 m. ev.		
'th d. 11 h. 19 m. mo.		
d. 1 h. 22 m. mo.		
st d. 5 h. 41 m. mo.		
H M	H M	
0 56	4 41	legs
1 24	5 37	legs
1 47	6 31	feet
2 9	7 22	feet
2 30	8 9	feet
2 51	8 54	head
3 13	9 37	head
3 38	10 19	neck
4 6	11 0	neck
sets	11 40	neck
9 15	0 1	arms
10 7	0 43	arms
10 52	1 28	breast
11 30	2 15	breast
morn	3 2	heart
0 3	3 51	heart
0 32	4 45	heart
0 58	5 41	bowels
1 23	6 40	bowels
1 49	7 39	reins
2 18	8 39	reins
2 53	9 38	secrets
3 33	10 35	secrets
rises	11 30	thighs
9 23	——	thighs
10 13	0 48	knees
10 52	1 42	knees
11 23	2 32	legs
11 49	3 19	legs
morn	4 6	feet
0 12	4 54	feet

MEMORANDA

1
2
3
4
5
6
7
8
9
10
11
12
13
14
15
16
17
18
19
20
21
22
23
24
25
26
27
28
29
30
31

CALENDAR. **JUNE, 1861.** MEMORANDA.

Moon's Phases.

New Moon, 8th d. 8 h. 54 m. mo.
First Quarter, 15th d. 5 h. 32 m. ev.
Full Moon, 22d d. 9 h. 39 m. mo.
Last Quarter, 29th d. 9 h. 56 m. ev.

D. M.	D. W.	Sun rises	Sun sets	Moon sets	H.W. Bost'n	Moon's place.
		H M	H M	H M	H M	
1	Sa	4 25	7 30	0 33	5 42	feet
2	G	4 25	7 31	0 54	6 31	head
3	M	4 25	7 31	1 16	7 21	head
4	Tu	4 24	7 32	1 40	8 11	neck
5	W	4 24	7 33	2 7	8 59	neck
6	Th	4 24	7 33	2 39	9 46	neck
7	Fr	4 23	7 34	3 19	10 34	arms
8	Sa	4 23	7 35	sets	11 19	arms
9	G	4 23	7 35	8 51	——	breast
10	M	4 22	7 36	9 31	0 26	breast
11	Tu	4 22	7 36	10 6	1 12	breast
12	W	4 22	7 37	10 35	1 57	heart
13	Th	4 22	7 37	11 1	2 42	heart
14	Fr	4 22	7 38	11 27	3 27	bowels
15	Sa	4 22	7 38	11 53	4 16	bowels
16	G	4 22	7 38	morn	5 9	reins
17	M	4 22	7 39	0 20	6 8	reins
18	Tu	4 22	7 39	0 50	7 12	secrets
19	W	4 23	7 39	1 26	8 17	secrets
20	Th	4 23	7 40	2 11	9 21	thighs
21	Fr	4 23	7 40	3 5	10 23	thighs
22	Sa	4 23	7 40	rises	11 19	knees
23	G	4 23	7 40	8 45	——	knees
24	M	4 24	7 40	9 21	0 34	legs
25	Tu	4 24	7 40	9 50	1 20	legs
26	W	4 24	7 40	10 15	2 4	legs
27	Th	4 25	7 40	10 37	2 46	feet
28	Fr	4 25	7 40	10 59	3 25	feet
29	Sa	4 26	7 40	11 20	4 7	head
30	G	4 26	7 40	11 42	4 53	head

Memoranda: 1–30

Moon's Phases.

New Moon, 7th d. 9 h. 28 m. ev.
First Quarter, 14th d. 10 h. 4 m. ev.
Full Moon, 21st d. 7 h. 22 m. ev.
Last Quarter, 29th d. 3 h. 7 m. ev.

D. M.	D. W.	Sun rises	Sun sets.	Moon sets.	H. W. Bost'n	Moon's place.	
		H M	H M	H M	H M		1
1	M	4 27	7 40	morn	5 42	head	2
2	Tu	4 27	7 40	0 8	6 34	neck	3
3	W	4 28	7 40	0 39	7 28	neck	4
4	Th	4 28	7 40	1 16	8 24	arms	5
5	Fr	4 29	7 39	1 59	9 18	arms	6
6	Sa	4 29	7 39	2 51	10 11	arms	7
7	G	4 30	7 39	sets	11 1	breast	8
8	M	4 31	7 38	8 6	11 47	breast	9
9	Tu	4 31	7 38	8 37	0 9	heart	10
10	W	4 32	7 37	9 6	0 52	heart	11
11	Th	4 33	7 37	9 32	1 35	bowels	12
12	Fr	4 34	7 37	9 57	2 19	bowels	13
13	Sa	4 35	7 36	10 23	3 3	reins	14
14	G	4 35	7 35	10 52	3 50	reins	15
15	M	4 36	7 35	11 25	4 43	secrets	16
16	Tu	4 37	7 34	morn	5 45	secrets	17
17	W	4 38	7 33	0 5	6 55	secrets	18
18	Th	4 39	7 33	0 55	8 5	thighs	19
19	Fr	4 39	7 32	1 54	9 12	thighs	20
20	Sa	4 40	7 31	3 0	10 12	knees	21
21	G	4 41	7 30	rises	11 5	knees	22
22	M	4 42	7 29	7 49	11 50	legs	23
23	Tu	4 43	7 29	8 15	0 11	legs	24
24	W	4 44	7 28	8 39	0 52	feet	25
25	Th	4 45	7 27	9 1	1 31	feet	26
26	Fr	4 46	7 26	9 22	2 9	feet	27
27	Sa	4 47	7 25	9 44	2 46	head	28
28	G	4 48	7 24	10 9	3 25	head	29
29	M	4 49	7 23	10 37	4 8	neck	30
30	Tu	4 50	7 21	11 10	4 56	neck	31
31	W	4 51	7 20	11 51	5 51	neck	

MARLAND'S PATENT FIRE-PROOF SAFE.

Second. LACONIA, N. H., Dec. 14th, 1860.

MESSRS. M. B. BIGELOW & ANSON HARDY: GENTLEMEN:—We, in common with many of our neighbors, were burned out at the fire which occurred in this town on the morning of 21st November last. We had one of your Marland Patent Fire-Proof Safes, which we barely had time to roll out of the building on to the side walk, and there leave it. It stood some three to four feet from the building, exposed to the flames, became heated to a white heat on one side of the Safe. On opening the Safe some three hours after the fire, we found the books and papers as perfect as when put in, with the exception of a few papers that were on the side most heated, were stained with varnish from the wood work. (Enclosed is the worst sample we have.) The varnish on the soap stone forming the door, only shew evidence of having been heated but a narrow space.

Yours, Respectfully, PITMAN & TILTON.

Moon's Phases.

New Moon, 6th d. 8 h. 10 m. mo.
First Quarter, 13th d. 2 h. 32 m. mo.
Full Moon, 20th d. 7 h. 7 m. mo.
Last Quarter, 28th d. 8 h. 39 m. mo.

D. M.	D. W.	Sun rises	Sun sets.	Moon sets.	H.W. Bost'n	Moon's place.
		H M	H M	H M	H M	
1	Th	4 52	7 19	morn	6 50	arms
2	Fr	4 53	7 18	0 40	7 52	arms
3	Sa	4 54	7 17	1 37	8 52	breast
4	**G**	4 55	7 16	2 42	9 47	breast
5	M	4 56	7 14	3 51	10 39	heart
6	Tu	4 57	7 13	sets	11 25	heart
7	W	4 58	7 12	7 35	———	bowels
8	Th	4 59	7 11	8 1	0 29	bowels
9	Fr	5 1	7 9	8 27	1 11	bowels
10	Sa	5 2	7 8	8 55	1 55	reins
11	**G**	5 3	7 7	9 27	2 41	reins
12	M	5 4	7 5	10 5	3 30	secrets
13	Tu	5 5	7 4	10 52	4 27	secrets
14	W	5 6	7 2	11 47	5 33	thighs
15	Th	5 7	7 1	morn	6 46	thighs
16	Fr	5 8	6 59	0 49	7 57	knees
17	Sa	5 9	6 58	1 56	9 0	knees
18	**G**	5 10	6 56	3 5	9 56	legs
19	M	5 11	6 55	4 15	10 44	legs
20	Tu	5 12	6 53	rises	11 25	feet
21	W	5 13	6 52	7 4	———	feet
22	Th	5 14	6 50	7 27	0 20	feet
23	Fr	5 15	6 49	7 49	0 56	head
24	Sa	5 16	6 47	8 12	1 32	head
25	**G**	5 17	6 46	8 39	2 9	neck
26	M	5 19	6 44	9 11	2 49	neck
27	Tu	5 20	6 42	9 48	3 31	neck
28	W	5 21	6 41	10 32	4 20	arms
29	Th	5 22	6 39	11 24	5 16	arms
30	Fr	5 23	6 37	morn	6 18	breast
31	Sa	5 24	6 35	0 24	7 22	breast

Memoranda: 1 2 3 4 5 6 7 8 9 10 11 12 13 14 15 16 17 18 19 20 21 22 23 24 25 26 27 28 29 30 31

Moon's Phases.

New Moon, 4th d. 5 h. 29 m. ev.
First Quarter, 11th d. 8 h. 32 m. mo.
Full Moon, 18th d. 9 h. 18 m. ev.
Last Quarter, 27th d. 1 h. 40 m. mo.

D. M.	D. W.	Sun rises	Sun sets.	Moon sets.	H.W. Bost'n	Moon's place.	Memoranda
		H M	H M	H M	H M		1
1	G	5 24	6 34	1 29	8 23	breast	2
2	M	5 26	6 32	2 39	9 21	heart	3.
3	Tu	5 27	6 30	3 52	10 12	heart	4
4	W	5 28	6 29	5 7	10 59	bowels	5
5	Th	5 29	6 27	sets	11 43	bowels	6
6	Fr	5 30	6 25	6 57	0 4	reins	7
7	Sa	5 31	6 24	7 30	0 48	reins	8
8	G	5 32	6 22	8 6	1 35	secrets	9
9	M	5 33	6 20	8 50	2 25	secrets	10
10	Tu	5 34	6 18	9 43	3 19	thighs	11
11	W	5 36	6 17	10 43	4 18	thighs	12
12	Th	5 37	6 15	11 49	5 26	knees	13
13	Fr	5 38	6 13	morn	6 36	knees	14
14	Sa	5 39	6 11	0 57	7 42	legs	15
15	G	5 40	6 10	2 5	8 40	legs	16
16	M	5 41	6 8	3 12	9 29	legs	17
17	Tu	5 42	6 6	4 16	10 14	feet	18
18	W	5 43	6 4	5 18	10 54	feet	19
19	Th	5 44	6 2	rises	11 30	head	20
20	Fr	5 45	6 1	6 16	——	head	21
21	Sa	5 46	5 59	6 42	0 22	head	22
22	G	5 47	5 57	7 12	0 59	neck	23
23	M	5 48	5 55	7 47	1 38	neck	24
24	Tu	5 49	5 54	8 28	2 20	arms	25
25	W	5 50	5 52	9 16	3 3	arms	26
26	Th	5 52	5 50	10 12	3 52	arms	27
27	Fr	5 53	5 48	11 14	4 47	breast	28.
28	Sa	5 54	5 47	morn	5 47	breast	29
29	G	5 55	5 45	0 21	6 49	heart	30
30	M	5 56	5 43	1 30	7 50	heart	

Moon's Phases.

New Moon, 4th d. 2 h. 13 m. mo.
First Quarter, 10th d. 5 h. 25 m. ev.
Full Moon, 18th d. 1 h. 54 m. ev.
Last Quarter, 26th d. 5 h. 10 m. ev.

D. M.	D. W.	Sun rises	Sun sets	Moon sets	H.W. Bost'n	Moon's place	
		H M	H M	H M	H M		1
1	Tu	5 57	5 41	2 41	8 48	bowels	2
2	W	5 58	5 40	3 55	9 40	bowels	3
3	Th	5 59	5 38	5 10	10 30	reins	4
4	Fr	6 0	5 36	sets	11 17	reins	5
5	Sa	6 1	5 35	6 1	——	secrets	6
6	G	6 3	5 33	6 45	0 27	secrets	7
7	M	6 4	5 31	7 37	1 19	thighs	8
8	Tu	6 5	5 29	8 36	2 14	thighs	9
9	W	6 6	5 28	9 41	3 10	knees	10
10	Th	6 7	5 26	10 49	4 9	knees	11
11	Fr	6 9	5 25	11 57	5 12	knees	12
12	Sa	6 10	5 23	morn	6 14	legs	13
13	G	6 11	5 21	1 4	7 13	legs	14
14	M	6 12	5 20	2 9	8 6	feet	15
15	Tu	6 13	5 18	3 11	8 54	feet	16
16	W	6 14	5 16	4 12	9 38	head	17
17	Th	6 16	5 15	5 13	10 18	head	18
18	Fr	6 17	5 13	6 14	10 58	head	19
19	Sa	6 18	5 12	rises	11 34	neck	20
20	G	6 19	5 10	5 46	——	neck	21
21	M	6 20	5 9	6 27	0 31	arms	22
22	Tu	6 21	5 7	7 12	1 12	arms	23
23	W	6 22	5 6	8 4	1 56	arms	24
24	Th	6 24	5 4	9 2	2 41	breast	25
25	Fr	6 25	5 3	10 6	3 28	breast	26
26	Sa	6 26	5 1	11 12	4 19	heart	27
27	G	6 27	5 0	morn	5 15	heart	28
28	M	6 29	4 59	0 20	6 13	heart	29
29	Tu	6 30	4 57	1 30	7 12	bowels	30
30	W	6 31	4 56	2 43	8 11	bowels	31
31	Th	6 32	4 55	3 58	9 7	reins	

Moon's Phases.

New Moon, 2d d. 11 h. 20 m. mo.
First Quarter, 9th d. 6 h. 0 m. mo.
Full Moon, 17th d. 8 h. 23 m. mo.
Last Quarter, 25th d. 6 h. 23 m. mo.

D. M.	D. W.	Sun rises	Sun sets.	Moon sets.	H. W. Bost'n	Moon's place.
		H M	H M	H M	H M	
1	Fr	6 34	4 53	5 16	10 1	reins
2	Sa	6 35	4 52	6 36	10 55	secrets
3	G	6 36	4 51	sets	11 46	secrets
4	M	6 37	4 50	6 19	0 12	thighs
5	Tu	6 39	4 48	7 26	1 8	thighs
6	W	6 40	4 47	8 36	2 3	knees
7	Th	6 41	4 46	9 47	2 57	knees
8	Fr	6 42	4 45	10 56	3 51	legs
9	Sa	6 44	4 44	morn	4 45	legs
10	G	6 45	4 43	0 2	5 39	feet
11	M	6 46	4 42	1 5	6 32	feet
12	Tu	6 48	4 41	2 6	7 24	feet
13	W	6 49	4 40	3 6	8 12	head
14	Th	6 50	4 39	4 6	8 58	head
15	Fr	6 51	4 38	5 7	9 43	neck
16	Sa	6 53	4 37	6 7	10 26	neck
17	G	6 54	4 36	rises	11 8	neck
18	M	6 55	4 36	5 10	11 49	arms
19	Tu	6 56	4 35	6 0	0 10	arms
20	W	6 57	4 34	6 57	0 52	breast
21	Th	6 59	4 33	7 58	1 36	breast
22	Fr	7 0	4 33	9 2	2 21	breast
23	Sa	7 1	4 32	10 9	3 5	heart
24	G	7 2	4 32	11 17	3 52	heart
25	M	7 3	4 31	morn	4 41	bowels
26	Tu	7 5	4 31	0 25	5 36	bowels
27	W	7 6	4 30	1 36	6 34	reins
28	Th	7 7	4 30	2 50	7 34	reins
29	Fr	7 8	4 29	4 6	8 36	secrets
30	Sa	7 9	4 29	5 24	9 37	secrets

Memoranda: 1 2 3 4 5 6 7 8 9 10 11 12 13 14 15 16 17 18 19 20 21 22 23 24 25 26 27 28 29 30

Moon's Phases.

New Moon, 1st d. 9 h. 33 m. ev.
First Quarter, 8th d. 10 h. 25 m. ev.
Full Moon, 17th d. 3 h. 24 m. mo.
Last Quarter, 24th d. 5 h. 8 m. ev.
New Moon, 31st d. 9 h. 10 m. mo.

D. M.	D. W.	Sun rises	Sun sets.	Moon rises.	H.W. Bost'n	Moon's place.		
		H M	H M	H M	H M			
1	G	7 10	4 29	6 42	10 37	thighs	1	
2	M	7 11	4 28	sets	11 34	thighs	2	
3	Tu	7 12	4 28	6 11	0 1	knees	3	
4	W	7 13	4 28	7 26	0 54	knees	4	.
5	Th	7 14	4 28	8 38	1 46	legs	5	
6	Fr	7 15	4 28	9 47	2 35	legs	6	
7	Sa	7 16	4 28	10 53	3 21	legs	7	
8	G	7 17	4 28	11 57	4 7	feet	8	
9	M	7 18	4 28	morn	4 56	feet	9	
10	Tu	7 19	4 28	0 59	5 45	head	10	
11	W	7 20	4 28	1 59	6 36	head	11	
12	Th	7 20	4 28	2 59	7 27	neck	12	
13	Fr	7 21	4 28	3 59	8 19	neck	13	
14	Sa	7 22	4 28	4 59	9 8	neck	14	
15	G	7 23	4 29	5 57	9 57	arms	15	
16	M	7 23	4 29	6 51	10 45	arms	16	
17	Tu	7 24	4 29	rises	11 29	breast	17	
18	W	7 25	4 29	5 53	——	breast	18	
19	Th	7 25	4 30	6 56	0 32	breast	19	
20	Fr	7 26	4 31	8 2	1 15	heart	20	
21	Sa	7 26	4 31	9 9	1 57	heart	21	
22	G	7 27	4 31	10 17	2 40	bowels	22	
23	M	7 27	4 32	11 25	3 24	bowels	23	
24	Tu	7 27	4 33	morn	4 10	reins	24	
25	W	7 28	4 33	0 35	5 3	reins	25	
26	Th	7 28	4 34	1 47	6 1	reins	26	
27	Fr	7 29	4 35	3 1	7 7	secrets	27	
28	Sa	7 29	4 35	4 16	8 16	secrets	28	
29	G	7 29	4 36	5 28	9 22	thighs	29	
30	M	7 29	4 37	6 34	10 25	thighs	30	
31	Tu	7 30	4 38	7 30	11 22	knees	31	

GOVERNMENT FOR 1861.

:lected December 10, 1860.

.R.

)AVIS.

.EN.

Bemis.
& Bliss.
W Sturtevant.
B. Pratt.
)DDARD.
Taft.
R. Heywood.
Hobbs.

)UNCIL.

.h H. Clark, J. Waldo

oodward, S.J.Brimhall.
alter Henry, F. B. Nor-

ank H. Kelley, M. S.

nes Mclanefy, Richard

nsend, Lorin Wetherell.
. Estey, Henry C. Rice.
Ball, Samuel A. Porter.

(MITTEE.

W. Russell, N. H. An-

h, O. K. Earle.
is Bartlett, J. J. Power-
ng, A. B. Capron.
ie, Thos. Magennis.
C. Newton, Albert W.

allard, J. D. E. Jones.
. Shippen, Wm. Work-

:cretary—Rev. J. D. E.

OVERSEERS OF THE POOR.

Ward 1—Tyler C. Kirby. 2—Geo. G. Burbank. 3—Lyman Brown. 4—James McFarland. 5—Vernon A. Ladd. 6—Thomas Pierce. 7—George Goer. 8—Levi Jackson.

ASSISTANT ASSESSORS.

Ward 1—N. T. Bemis. 2—W. A. S. Smith. 3—Patrick Nugent. 4—Walter R. Bigelow. 5—John Simmons. 6—Hiram French. 7—Gerry Hutchinson. 8—Warren Williams.

WARDENS.

Ward 1—Wm. M. Johnson. 2—Luther Ross. 3—Hollis Eaton. 4—Moses Taft. 5—Wm. C. Whiting. 6—Constant Shepard. 7—Putnam W. Taft. 8—Austin L. Rogers.

WARD CLERKS.

Ward 1—Geo. F. Rice. 2—Geo. W. Gale. 3—Geo. Holmes. 4—Charles A. Tenney. 5—Henry J Murray. 6—Brigham Balcom. 7—James H. Bancroft. 8—W. A. Brigham.

INSPECTORS.

Ward 1—Geo. L. Bliss, J. A. Andrews, H. O. Lee.
2—Sewall Rice, Geo. R. Peckham, Thos. McKeon.
3—Chas. H. Knowlton, Samuel McFaden, Thos. B. Underwood.
4—Samuel Clark, Henry M. Conville, Elliot Swan.
5—Wm. G. Strong, J. J. McCormick, Benj. F. Stowell.
6—P. H. Carpenter, Isaac G. Larned, John S. Baldwin.
7—Loring Eddy, Jacob Childs, H. W. Babbit.
8—Dexter Rice, Wm. A. Ayers, James L. Estey.

CHOOLS.

Torcester, have long en-
ion for their excellence;
ell deserving that repu-
e in number, taught by
l located in all parts of
all the children within
n the center and New
d admission to their ad-
pplication to the Super-
City Hall. The schools
irge of a Committee of
elected each year, and
se deliberations are pre-
. Besides the supervis-
e schools have the ben-
of the Superintendent,
iich have proved most
ill as economical.
zlish High School is de-
in all the higher English
Latin, Greek and French
s also kept during the
inefit of lads and young
n summer. And

A FREE EVENING SCHOOL

is opened during the winter, for persons of all ages, and both sexes, who are employed during the day. Domestics and other persons, here have an excellent opportunity to commence or pursue their studies under competent teachers, free of cost; and many wisely avail themselves of it.

The commencement of the School year, and the arrangement of the terms and vacations, have been recently changed, and are as follows:

The school year commences on the second Monday in May, and is divided into four terms, comprising forty-three weeks, and commencing respectively on the second Monday in May, the first Monday in September, the Monday after Thanksgiving and the last Monday in February.

The Annual Examination is made at the close of the Spring term, and all promotions are made by the Visiting Committee at that time, and at no other, except in especial cases, to be voted by the Board.

The Vacations in all the schools, exc-pt the Suburban, are as follows: six weeks preceding the first Monday in September; Thanksgiving week; one week preceding the last Monday in

February; and one week preceding the second Monday in May.

Therefore the Fall term will comprise eleven weeks; the Winter term twelve; the Spring, ten, and the Summer, ten.

Hon. A. H. Bullock having presented the city the sum of $1000, as a fund from the income of which to present annually Medals for excellence in the High School, it has been decided to award twenty SILVER MEDALS to as many of the pupils, who shall excel in the several branches pursued in the school,—the award to be made by a Board of five Judges, to be elected annually by the School Committee, from citizens outside of their own number.

PRIVATE SCHOOLS,

of various grades, abound in the city. Among the more prominent of these are Mr. Metcalf's "Highland School," for boys, on Salisbury street; Mr. Lombard's "Salisbury Mansion School," Lincoln Square; Rev. Dr. Pattison's "Oread Institute," on a romantic eminence west from City Hall; the Worcester Academy, located in the old Antiquarian Hall, Summer street, Rev. J. R. Stone, principal,—Prof. Bushee's Young Ladies Institute, in Clark's Block, and Mr. Eaton's College of Commerce, Science and Literature, in Bank Block—which are wholly or partially boarding schools of high grade, and receive many scholars from abroad. There are besides, several private schools for smaller scholars, which are well sustained.

Misses Robinson and Gardner's School of Design and French Institute, in Clark's Block, is a valuable addition to our educational advantages, and is meeting with encouraging success.

THE COLLEGE OF THE HOLY CROSS,

Situated on the beautiful eminence known as Mt. St. James, is designed exclusively for the education of young persons of the Catholic faith. Rev. Anthony Ciampi, S. J., is President; and he is assisted by a full board of Professors.

THE FEMALE COLLEGE,

on Union Hill, was established and opened for students on the first of Sept. 1856, and now has about 100 students. It is intended to furnish for young women the advantages of a full classical and collegiate education; and the expenses are materially reduced by the performance of the domestic duties of the boarding department, by the pupils. Werdon Reynolds, the President, is assisted by a full board of teachers. Rev. Joseph Smith, Steward. Rev. E. A. Cummings, Financial Secretary. Rev. J. M. Rockwood, Rec. Secretary.

WORCESTER LYCEUM AND LIBRARY ASSOCIATION.

A course of Thursday evening Lectures is sustained by this Association, as heretofore. Edward Earle, President; Geo. Chandler, Vice President; James S. Rogers, Recording Secretary; Richard Hammant, Treasurer.

THE NATURAL HISTORY DEPARTMENT,

is composed of such members as choose to unite for the purpose of studying Natural History. This department has a valuable collection of specimens, and its meetings have been attended with great interest. Dr. Rufus Woodward, President; Stephen C. Earle, Secretary; Nathaniel Paine, Treasurer.

THE WORCESTER RHETORICAL SOCIETY,

incorporated in 1853, meets every Tuesday Evening in South Warren Hall, "for mental and moral improvement, by means of Essays, Debates, and various Rhetorical exercises." Clark Jillson, Corresponding Secretary; the other officers are chosen quarterly.

FRANKLIN LITERARY SOCIETY,

organized in October 1859. Object, mental and moral improvement, by Debates, and Rhetorical exercises.—Officers chosen quarterly. Meets Friday evenings, at Franklin Hall, 263 Main St.

WORCESTER CO. MECHANICS ASSOCIATION.

This Association provides a course of Lectures each winter, and the use of a choice library of more than 1400 volumes, besides other valuable privileges, to its members. Richard Ball, President; Phineas Ball, Secretary; A. Marsh, Treasurer.

The Mechanics Hall, erected by this Association, is one of the most spacious and beautiful in New England, and will furnish seats for about 2400 persons. There are eight entrances to the hall, and six stair-cases communicating with the floor below. Washburn Hall, in the same building, is a very accessible and convenient Hall for an audience of five or six hundred persons. Dea. Z. E. Berry, Janitor.

WORCESTER CHILDREN'S FRIEND SOCIETY.

This Society still continues its efforts to "rescue from evil and misery such children as are deprived of their natural parents," and provides for them, at its HOME on Shrewsbury street, until homes are found for them in suitable families. Donations of money or provisions always thankfully received, and judiciously used. Miss Tamerson White, Matron; Miss Harriet Knight, Assistant Matron.

FEMALE EMPLOYMENT SOCIETY.

This is another public Institution of much value. Its design is to furnish work, chiefly sewing, at fair prices, to the industrious poor, finding a market for the various articles manufactured, through its store, 100 Main street, and in other ways.

WORCESTER MECHANICS MUTUAL LOAN FUND ASSOCIATION.

A Corporation for the aid of mechanics and other workers in securing homes, by the regular monthly investment of small sums. A. L. Burbank, Sec'y, 205 Main St.

WORCESTER CO. HORTICULTURAL SOCIETY.

A. H. Bullock, President; J. Henry Hill, Secretary; F. Wm. Paine, Treasurer; Clarendon Harris, Librarian. The Annual exhibition of Flowers and Fruits in the Hall of this Society, in October, has attracted much attention, and given a great impulse to the cultivation of good fruit in this vicinity.

WORCESTER AGRICULTURAL SOCIETY.

Wm. S. Lincoln, President; Chas. M. Miles, Treasurer; John M. Washburn, Cor. and Rec. Secretary.

The society has nearly twenty acres of land on Highland St, west of the Court House, for the accommodation of its Annual Exhibitions, (including a half-mile trotting course,) on which is erected a spacious hall. Its annual exhibition is now fixed by law on the first Tuesday of October.

REV. THEOBALD MATHEW TOTAL ABSTINENCE SOCIETY.

John Faby, President; Richard O'Flinn, Vice President; Edward Leahy, Treasurer; John Quinn, Secretary; Committee, Thomas Britt, Thomas Crowley, Wm. Millea, Edward Cunningham, Michael Garvey.

ST. JOHN'S CHRISTIAN DOCTRINE ASSOCIATION, devoted to the promotion of Sunday-School Instruction in St. John's Church, in Worcester. Robert Laverty, President; Thomas L. Magennis, Rec. Secretary.

WORCESTER CATHOLIC LIBRARY AND DEBATING ASSOCIATION.—Object, Mutual Improvement. John McDonald. President; H. McConville, Secretary; S. Dodd, Librarian.

AMERICAN ANTIQUARIAN SOCIETY.

Library in Antiquarian Hall, Lincoln Square, Worcester. President, Hon. S. Salisbury; Vice Presidents, Rev. Wm. Jenks, D. D., Hon. Levi Lincoln, LL. D.; Secretaries. Jared Sparks, LL. D., Foreign; Hon. Benj. F. Thomas, LL. D., Domestic; Hon. A. H. Bullock, Recording; Treasurer, Hon Henry Chapin; Committee of Publication, Sam'l F. Haven, Esq , Rev. E. E. Hale, Chas. Deane, Esq.; Librarian, Sam'l F. Haven, Esq.

WORCESTER MOZART SOCIETY.

This is a musical association, composed of the principal professors of music and members of the several choirs of the city. The society meets for the rehearsal of sacred music &c., at Washburn Hall, every Monday evening during the winter, and occasionally favors the public with concerts. A. L. Benchley, President; A. Firth, Vice President; E. H. Frost, Conductor; J. A. Dorman, Secretary and Treasurer; S. Brown, Librarian.

THE WORCESTER TEMPERANCE LEAGUE.

This is a new association, whose object is to promote, by all proper means, total abstinence from the use of intoxicating liquors as a beverage. Any person may become a member by signing the pledge; and all over 16 years of age, who pay annually at least 50 cents, may vote at its meetings. The officers elected in October last are as follows: President—Hon. William W. Rice; Vice Presidents—Rev. Drs. A. Hill and S. Sweetser, Dr. Geo. Chandler, Hon. Dexter F. Parker, P. L. Moen, Edward Earle; Secretary—Rev. Horace James; Treasurer—Albert Tolman: Directors—The secretary and treasurer, ex officio, Rev. J. H. Twombly. Rev. H. L. Wayland, Charles Ballard, Abraham Firth, Wm. Mecorney, Geo. W. Russell, S. R. Heywood.

WORCESTER GYMNASTIC CLUB.

Consists of forty members. Established in 1858. The club has a gymnasium in Foster's block, opposite R. R. station. Transient subscribers also admitted. Regular classes at 5 and 8 p m., daily. T. W. Higginson, President; Dr. O. F. Harris, Vice President; L. H. Bigelow, Secretary; C. W. Gilbert, Treasurer; Samuel H Putnam, R. H. Southgate, and Edward A. Rice, Executive Committee.

THE FREE PUBLIC LIBRARY.

The new building erected for the use of the Free Public Library, on Elm street, will be completed and occupied during the coming spring. In the mean time, the library remains in the rooms in Bank Block. Foster street. Many new books have been added during the year, and a very large number have been taken out by readers. The following are the standing committees of the Board of Directors:—On the Library—Dr. John Green, Isaac Davis, Stephen Salisbury, Wm. A. Smith, Henry Chapin, Dwight Foster ; On Building and Library Rooms—A. H. Bullock, Isaac Davis, D. S. Messinger; On Finance—W. W. Rice, Albert Tolman, J. J. Power. Z. Baker, librarian. Miss C. Barnes, asst. librarian. Open from 9 to 12½. 2½ to 5, 6½ to 8, daily, Sundays and holidays,excepted.

SONS OF TEMPERANCE.

WORCESTER DIVISION, No. 39, meet every Thursday evening at their rooms in Warren Hall.

RAINBOW DIVISION, No. 117, meet every Monday Evening in Warren Hall.

NEW WORCESTER DIVISION, No. 149, meet at Union Hall,New Worcester, every Friday evening.

The officers of these Divisions are elected quarterly.

FREE MASONS.

MORNING STAR LODGE. Joseph B. Knox, W. M; Charles G. Reed, S. W.; H. C. Bigelow, J. W.; Wm. L. Clark, Treasurer; Thomas M. Lamb, Secretary; Charles J. Tickford, S. D.; Lewis C. Stone, J. D.; E. D. McFarland, S. S.; Rolla N. Start, J. S.; Horace Chenery, C.; George J. Morey, M.; Albert S. Coffin. I. S; Hollis Bali, T.

Regular communications at Masonic Hall, Waldo Block, 1st Tuesday in each month.

MONTACUTE LODGE. G. W. Bentley, W. M., J. H. Osgood, S. W., J. D. Washburn, J. W., T. W. Wellington, Treasurer, J. L. Burbank, Secretary, E. P. Woodward, S. D., Jonathan Barnard, J. D., H. E. Knapp, S. S., A. Y. Thompson, J. S., W. A. Smith, C., J. E. Wood, M., R. Fiske, I. S., M. Church, Tyler. Communications are held at Masonic Hall, the 2d Tuesday in each month.

ROYAL ARCH CHAPTER. Henry Goddard, H. P., 2d Friday in each month, July and August excepted.

HIRAM COUNCIL, R. & S. M. Meets quarterly, on the 2d Thursdays of September, December, March and June. G. W. Bentley, T. I. G. M.

WORCESTER COUNTY ENCAMPMENT OF KNIGHTS TEMPLAR. Seth P. Miller, M. E. G. C. 1st Thursday in each month.

ODD FELLOWS.

QUINSIGAMOND LODGE. Alonzo M. Driscoll, N. G , meet every Monday evening at Masonic Hall, Waldo Block.

BANKS IN WORCESTER.

WORCESTER BANK. Foster Street, Capital, $300,000. STEPHEN SALISBURY, President. WM. CROSS, Cashier, Charles B. Whiting, Assistant Cashier. Charles M. Bent, Book-keeper. Levi Lincoln, Geo. T. Rice, Rejoice Newton, Benj. F. Heywood, Dwight Foster, R. L. Hawes, Directors. Solicitor—Dwight Foster. Discount Day, Tuesday.

CENTRAL BANK. Corner of Main and Front Streets, up stairs. Capital $350,000. JOHN C. MASON, President. GEO. F. HARTS-HORN, Cashier. Henry A. Marsh, Teller. W. J. Hapgood, Book-keeper. John C. Mason, Ichabod Washburn, Chas. G. Prentiss, P. L. Moen, Joseph Mason, George F. Hoar, Samuel Woodward, Geo. Chandler, Albert Curtis, Directors. Solicitor—G. F. Hoar. Discount day, Monday.

QUINSIGAMOND BANK. 137 Main Street. Capital $250,000. ISAAC DAVIS, President. J. S. FARNUM, Cashier. Isaac Davis, Samuel H. Colton, E. B. Stoddard, Wm. Dickinson, Jos. Walker, C. L. Putnam, Draper Ruggles, Directors. Solicitor—E. B. Stoddard. Discount day, Monday.

MECHANICS BANK. Central Exchange, Capital $350,000. H. BLISS, President. SCOTTO BERRY, Cashier. J. M. Barker, Teller. George E. Merrill, Book-keeper. Henry Goulding, F. H. Dewey, Wm. M. Bickford, Harrison Bliss, D. S. Messinger, J. M. C. Armsby, Merrick Bemis, Directors. Solicitor—F. H. Dewey. Discount day, Tuesday.

CITY BANK. Corner of Main and Pearl Sts. Capital, $400,000. GEO. W. RICHARDSON, President. NATH'L PAINE, Cashier. L. W. Hammond, Book-keeper. A. A. Goodell, Teller. Geo. W. Richardson, Calvin Foster, Lewis Barnard, Wm. B. Fox, H. N. Bigelow, Geo. M. Rice, Jas. B. Blake, Chas. Devens, Jr., Directors. Solicitor—Charles Devens, Jr. Discount day, Monday.

CITIZENS BANK. 190 Main Street. Capital, $150,000. F. H. KINNICUTT, President, JOHN C. RIPLEY, Cashier. Francis T. Merrick, Anthony Chase, Francis H. Kinnicutt, D. Waldo Lincoln, Geo. A. Trumbull, A. H. Bullock, Worcester, and H. E. Bugbee, Webster, Directors. Discount day, Monday.

Bank hours, from 9 to 1, and from 2 to 4 o'clock in Summer; from 9 1-2 to 1, and from 2 to 4 in Winter. The Banks are not open for business on Saturday afternoons.

SAVINGS BANKS,

Worcester Co. Institution for Savings.

Office in the rear of Worcester Bank, Foster Street. Stephen Salisbury, President ; J. Henry Hill, Secretary; Chas. A. Hamilton, Treasurer ; Edward Hamilton, Assistant Treasurer; Committee of Investment, the Treasurer, Secretary and Henry Chapin, John C. Mason, D. Waldo Lincoln, A. H. Bullock and Stephen Salisbury.

Worcester Mechanics Savings Bank.

Office in Central Exchange. J. S. C. Knowlton, President; Andrew McF. Davis, Secretary; H. Woodward, Treasurer.

Worcester Five Cents Savings Bank.

Office No. 98 Main street. Charles L. Putnam, President; E. B. Stoddard, Secretary: Clarendon Harris, Treasurer; Geo. W. Richardson, D. S. Messinger, James Green, Charles L. Putnam, E. B. Stoddard, Clarendon Harris, Financial Committee.

RAILROADS.

BOSTON AND WORCESTER. Passenger Cars leave Worcester 6 times every week day, Fare to Boston $1.25.

NORWICH AND WORCESTER. Accommodation Cars leave in the morning and afternoon, daily. The Steamboat train leaves for New York every night, most of the year, not far from 7 o'clock. Fare to Norwich, $1.80, to New York, $3.00.

WESTERN. Passenger Cars leave Worcester 4 times daily. Fare to Springfield, $1.35, to Albany, $4.00, to New York, $4.00.

PROVIDENCE AND WORCESTER. Passenger and Freight trains pass over the road daily, from Green Street. Fare to Providence, $1.35.

WORCESTER AND NASHUA. Cars pass over the road daily, three times each way, connecting at Groton Junction with trains for Lowell, Fitchburg, Boston, and Townsend. Fare to Nashua, $1.40. Office in Worcester Bank Block, Foster Street. Geo. T. Rice, President; Geo. W. Bentley, Superintendent; T. W. Hammond, Treasurer.

FITCHBURG AND WORCESTER. Cars run to and from Worcester in connection with all the trains on the Worcester and Nashua Railroad. Fare 85 cents. Ivers Phillips, Superintendent.

STAGES AND OMNIBUSES.

BARRE. Arrives in Worcester 9,30 A. M. and 3,45 P. M.—Leaves Bay State House, 10 A. M. and 4 P. M.

GRAFTON. Arrives at 9 A. M. and 2,15 P. M. —Leaves office, 207 Main St. at 10,15 A. M. and 4,30 P. M.

HOLDEN, RUTLAND AND HUBBARDSTON. Arrives at 9,30 A. M.—Leaves Bay State House at 4 P. M.

LEICESTER & SPENCER. Arrives at 9 A. M. and 2,30 P. M.—Leaves Flagg's Block at 10,30 A. M. and 5 P. M. Tuesday, Thursday and Saturday Evenings. Leave Leicester at 6,30, and No. 1 Flagg's Block, at 9 o'clock.

MILLBURY AND SUTTON. Arrives at 8,45 A. M. and 2 P. M.—Leaves 82 Main St. Stage Office at 10,00 A. M. and 4,30 P. M.

NEW WORCESTER. Leaves 1 Flagg's Block at 9,30, 10,30, and 12 A. M. and 2,30, 5 and 9 P. M. —Leaves New Worcester at 8,30 and 10 A. M. and 1,30, 3,30 and 7,10 P. M.

SHREWSBURY, NORTHBORO' AND MARLBORO', Arrives at 9,30 A. M.—Leaves Bay State House at 3,45 P. M.

QUINSIGAMOND OMNIBUS, between Main St. and Quinsigamond Village.

PLEASANT ST. OMNIBUS, between Main St. and Pleasantville.

COUNTY OFFICERS.

COUNTY COMMISSIONERS. Asaph Wood, Gardner, Velorous Taft, Upton, Amory Holman, Bolton.

SPECIAL COMMISSIONERS. Thomas Billings, Lunenburg; Bonum Nye, North Brookfield. Sessions in the Brick Court House, March 20, June 18, Sept. 10, and Dec. 24.

County Treasurer, Anthony Chase. Office in Court House.

Register of Deeds, Alex. H. Wilder. Office in Court House.

Clerk of the Courts, Jos. Mason. Office in Court House.

Asistant Clerk, William A. Smith. Office in Court House.

Sheriff, John S. C. Knowlton. Office in Central Exchange, and Brick Court House.

Overseers of the House of Correction, J. S. C. Knowlton and Edward Lamb. Rufus Carter, Keeper.

Commissioners under the Personal Liberty act, Henry Chapin, Worcester; Chas. Mason, Fitchburg.

William Jennison. Jos. Mason, Wm. A. Smith, Commissioners to fix and take bail in criminal cases.

Masters in Chancery, Henry C. Rice, Hartley Williams, J. Henry Hill, W. S. Davis.

Commissioners of Insolvency, W. A. Williams, Worcester, David H. Merriam, Fitchburg, T. G. Kent, Milford, D. L. Morrill, Worcester.

COURTS.

COURTS OF PROBATE AND INSOLVENCY. Henry Chapin, Judge; John J. Piper, Register: Chas. E. Stevens. Assistant Register.

Courts are held for Probate business in the Brick Court House, on the first Tuesday of every month. At West Brookfield, 2d Tuesday of May and Oct. At Clinton. 2d Tuesday in May and Oct. At Fitchburg, Wedn. next after 3d Tuesday in May and Oct. At Templeton, Thursd. next after 3d Tuesday in May and Oct. At Barre, Friday next after 2d Tuesd. in May and Oct. At Milford 4th Tuesd. in May. At Uxbridge, 4th Tuesd. in May and Oct.

For Insolvent business, in the Brick Court House, Worcester, the 2d and 4th Tuesdays in each month. At Fitchburg, the last Saturdays of January, March, May, July, September and November.

SUPREME JUDICIAL COURT. Geo. T Bigelow, of Boston, Chief Justice; Charles A. Dewey, of Northampton. Theron Metcalf, and Pliny Merrick, of Boston, E. R. Hoar, of Concord, and Reuben Chapman, of Springfield, Associate Justices.

Sessions in Worcester, Jury Term, April 9: Law Term, Oct. 1.

SUPERIOR COURT. Charles Allen, Worcester, Chief Justice; Julius Rockwell, Pittsfield; Otis P. Lord. Salem; Marcus Morton, Jr., Andover; Ezra Wilkinson, Dedham; John P. Putnam, Boston; Henry Vose, Springfield; Seth Ames, Cambridge; Thos. Russell, Boston; Lincoln F. Brigham, New Bedford, Associate Justices. P. Emory Aldrich, Worcester, District Attorney.

Sessions in Worcester, for Criminal cases, Jan. 21, May 13, and Oct. 21: for Civil cases, March, 4, Sept. 2, and Dec. 9.

Sessions in Fitchburg, June 10 and Nov. 11, for Civil business; Aug. 12 for Criminal.

COMMISSIONERS APPOINTED TO QUALIFY CIVIL OFFICERS. Henry Chapin, William Jennison, Charles W. Hartshorn, Levi Lincoln, Wm. A. Smith, Calvin Willard, Joseph Mason, G. W. Richardson.

DEPUTY SHERIFFS.

Ashburnham,	Marshall Wetherbee.
Athol,	Gardner Lord, Jr.
Barre,	Daniel Cummings.
Blackstone,	Sylvanus H. Benson.
Clinton,	Enoch K. Gibbs.
Fitchburg,	Alpheus P. Kimball.
Gardner,	George W. Dodd.
Grafton,	Jonathan B. Sibley.
Hubbardston,	Appleton Clark.
Milford,	Samuel W. Hayward.
Oxford,	Orrin W. Chafee.
Petersham,	Cephas Willard.
Southbridge,	Solomon Thayer.
Spencer,	Francis Adams, Jr.
Templeton, (Baldwinville),	John Stearns.
Uxbridge,	Thomas Aldrich.
Webster,	Solomon Shumway.
W. Brookfield,	Silas D. Cooke.
Westborough,	Daniel F. Newton.
Winchendon,	Joseph S. Watson.
Worcester,	Jonathan Day.
	Jonathan B. Sibley.

JAILORS.—Rufus Carter, Worcester; Alpheus P. Kimball, Fitchburg.

POLICE COURT.

IN EAST CITY HALL.

WM. N. GREEN, Justice. J. W. WETHERELL and W. RICE, Associate Justices. CLARK JILLSON, Clerk.

Sessions for Criminal business, daily, at 9 A. M. For civil business, every Saturday, Trials 1st and 3d Saturdays of each month.

By the new General Statutes, it is required that all *civil* cases, in which all the parties reside in Worcester, shall be brought before the Police Court for trial.

TRIAL JUSTICE for Worcester, ADIN THAYER, 218 Main Street.

POST OFFICE.

In Central Exchange. Emory Banister, Postmaster. Theodore H. Bartlett, Asst. Post Master. Francis C. Bigelow, Samuel Pierce, T. L. Mason, and A. A. Lovell, Clerks. E. W. Bartlett, Charles L. Redding, Penny Posts.

TELEGRAPH OFFICE.

The office of the American Telegraph Co. is in the Insurance building, opposite Elm street, from which despatches may be sent to almost any part of the country, during business hours.

GENERAL EXPRESS OFFICE, 2 Lincoln House Block, cor. Main and Maple Sts. All Railroad Express business is now done at this Office.

FIRE INSURANCE.

The Worcester Mutual Fire Insurance Co., is one of the oldest and safest Mutual Companies in the country. Anthony Chase, President; Fred. Wm. Paine, Treasurer; Chas. M. Miles, Secretary. Office in the Stone Court House.

Merchants and Farmers Mutual Fire Insurance Co. 98 Main Street. Isaac Davis President; Charles L. Putnam, Secretary.

People's Mutual Fire Insurance Co. 229 Main street. Henry Chapin, President; A. N. Currier, Sec'y; Samuel H. Colton, Treasurer.

Mechanics Mutual Fire Insurance Co. Office in Waldo Block, Main Street. A. H. Bullock, President. P. Hammond, Secretary.

Bay State Fire Insurance Co. Office in Clark's Block, cor. Main and Mechanics Streets. Charles L. Putnam, President; Calvin Foster, Secretary.

LIFE ASSURANCE.

State Mutual Life Assurance Co. Office, 98 Main street, Worcester. Hon. Isaac Davis, is President. Hon. E. Washburn and Hon. John Brooks, Vice Presidents; Benj. F. Heywood and Joseph Sargent, Consulting Physicians; William Dickinson, Treasurer; Clarendon Harris, Sec'y.

MASS. VOLUNTEER MILITIA.
Third Division.

Major General, Augustus Morse, Leominster.
Division Inspector, Charles H. Merriam, "
Quarter Master, Theron E. Hall, Holden.
Aid, William B. Wood, Fitchburg.
Aid, John W. Wetherell, Worcester.
Judge Advocate, Joel W. Fletcher, Leominster.

Fifth Brigade.

Brigadier General, (not filled.)
Brigade Inspector, A. B. R. Sprague, Worcester.
Quarter Master, Henry Phelps, "
Engineer, John Boyden, "
Aid, Edwin Bynner, "

Third Battalion of Rifles.

Major, (not filled.)
Adjutant, Samuel V. Stone, Worcester.
Quarter Master, David F. Parmenter, Holden.
Surgeon, Samuel Flagg, Worcester.

Company A—Worcester City Guards.
Captain, George H. Ward. 1st Lt., Edwin A. Wood. 2d Lt., Josiah Picket. 3rd Lt., Samuel Hathaway. 4th Lt., Geo. C. Joslin.

Company B—Holden.
Captain Chas. Knowlton. 1st Lt., Chas. W. Gleason. 2d Lt., Joseph H. Gleason. 3d Lt., A. F. Gleason. 4th Lt., Silas Flagg, Jr.

Third Battalion of Infantry.

Major, Edward Lamb, Worcester.
Adjutant, John M. Studley, "
Quarter Master, Wm. H. Comstock, Jr., Milford.
Surgeon, Frank H. Kelley, Worcester.

Company B—Worcester Light Infantry.
Captain, Harrison W. Pratt. 1st Lt., George W. Prouty. 2d Lt., Geo. W. Hobbs. 3d Lt., Salisbury Hyde. 4th Lt., J. Waldo Denny.

Company C—West Boylston.
Captain, D F. Prescott. 1st Lt., Chas. A. Pratt, 2d Lt., T. A. Norcross. 3d Lt., Joel H. Howe.

CEMETERIES.

The HOPE CEMETERY, near New Worcester, is owned by the city. Its beautiful location and fine natural advantages, have rendered it an attractive place of resort for citizens and strangers, and it is more and more visited, as it becomes better known. Persons who wish, may secure lots by purchase at a low price, by application to the City Treasurer, while ample provision is made for the accommodation of families not wishing to purchase, without charge.

The RURAL CEMETERY, on Grove street, is the property of a Corporation, which includes a large proportion of our older citizens. Constant improvements are going forward there, quite creditable to the good taste of those having them in charge. A new iron fence on the Grove street front is to be erected; and provision is made by which money may be invested for the permanent care of the lots. It is managed by a Board of Trustees, consisting of Levi Lincoln, President; Geo. T. Rice, S. Salisbury, H. W. Miller, F. W. Paine, and F. H. Dewey. C. Harris is Clerk, and Geo. Chandler, Treasurer.

MEETING-HOUSES AND MINISTERS.

Advent Church, Warren Hall, Rev. Albion Ross.
All Saints Church, (Episcopal) Pearl St., Rev. E. W. Hager.
Calvinist, Main Street, Rev. S. Sweetser, D. D.
Church of Christ, Thomas Street, W. A. S. Smyth and P. Blaisdell, Elders.
Church of the Unity, (Unitarian,) Elm Street, Rev. R. R. Shippen.
Chapel at County House, Rev. S. Souther.
First Baptist, East of Common, Rev. Lemuel Moss.
First Congregational, (Old South,) Rev. H. James.
Friends, corner of Chatham and Oxford Streets.
Hospital Chapel, Rev. S Souther.
Methodist, Park Street, Rev. J. H. Twombly.
Mission Chapel, Summer St, Rev. W. P. Reynolds.
New Worcester Methodist, in Union Hall, Rev. Daniel Dorchester.
Pleasant Street Baptist, Rev. J. J. Tucker.
Salem Street Church, east of Common, Rev. Merrill Richardson.
Second Congregational, (Unitarian,) Rev. A. Hill, D. D.
Second Methodist, Laurel St, Rev. J. C. Cromack.
St. John's Church, (Catholic,) Temple St, Revs. John Boyce and P. T. O'Reilley.
St. Anne's Church, Shrewsbury Street, Rev. J. J. Powers.
Third Baptist, Main Street, corner Hermon, Rev. H. L. Wayland.
Union, (Congregational,) Front St. Rev. E. Cutler.
Universalist, Foster St, Rev. L. M. Burrington.
Zion Methodist, Exchange St, Rev. Joseph Hicks.

STATE LUNATIC HOSPITAL.

Trustees, Jos. N. Bates and Wm. T. Merrifield, of Worcester, Chas. H. Stedman, of Boston; Thomas Colt, of Pittsfield, and Robert W. Hooper, of Boston; Superintendent, Merrick Bemis, M. D.; Assistant Physician, Franck H. Rice; Clerk and Apothecary, Henry C. Prentiss, M. D.; Treasurer, H. Woodward, (office in Mechanics Bank); Matron, Mrs. Caroline A. Bemis; Chaplain, Rev. S. Souther.

REPRESENTATIVES DISTRICTS, and Representatives for 1860. No. 26, Ward 6 in Worcester and the town of Auburn—Benj. F. Otis, of Worcester. No. 27, Wards 1 and 2 in Worcester—Dexter F. Parker. No. 28, Wards 3 and 8, Worcester—Jos. D. Daniels. No. 29, Wards 4 and 5, Worcester—Patrick O'Keefe. No. 30, Ward 7, Worcester—Alex. H. Bullock.

SENATOR for Worcester Center District, Ichabod Washburn, of Worcester.

Representative in Congress, ninth District, Eli Thayer, of Worcester, till March 4,—for two years following, Goldsmith F. Bailey, of Fitchburg.

JUSTICES OF THE QUORUM IN WORcester. Rejoice Newton, Wm. N. Green, William Jennison. Charles W. Hartshorn, Charles Allen, Ira M. Barton, Isaac Davis, Calvin Willard, Joseph Mason, J. Henry Hill, Wm. Greenleaf, John A. Dana, L. A. Maynard and W. A. Smith.

CORONERS IN WORCESTER. Lovell Baker, Jona. Day, Levi Jackson, J. E. Hathaway and J. M. Rice.

PUBLIC ADMINISTRATOR. Wm. Jennison.

PRINTING.

The undersigned would again invite the attention of his friends and fellow citizens to his increased facilities for doing every variety of

PRINTING

that may be called for. Fine Book and Pamphlet work done in a superior manner, on nice, thick paper, or on cheaper paper, as desired; and for a lower price than the same quality work can be obtained in Boston. Cards and Bill Heads, Posters and Showbills, Circulars and Labels, Checks, Notes and Receipts, new style Cloth Direction Tags, and all kinds of

PRINTING,

required for Business, Social or Wedding purposes, promptly done, in superior style.

HENRY J. HOWLAND, **212** Main Street.

The following notice was written by J. L. CLARKE, Esq., (now of the State Auditor's Office,) and published editorially in the Worcester Transcript, some years since, and the facts there stated are still worthy of attention.

ELEGANT TYPOGRAPHY.—It seems to have been the impression in many minds, that book printing cannot be done in a superior style, except in Boston or some of the larger cities. It is altogether a mistaken opinion, as some of the most perfect and elegant book work we have ever seen is executed at the office of Henry J. Howland, of this city. We have a specimen just now before us, the pamphlet containing a recent sermon occasioned by the death of a distinguished citizen. Its typography cannot be excelled, nor can it suffer by comparison with the most elegant English and American specimens of printing. Those desiring work of this kind, are referred to Mr. Howland.   (212 Main Street, Worcester.)

VILLAGES, &c.

Fairmount, the hill north of Rural Cemetery.
Hopeville,—on Sutton lane.
Jamesville,—South of Stafford St, near Auburn.
New Worcester,—at the junction of Main with Leicester, Webster and Cambridge sts.
Northville,—on and near West Boylston st., two miles north of Court House.
Quinsigamond Village,—2 miles S. E. of City Hall, on Millbury st.
South Worcester,—at the intersection of Southbridge st. with Cambridge st.
Tatnuck.—at the intersection of Mill and Mower sts. with Pleasant st., 3 miles from City Hall.
Valley Falls,—on Leicester st. near Leicester.

PUBLIC STREETS.

Adams st, from Shrewsbury st. to Belmont st
Agricultural st, from Highland st to Elm st, (private from Highland st to Sunnyside)
Apricot st, from Leicester st to Leicester line
Ararat st, from Brooks st to Brattle st
Arch st, from Summer to Carroll st
Ashland st, from Elm to Pleasant st
Austin st, from 266 Main st westerly to Mason st
Bailey st, from Pleasant st to Leicester line
Beaver st, from Main st to Lovell st
Belmont st, from Lincoln Square eastwardly to Shrewsbury,
Bigelow lane, from Plantation st to Bigelow's farm
Blithewood avenue, from Millbury avenue to Grafton st
Bloomingdale road, from Grafton to Plantation st
Bowdoin st, from Harvard to Chestnut st
Boylston st, from Lincoln st to Boylston
Brattle st, from Holden st to Holden line
Bridge st,from Front st north westerly to Summer
Brooks st, from West Boylston st to Malden st
Burncoat st, from Lincoln st to West Boylston line
Cambridge st, from Millbury st to N. Worcester
Carroll st, from Prospect st to Glen st
Cataract st, from Mower st to Holden line
Cedar st, from Chestnut to West st
Central st, from Main st eastwardly to Summer
Chandler st, from Irving to Newton, (private,from Main to Irving)
Charles st, from Summer to Blackstone st
Chatham st, from High st to Crown
Chelsea st, from Cambridge st to Southbridge st
Chester st, from Holden st to Holden
Chestnut st, from Pleasant st to Bowdoin
Church st, from Mechanic st to Front st
Clark st, from Burncoat st to Mountain st
Cliff st, from Granite st to Millbury st
Clinton lane, from Burncoat st to Mountain st
College st, from Southbridge st to Auburn
Concord st, from Grove st to Prescott st
Corbett st, from 258 Main to High st
Crown st, from Pleasant to Chatham st
East Central st, from Summer to Shrewsbury st
East Worcester st, from Shrewsbury st to Railroad
Edward st, from Laurel to Belmont st
Elm st, from Main to Hudson st
Endicott st, from Vernon st to Millbury st
Everett st, from Cedar to William st
Exchange st, from Main to Summer st
Flagg st, from Salisbury to Pleasant st

Forest st, from Salisbury to Holden st
Foster st, from 215 Main to Waldo or B.R.R.Depot
Fowler st, from Mill st to Leicester line
Foyle st, from Millbury st to Ward
Franklin st, from Park st eastwardly to Grafton st
Front st, from Main st eastwardly to Wash. Sq'r
Garden st, from Lincoln to Prescott st
Gates lane, from Leicester st to h of D. R. Gates
George st, from 76 1-2 Main to Harvard st
Glen st, from Orchard to Edward st
Goddard lane, from Cambridge st to Wire Factory
Grafton st, from Wash. Sq'r southeast to Grafton
Granite st, from Winthrop st to Millbury
Green st, from Park st, southwardly to Vernon st
Green's lane, from Lincoln st to h of W. E.Green
Greenwood st. from Millbury st to Millbury
Grove st, from Salisbury st northwardly to West Boylston st
Hadwin lane, from Pleasant st south
Hanover st, from Prospect to Arch st
Harrington st, from Millbury av. to Shrewsbury
Harrington court, leads from Bigelow lane
Harrison st, from Water to Barclay st
Harvard st, from Highland to Sudbury st
Heard st, from Stafford st to Auburn
Heywood st, from Millbury av. to Winthrop st
High st, from Pleasant to Austin st
Highland st, from Lincoln square west to Pleasant
Holbrook st, from Pleasant st to Mill st
Holden st, from Grove st to Holden line
Howard lane, from Fowler st west
Irving st, from Pleasant to Chandler st
Jackson st. from Main to Southbridge st
James st, from Stafford st to Jamesville
Jo Bill road, from Salisbury st westwardly to Sunny Side
Laurel st from Summer st to Wilmot
Leicester st, from New Worcester to Leicester
Liberty st, from Belmont to Arch st
Lincoln st, from Lincoln square northeast to Shrewsbury
Lincoln square is between the entrances of Highland, Lincoln, Main, Salisbury, Summer, and Belmont sts
Lovell st, from May st to Mill st
Lexington st, from Grove st east
Madison st, from Beacon st to W. R. R. (private to Main)
Main st, from Lincoln Square southwestwardly to N. Worcester
Malden st, from W. Boylston st to W.Boylston line
Manchester st, from Union st to Bridge st
Maple st, from Main st to Walnut st
Market st, from 39 Main to Summer st
May st, from Main to Pleasant st
Mechanic st, from Main st eastwardly to Bridge
Melrose st, from Burncoat st to Lincoln st
Mill st, from N. Worcester to Tatnuck
Millbrook st, from Burncoat to W. Boylston st
Millbury st, from Green st to Millbury
Millbury av., from Grafton st to Millbury
Mountain st, from Shrewsbury line to Holden line
Mower st, from Pleasant st to Paxton line
Myrtle st, from Main st eastwardly to Orange st
Nelson place, from Holden st to the Nelson farm
Nixon st, from Mountain st to West Boylston line
Oak st, from Elm st to Cedar st
Olean st, from Mower st to Holden line
Orange st, from Park st to Madison st

Oxford st, from Pleasant st to Austin st (thence private to Chandler)
Park st, from Main to Franklin st
Pearl st, from Main st west to Chestnut
Plantation st. from Grafton st to Lincoln st
Pleasant st, from Main st westwardly to Paxton
Pleasant place, from Pleasant st to Pickford's factory, Tatnuck
Plymouth st, from Green to Orange st
Portland st, from Park st southwardly to Myrtle st, (thence private to Madison
Pratt st, from Salisbury st to Grove st
Prescott st, from Concord to North st
Prospect st, from Summer st east
Prouty lane, from Pleasant st to b of E. Prouty
Providence st, from Grafton st to Winthrop
Ranks lane, from Pleasant st to Salisbury
Rice court, from Mountain st to Nixon st
Salem st, from Park to Southbridge st
Salisbury st. from Lincoln square to Holden
School st, from Main to Summer st
Shelby st, from Carroll to Wilmot st
Shrewsbury st, from Wash. square to Belmont st
Smith lane, from Holden st west
Southbridge st, from Main southwardly to Auburn
Spring st, from Front to Mechanic st
Stafford st, from Leicester st to Clappville
State st, from Main st to Harvard st
Stow place, from Chester st west
Summer st, from Lincoln sq'r to Wash. sq'r
Sutton lane, from Cambridge st to Sutton's Mills, and back (Hopeville)
Tatnuck st, from May to Mill st
Temple st, from Green to Grafton st
Thomas st, from Main to Summer st
Tracy place, from Southbridge st west
Trumbull st, from Front to Park st
Union st, from Mechanic st northwardly to Lincoln square
Upland st, from Greenwood to College st
Vernon st, from Green southwardly to Millbury st
Waldo st, from Foster st north
Walnut st, from Main to Chestnut st
Ward st, from Vernon southwardly to Millbury st
Washington st, from Park to Lamartine st, (thence private to Lafayette)
Washington square is located between the entrances of Front, Grafton, Pine and Summer sts
Water st, from Grafton st to Vernon st
Webster st, from New Worcester to Auburn
Wellington st, from Main to Chandler st
West st, from Pleasant to John st
Westboro' st, from Harrington st to Shrewsbury
West Boylston st, from Grove st to West Boylston
William st, from Chestnut st across N. Ashland st
Willow lane, from Prouty lane to Pleasant st
Winthrop st, from Vernon st to Granite st
Woodland place, from Grafton st to Sam'l Allen's

PRIVATE STREETS.

Abbott st, from Pleasant to Border st
Ætna st, from Providence to Barclay st
Agricultural st, from Highland st to Sunny Side
Allen st, from Main to Mt. Pleasant st
Armory st, from So'bridge st westerly to Southgate
Ash st, from Green to Washington st
Assonet st, from Plymouth across Gold st
Auburn st, from Catherine st to Harrington av.
Auburn st, from May to King st
Auburn place, north from Kendall st
Barclay st, from Union av. to Grafton st

Bartlett place, from Front st south
Barton court, from 254 Main st west
Beacon st, from Madison to Benefit st
Beech st, from Winter to Pond st
Belknap st, from Washington to Plymouth st
Bellevue st, from Pleasant to Bluff st
Benefit st, from 375 Main to Beacon st
Benefit court, from Benefit st west
Benson court, from Cambridge st south
Berkley st, from Millbury to Ward st
Bigelow's court, from Front st north
Blackstone st, from Exchange st south by Canal
Bliss st, from Highland to Salisbury st
Blossom st, from Russell to Hudson st
Bluff st, from King st west
Border st, from Chandler to Winfield st
Bowdoin st, from Chestnut to N. Ashland st
Bremer st, from Dryden to Whittier st
Brown's block, cor. Salem and Myrtle sts
Brown st, from Beech across Pond st
Bryant st, from Bremer to Hemans st
Burnside court, from 297 Main st east
Burt st, from Grafton st to Temple
Butman alley, from 252 Main to High st
Byron st, from Nashua to Millbrook st
Canal st, from Front st to Western Railroad
Canterbury st, from Hammond across Goddard st
Carlton st, from Belmont st north—rear of Gas works
Carlton st, from Front to Mechanic st
Catherine st, from Lincoln st southeast to Belmont
Central court, from Exchange st south
Chandler court, from 25 Chandler
Chandler st, from Main to Irving st (thence public to Mason)
Channing st, from Catharine to Mt. Vernon st
Chapin st, from Winthrop to Ætna st
Charlton st, from Beacon to Main st
Chatham st, from Crown to Newbury st
Chatham st place, from Chatham st south
Cherry st, from Bartlett place to Canal st
Claremont st. from Main to Woodland st
Clarkson st, from Providence to Barclay st
Clinton st, from Pleasant to Chatham st
Columbia st, from Water to Winthrop
Columbian court, from Exchange st south
Congress st, from Crown to Newbury st
Coral st, from Providence to Grafton st
Coral st, from Millbury to Ward st
Cottage st, from West to Fruit st
Crescent st, from Henchman to Nashua st
Cross st, from Shrewsbury st to E. Worcester
Cypress st from Exchange st south
Dewey st, from Pleasant to May st
Dix st, from Harvard to N. Ashland st
Downing st, from Main to Woodland st
Dryden st, from Edgeworth to Hemans st
Earle st, from Edward to Elizabeth st
East st, from Belmont to Reservoir st
Eaton place, from Front st south
Eden st, from Sudbury st north
Edgeworth st, from Milton to Byron st
Elliot st, from Carroll st to Wilmot
Elizabeth st, from Belmont st to Reservoir
Florence st, from Beaver to Maywood st
Forest Avenue, from 35 Lincoln st east
Foundry st, from Franklin st to Canal st
Fountain st, from Belmont to Arch st
Franklin court, north from 10 Shrewsbury st.
Freeland st, from Main to Tirrell (New Worcester)
Fremont st, from Cambridge st to Sutton lane.
Fruit st, from Pleasant to Elm st

Fulton st, from Summer to Mulberry st
Gardner st, from Main st to Western Railroad
Gertrude av., from Main st west opp. School st
Goddard st, from Green st east
Goddard st, from Main to Cambridge st
Goddard place, from Pleasant st north
Gold st, from Green to Southbridge st
Gold court, from Gold st
Grosvenor st, from Layfayette to Lamatine st
Hamilton square, east of Prescott st
Hamilton st, from Grafton to Plantation st
Hammond st, from Main to Kanzas st
Hancock st, from Lexington to Grafton st
Harrington avenue, from Lincoln st east
Harris st, from Jackson to Taylor st
Harvard place, from Harvard st east
Hawthorne st, from Main to Woodland st
Hemans st, from Dryden to Whittier st
Henchman st, from Lincoln to Margin st
Hermon st, from Main to Beacon st
Hibernia st, from Washington square north
Highland court, from Highland st south
High st court, from High st west
Hill st, from E. Central to Shrewsbury st
Hinds court, from Maple st north
Holley st, from Austin st north
Hollis st, from Kilby to Goddard st
Home st, from N. Ashland to Wachusett st
Houchin avenue, from Chatham st south
Howard st, from Summer to Blackstone st
Hudson st, from Elm to Pleasant st
Jefferson st, from Vernon to Providence st
John st, from Harvard across N. Ashland st
Kanzas st, from Southbridge to Cambridge st
Kendall st, from Lincoln st to Oak avenue
Kendall hill, from north end of Orchard st
Kilby st, from Main to Gardner st
King st, from Main to Chandler st
Lafayette st, from Southbridge to Millbury st
Lagrange st, from Main to Beacon st
Lamartine st, from Lafayette to Washington st
Langdon st, from Lafayette to Lamartine st
Larkin st, from Shrewsbury st to E. Worcester st
Laurel lane, from Laurel st to Shelby st
Lee st, from Highland st to Sunny Side
Linden st, from Elm to Pleasant st
Linwood place, east from Lincoln st
Locust st, from Southbridge to Railroad
Lodi st, from Lafayette to Lamartine st
Loudon st, from Main to Woodland st
Lovell court, from S. Irving st
Lowell st, from Main to Freeland st, N. Worcester
Lucus place, from Central st south
Lynn st, from Salem to Orange st
Lynde st, from Belmont to Kendall st
Madison st, from Main to Beacon st
Maple place, from Maple st west
Margin st, from Garden to Henchman st
Mason st, from Pleasant to May st
Maywood st, from Main st northwest
Mendon st, from Union av. to Grafton st
Milk st, from Franklin st south, by Canal
Milton st, from North st to Millbrook
Mott st, from Penn av. to Barclay st
Mt. Pleasant st, from Benefit to Allen st
Mt. Vernon st, from Westminster st east
Mulberry st, from Pine to Shelby st
Mullberry court, east from 16 Mulberry st
Nashua st, from Crescent to Byron st
Newbury st, from Pleasant to Chandler st
Newport st, from Liberty to Edward st
Newton st, from Pleasant to May st

North Ashland st, from Highland across William
North st, from Grove to Prescott st
Norwich st, from Foster to Mechanic st
Oak avenue, from Belmont to Catharine st
Olive st, from Mason to Dewey st
Orchard st, from Belmont across Arch st
Otis st, from Prescott to Hancock st
Oxford place, from Oxford st west
Palmer st, from Liberty to Edward
Parker st, from Winfield to Mason st
Parsons lane, from Apricot st south
Penn avenue, from Union avenue to Grafton st
Piedmont st, from Main to Pleasant st
Pink st, from Highland to N. Ashland st
Pond st, from Green to Winter st
Portland st, from Myrtle to Madison st (public
   from Park to Myrtle)
Prince st, from King to Queen st
Quarry st, from Belmont st to stone quarry
Queen st, from Chandler to King st
Quincy st, from Chatham to Austin st
Reservoir st, from Edward to East st
Russell st, from Pleasant to Elm st
Russell place, from Russell st west
Salem st, from Myrtle to Southbridge st, (public
   from Park to Myrtle)
Seaver st, from Pleasant to Elm st
Seymore st, from Millbury to Ward st
Sigourney st, from North to Edgeworth st
Slater's court, from Thomas st south
So. Irving st, from Chandler to Wellington st
Southgate st, from Cambridge st north
Sudbury st, from Chestnut to Main st
Suffolk st, from Bloomingdale road south
Summer st court, rear of 99 Summer
Summit st, from Gold to Ash st
Sunny Side, on the Jo Bill road
Sycamore st, from Main to Beacon st
Taylor st, from Millbury to Ward st
Taylor st, from Main to Harris st
Tirrell st, from Main to Freeland st, (N. Worcester)
Tow Path, from Green near Millbury st southerly
Townsend st, from Russell to Hudson st
Tremont st, from Front to Mechanic st
Troy st, from Belmont st north
Tufts st, from Chandler to Winfield st
Union avenue, from Vernon to Grafton st
Vine st, from Front to Cherry st
Wachuset st, from Dix to Home st
Waldo st, from Highland st to Salisbury
Wall st, from Grafton st north
Warren st, from Front to Cherry st
Waverly st, from Providence to Grafton st
Westminster st, from Catharine to Mt. Vernon st
Whittier st, from Edgeworth to Hemans st
White st, from Chandler to Bluff st
Willis st, from Bremer to Hemans st
Wilmot st, from Reservoir to Shelby st
Winfield st, from Border to May st
Winter st, from Green st to the Canal
Winter st court, from Winter st south
Woodland st, from King st across May to Down-
   ing st
Worth st, from Millbury to Ward st
Wyoming Site, between Main, State, Harvard and
   George sts, entrance from Gertrude avenue

LEGAL HOLIDAYS IN MASS.—22d of February,
Fast Day, Fourth of July, Thanksgiving, and
Christmas days.

DIRECTORY.

The names printed in Capitals, are those of persons doing business which they think worthy of announcing to the public by means of Advertisements, to which the reader is referred. See Index, pages 8 and 9.

Aborn Frederick W. shoemaker, h Tatnuck
Aborn Sam'l C. T. shoemaker, bds 11 Liberty
Abbott Caleb F. painter, h 25 Central
Abbott Chas. B. shoemaker, 58 Southbridge
ABBOTT E. E. real estate broker, 4 Bay State bl'k h cor. Pleasant and Hudson
Abbott Ezra, bootbottomer, bds Apricot
ABBOTT FREDERIC E. hat store, 4 Bay State block, bds at E. E. Abbott's, Pleasant
Abbott Hubbard, bootbottomer, h Apricot
Abbott Merrill, slater, h 45 Pleasant
Abercrombie Austin, farmer, Plantation
Acharton Chas. H. machinist, h 22 John
Adams Asa B. printer at Howland's, bds 410 Main
Adams Charles B. machinist, h 5 Gold
Adams Mrs. Cylena, h 2 Highland court
Adams Edward W. silk dyer, bds Grove
Adams Ephraim, clicker, h 29 Newbury
Adams Frances, boarding house, Webster
ADAMS HENRY B. silk dyer, Grove
Adams Henry C. manuf'r of Ind. Veg. Ointment, 207 Main, h 37 Salem
Adams Hezekiah, farmer, Millbury av.
Adams James H. h 16 Chandler
Adams J. Henry, machinist, bds 2 Maple place
Adams James M. machinist, bds 5 High
Adams John, confectioner, 71½ Main. h 2 Maple
Adams John Q., W. Ashland cor Bowdoin [place
Adams John Q. book-keeper, h 23 Hanover
Adams John Q. h Mason
Adams John Q. h 4 Belknap
Adams Mrs. Mary H. physician, h 39 Summer
Adams Nathan S. farmer, h 147 Pleasant
Adams Wm. supt. Washburn's foundry, h 6 Vine
Adams Wm. shoemaker, h 85 Summer
Adams Wm. machinist, h Austin cor. Bellevue
Adams Wm. A. jobber, h Abbott
Adams Wm. F. painter and grainer, h 53 Summer
Adams Wm. H. wire drawer. h Vernon
Adams Wm. W. machinist, bds 20 Thomas
Agan Thos. laborer, h Foundry cor. Vine
Ager John, paper manuf'r. Leicester, V. F.
Agin John, farmer, h Lovell
Agnew Peter, tailor, h 9 Bridge
Ainsworth Mrs. M. N. h 41 Pleasant
Aitchison Geo. T. carriage manul'r,6 Bridge,h 55 Front [ces, &c., h 11 Irving
ALBEE AMOS P. manuf'r soluble blueing, essen-
Albee Edwin, painter, h 17 Lamartine
Albee John N. overseer at Hopeville, h Cam-bridge, S Worcester [Bay State House
Albee Miss R. A. teacher. 6 Warren block, bds
Albro Isaac, carpenter, h 19 Beacon
Alcock James, peddler, bds Langdon
Alden Addison F. painter, h 6 Newbury
Alden Edward W. printer, bds 7 Carroll
Alden John B. painter, bds 23 Exchange
Alden Mrs. Persis, h 7 Carroll
Aldrich Aaron, carpenter, h 24 Madison
Aldrich Cyrenus, manuf'r turn'g tables, h 10 High
Aldrich Elbridge, carpenter, h 9 Providence
Aldrich Franklin A, book-keeper, 3 Pearl
Aldrich George W. clerk, bds 1 Goddard

Aldrich Henry W. tin peddler, h Highland Court
Aldrich Horace, mechanic, h Stafford
Aldrich J. M. musician, h 20 Thomas [3 Crown
Aldrich Rev. Jonathan, ag't Missionary Union, h
Aldrich Luther, box maker, bds 30 Mulberry
Aldrich Paine, manufacturer of turning tables, 8 High, h 1 High [change, h 38 Elm
Aldrich P. Emory, Dist. Attorney, 1 Central Ex-
Aldrich Pardon W. & Co. flour &c. 43 Front, bds 15 Main
Aldrich Thomas P. carpenter, h 81 Chandler
Aldrich Warren L. brakeman B. R, R. h 13 Ash
Aldrich Mrs. Wm. D. h 1 Goddard
Aldrich Wm. H. clerk at Davis', bds 2 Sudbury
Alexander Wm. R. farmer, h May
Alexander Charles P. clerk Swan's Hotel
Alger Warren A. mach:nist, bds 24 Thomas
Allen Albert S. organist and music teacher, 263 Main, h 20 Portland
Allen Alfred D. student, bds cor. Edward & Earle
Allen Asa M. (Prouty & A.) h 2 Prospect
Allen Benj. D. organist and music teacher, 263 Main, h 8 Trumbull
Allen Charles, judge, 285 Main, h 39 Elm cor West
Allen Charles, jr. at C. A. Harrington & Co.'s, bds 39 Elm
Allen Charles H. rolling mill, bds 3 Lynn
Allen Charles F. real estate trader. h 11 Fruit
Allen Charles L. armorer, h Salisbury
Allen Dwight D. & Co. (Lowe Emerson) boot form manuf'rs, Cypress, bds 2 Clinton
Allen (Ethan) & Wheelock, (T. P.) manuf'rs of fire arms, at Junction, h 320 Main
Allen Fred'k. blacksmith, Armsby's building, h
Allen Rev. Geo. bds 83 Summer [11 Lincoln
Allen G. F. (Austin & A.) h 20 High [Pleasant
Allen George L. boots and shoes, 176 Main, h 43
Allen Henry W., Peaslee & Co.'s, bds 61 Pleasant
Allen Hugh J. clicker, h 9 Austin
Allen Ira T. h 2 Carroll
Allen James E. bootmaker, h Auburn
Allen James F. acct. at Wheeler's, h 1 Everett
Allen Jared, blacksmith, Pleasant, Tatnuck
Allen John, shoemaker, bds 26 Mechanic
Allen Jonas B. carpenter, bds 6 Sycamore
Allen John, harness maker, h 1 Chandler court
Allen Joseph, chemist, bds 11 Fruit
Allen Joseph M. farmer, h Salisbury
Allen J. W. mason, h 31 Myrtle
Allen M. D. h Dewey
Allen Owen W. boot manuf'r, bds 6 High
Allen Samuel, h 36 Elm
Allen Thomas, roller, Quinsigamond
Allen Willard F. trunk and harness maker, Bank block, Foster, h 8 Sycamore
ALLEN WM. bookseller and binder, 275 Main, h 22 Providence [avenue
Allen Wm form'n machinist at ct. mill, h Forest
Allen Wm. T. form'n at Walker's, h 13 Lincoln
Allis Phebe, tailoress, 1 Walnut
Allison Wm. carpenter, bds 74 Southbridge
Allman John, cigar maker, bds 5 Maple
Allyn Wm. R. lumber yard, Central, h East

Alton Alphonze A. carpenter, h 3 John
Alton James E. mason, h Quinsigamond
Alton James D. machinist, h Newport
Ames Edwin, mason, h 7 Quincy
Ames Hiram H. machinist, h 4 Central
Ames Mrs. Sarah, h 19 Hanover
Amidown Marcus M. machinist, bds 1 High st, ct.
Amidon Martin, carpenter, h 32 Beacon
Ammidon John. (Dodge & Ammidon) h 8 Union
ANDREWS DANIEL F. pattern maker, Junction shop, h 2 Harris
Andrews E. F. clerk, bds rear Mulberry
Andrews Geo. B. milk dealer, h Lincoln
Andrews Geo. W. painter, bds 7 Maple
Andrews Henry, pattern maker, Junction shop
Andrews John A. physician, office 105 Main, h 47 Summer   [mer
Andrews John A Jr. brass moulder, bds 47 Sum-
Andrews Nahum H. (Gould & A.) h 59½ Main
Andrews Mrs. Persis H. h 6 Congress
Andrews Wm. H. pattern maker, bds 2 Harris
Anderson Edward, bds 3 Pearl
Anger Augustus, blacksmith, h 32 Thomas
Anger Francis, musical instrument maker, h 12
Angier Austin, laborer, h 8 Arch   [Pleasant
Angier Charlotte M. nurse, h 25 Shelby
Angier Calvin W. refreshment rooms, B. & W. R. R. station
Angier John, wiredrawer, bds rear of 8 Central
Anglum Daniel, laborer, h 3 E. Central
Anthony Arnold, teamster, h Quinsigamond
Anthony Chas. J. h Cedar
Apperson James, mason, h 15 Chandler
Arbuckle Matthew, musician, bds 9 Maple
Arnsby J. M. C. h 30½ Lincoln
Arnold Cyrus, soap maker, h 232 Pleasant
Arnold Daniel, (Farnum & Co.) boot manuf'r, 24 Front, h Mason
Arnold Jas.G. patents,4 Bangs block, h 7 Harvard
Arnold S. A. machinist, h 20 Summer
Ash Patrick, laborer, h Hill
Ashley Mrs. Eunice, h Bloomingdale
Ashly Wm. S. at D. W. Johnson's, bds Suffolk
Atherton Chas. H. machinist, court mill,h 22 John
Atherton David, carpenter, h 41 Washington
Athy Andrew, bootmaker, h Mechanic cor Spring
Atkins Wm. fireman P. & W. R. R. bds 90 South-
Aubertin Augustus, grocer, h 2 Tremont [bridge
AUSTIN (Alpheus B.) & ALLEN (G. F.) cabinet makers, 9 Southbridge, bds 27 Chatham
Austin Andrew, carpenter, bds 15 Chandler
Austin A. M. carpenter at Dennis & Lee's, bds Charlton
Austin Geo. W. at grove mill, bds Burncoat
Austin James, currier, h Winter
Austin James,woodsawyer,Nor. R. R. h Burnside ct.
Austin Morris, laborer, h 32 Winter
Austin Sampson, farmer, Millbury avenue
Avery Andre, mason, h Central
Avery Francis J. farmer, Salisbury
Avery Joseph. farmer, Salisbury
AYRES HORACE, grocer, 238 Main, h Corbett
Ayres Samuel, wireworker, h Holden
Ayres Warren, box maker, h 23 Salem
Ayers W. A. agent, h 92 Main
Ayers Wm. E. clerk Savings Bank   [chanic
Ayer Loron, watch Norwich ft. house, bds 30 Me-
Babbitt Harrison W. collector, h 91 Pleasant
Babbitt Lewis, dry goods peddler, h 6 Charlton
Babbitt Samuel F. carpenter, h John
Babbitt Thos. H. machinist, bds 7 Shelby
Babcock Chester K. building mover, h 2 Austin
Bachant Anthony, carriage maker, h 18 Thomas

Back Wm. machinist, h 32 Green
Bacon Albert J. bootmaker, h 45 Main
Bacon Chas. L. laundryman at Hospital
Bacon Frank J. music teacher, 48 Front
Bacon Henry, law student, bds 22 Elm
Bacon J. E. master transportation,Nash. R.R. bds
Bacon J. H. boxmaker, h 20 Carrol   [80 Main
Bacon John W. machinist, bds 14 Webster
Bacon Peter C. counsellor, 1 Cen. Ex. h 22 Elm
Bacon Wm. M. cabinet maker, h Woodland
Bailey Mrs. Addison. h 4 Brown's block
Bailey A. F. machinist, h Piedmont
Bailey Benj. F. farmer, Bailey   [ton
Bailey Geo. watchman at T. K. Earle's,h 24 Graf-
Bailey Geo. P. letter cutter & die sinker, 6 Cen. Ex. h 20 Thomas
Bailey Geo. W. carriage trimmer, bds 7 Orange
Bailey J. E. Brookfield & W. Ex. bds Waldo House
Bailey Nathan, bootmaker, h 15 Foundry
Bailey Nelson, carriage maker, h 3 Shrewsbury
Bailey Silas, h 49 Central
Bailey Sherman A. machinist, h 31 Laurel
Bailey Wm. laborer, h 2 Liberty
Bailey Wm. H. wiredrawer, bds 3 Prospect
Bailey Wm. H. clicker, h 15 Charlton
Baird Mrs. Mary, h Grafton
Baird Thos N. carpenter, court mill. h 1 Edward
Baker B. F. bootsider, at C. H. Fitch's
Baker Chas. lumber manufacturer and dealer, Manchester, bds 294 Main
Baker Cyrus, carpenter, h 15 Providence
Baker David, laborer, h Millbury
Baker David, moulder, h 54 Exchange
Baker David J. livery stable & saloon, 4 Webster
Baker Edward A. shoemaker, bds 27 Mechanic
Baker Healey,shoe manuf'r,305 Main, h 32 Pleas't
Baker Henry S. clicker, bds 18 1-2 Portland
Baker James H. carpenter, h 40 Portland
Baker John P. at H. Griffin & Co. h Clinton
Baker Joel, moulder, Armory
Baker J. L. 3 Brinley hall, h 19 Laurel
Baker Joseph, pistolmaker, bds 7 Mechanic
Baker Lovell. 3 Brinley hall, bds 19 Laurel
Baker Miss Nancy, teacher at C. B. Metcalf's
Baker Wm. J. boxmanufacturer, h 47 Austin
Baker Wm. G. carriagesmith, bds 76 Front
Baker Wm. E. carriagemaker, bds 1 Green
Baker Rev. Zepheniah, librarian Public Library, bds 29 Crown
Bakes Henry, fixer at Fox's, h 7 Millbury
Balcom Brigham, b'k k'r Peo. In. Co. h 28 Portl'd
Balcom Elias T. proprietor Lincoln House
Balcom Sumner W. bds 375 Main
Balcom Wm. H. clerk at Lincoln House
Baldwin Benj. hostler at A. M. Stockwell's
Baldwin Charles O. Spy office, bds 9 Orange
Baldwin Charles H. plumber, 6 Exchange
Baldwin Edward, laborer, h Gold
Baldwin Geo. W. (Foster & B.) bds Oak cor Cedar
Baldwin John D. & Co. editors and publishers of Spy, 212 Main, h 9 Orange
Baldwin John S, Spy office, bds 9 Orange
Baldwin John W. expressman, bds 14 Charlton
Ball Albert, machinist, h 1 Reservoir
Ball Charles A. H. at hospital
Ball David H. blacksmith, bds 74 Pleasant
Ball Edw. W. clerk for J. Firth, h 9 Crown
Ball Hollis, wire annealer, h 20 Prescott
Ball Homer J. wire drawer, h Quinsigamond
Ball Horatio, butcher at A. Peaslee & Co. bds 61
Ball Leroy D. machinist, bds 51 Summer [Pleas't
Ball N. A. shoemaker, h 74 Pleasant
Ball Phinehas, civil engineer, 14 Cen. Exchange

Ball (Richard,) & Williams (W.) manuf'rs of wood working machinery, 28 School, h Chestnut
Ballard Chas. insurance agt. h Goddard place
Ballard Chas. H. machinist at Ball & Williams, h 51 Summer [h Vernon
Ballard (John S.) & Spurr (E.) grocers, 227 Main,
Ballard John J. farmer, Grafton
Ballard Salem L. machinist, h 46 Orange
Ballard Thos. E. cabinetmaker, h 25 Orange
Ballord Marshall S. sash & blind dealer, h 16 Portland [Congress
Ballou Amasa, painter, 3 Pleasant, up stairs, h 11
Ballou F. M. wire temperer, bds 26 Thomas
Ballou Wesley, wire roller, h Kendall Hill
Bancroft Chas. S. teamster, h Webster
Bancroft Clarkson R. shoemaker, h 26 Mechanic
Bancroft Enoch, farmer, Lincoln
Bancroft E. W. clicker, h 40 Austin
Bancroft Isaac A. boxmaker, h 49 Chandler
Bancroft J. A. street sprinkler, h 45 Exchange
Bancroft James H. boot and shoe store, 301 Main h 54 Austin
BANCROFT JOHN A. & L. F. wood & stabling, Bancroft Lorey F. (J. A. & L. F.) [82 Front
Bancroft Peter M. farmer, h Webster
Bancroft Timothy, farmer, Lincoln
Bancroft Mrs. Timothy W. h 60 Front [Pleasant
Bancroft Truman G. saloon, 1 Mechanic, bds 17
Bangs Anson, dealer in eave troughs, &c. h Main cor Beaver [Bangs
Bangs E. P. puts up eave troughs, &c. h with A
Banister Emory, post master, h 3 Harvard
Banister Samuel, prop'r Exchange hotel
Banning Erastus M. h 5 Piedmont
Barber Mrs. Almon A. h 41 Summer
Barber Benjamin, pavior, h 15 Green
Barber Geo. (Bigelow & B.) k Southbridge, cor Cambridge
Barber Geo. A. bootcrimper, bds 15 Portland
Barber Isaac, carriagemaker at Breck's, h 6 Carriage
Barber John P. farmer, Granite [roll
Barber Josiah, blacksmith, ct. mill, h 18 Green
Barber Joseph, teacher Wor. Acad'y, bds 46 Front
Barber Levi H. machinist, h 2 Millbrook
Barber Mrs. Lucy A. dressmaker, h 20 Park
Barber Walter, forger, h 136 Southbridge
Barber Silas, farmer, West Boylston
Barber Wm. T. farmer, West Boylston
Barber Misses, h 15 Portland
Barbour I. R. jr. agt. Parkhurst's mill. h Leic'r
Barbour Wm. C. skate manufacturer Cypress, h
Barden Joel, hay cutters, h Lovell [May
Bardlow Wm. rolling mill, h Foyle [Harvard
Barker John M. teller Mechanics Bank, bds 21
Barker Josiah G. carriagemaker, 56 Union, h 7
Barker Levi, h 19 Park [Liberty
Barker Richard, carpenter, h 19 Park [tin
Barker Sam'l D. hat repairer, 233 Main, h 65 Austin
Barker Wm. acct. h 21 Harvard
Barnard A. B. agt. for Buckeye mowing machine, Union, cor Exchange, h 1 Crescent
Barnard Benajah, truckman, h 10 Catharine
Barnard Mrs. E. L. h 10 State
Barnard Franklin, thomsonian, 79 Main
Barnard Geo. A. farmer, Millbrook
Barnard G. Edwin, jeweller, 205 Main, bds 87
Barnard John, farmer, Millbrook [Summer
Barnard Jonathan, expressman, h 19 William
BARNARD (Lewis), SUMNER (Geo.) & CO. (O. E. Putnam) dry goods, &c. 191 Main, h 29 Lin'n
Barnes Mrs. Baxter, h 50 Mechanic [Portland
Barnes Calina, asst. librarian pub. library, bds 15
Barnes Francis, paperhanger, h 15 William

Barnes Mrs. Joseph, 66 Exchange
Barnes Norman E. carpenter, h Tatnuck
Barnes Peter R. gardener for Henry Gou'ding
Barnes Richard E. thman, bds 18 Central
Barnes Samuel S. painter, h 4 Newport
Barnes W. H. ticket cl'k B. R. R. h 10 Myrtle
Barney Raymond, painter, bds 56 Exchange
Barr Eldridge, machinist, bds cor Main & La-
Barr Wm. A. clicker, h 3 Seaver [grange
Barrett Albert H. machinist, bds 9 Salem
Barrett C. W. shoemaker, 20 Main
Barrett Geo. E. machinist, h 9 Salem
Barrett Henry, pattern maker, bds 11 Portland
Barrett Jos. & Co. (C. Cutting,) machinists, Junction mill, h 9 Salem
Barrett Joseph F. carder, Webster
Barrett Lyman B. stair builder, h 35 Washington
Barrett Marvin, machinist, bds 36 Front
Barrett Michael, laborer, h 42 Shrewsbury
Barrett Rufus, engineer, P. R. R. bds 5 Maple
Barrett Samuel D. patternmaker, bds 67 Main
Barrett Mrs. Wm. C. h 67 Main [Stafford
Barrows Alonzo M. machinist, h Leicester, cor
Barrows Albert, brakeman, bds 14 Goddard
Barrows Foster, B. R. R. h 33 Austin
Barrows Wm. D. machinist, h 5 Webster
Barry Daniel, armorer, h 15 Temple
Barry Edward, cook at Spurr & Priest's, h rear of
Barry John, laborer, h S. Irving [70 Mechanic
Barry John, bootmaker, h 20 Washington
Barry Richard, armorer, h 24 Millbury
Barry Russell W. carpenter, h 14 Chatham
Barry Thomas, boot treer, bds Salem
Barry Thomas, laborer, h 97 Summer
Barth Wm. tailor at Lewisson's, h 1 Burnside c't
Bartlett Albert M. machinist, h 29 Oxford
Bartlett Andrew, machinist, bds 13 Chandler
Bartlett C. S. printer, bds cor. Sum'r & Exchange
Bartlett Charles A. farmer, bds Belmont
Bartlett Dwight, truckman, h 5 Cherry
Bartlett Ephriam W. penny post, h 73 Summer
Bartlett Geo. H. shoemaker, h 7 Austin
Bartlett Mrs. Isaac, h 2 Glen
Bartlett J. W. sash & blinds, 73 Front, h 73 Front
Bartlett John, laborer, h Grafton
Bartlett Jonas, farmer, Belmont
Bartlett Perley, cookie shop, Front, h 8 Edward
Bartlett Phineas, farmer, Leicester
Bartlett Stephen, h 22 Orange
Bartlett Theodore H. asst. P. M. h 12 Chatham
Bartlett Thomas, blacksmith, h rear 11 Market
Bartley Michael, laborer, h Canal cor Winter
Bartley Thomas, blacksmith, h 11 Market
Barton Austin, carpenter, h 19 Prescott
Barton Charles H. shoemaker, h 3 Belknap
Barton Edmund M. bds 254 Main
Barton Mrs. Emerson, h 3 Lynn
Barton Geo. S. (Goddard, Rice & Co.) h 4 Crown
Barton Geo. W. mason, h 4 Belknap
Barton Ira M. counsellor, 254 Main
Barton J. H. machinist, h 13 Myrtle
Barton Martin, laborer, h 13 Vine
Barton Washington, roll coverer, h 26 Mechanic
Barton Wm. S. h 32 High
Bascom Lewis H. boot stitcher, h 21 Salem
Bassett (Ahaz) & Sawyer, (W. A.) produce dealers, 7 City Hall, h 36 Mulberry
Bassett Arthur, bag. mast'r, N. R. R. h 1 Carlton
Bassett Hiram, carpenter, h Plantation
Bassett Jos. M. acct. F. Willard & Co. 3 Elliot
Bassett L. J. carpenter, bds 13 Elliot [bridge
Batcheider Hiram W. shoemaker, bds 63 South-
Batchelder J. W. R. court mill, h 2 Market

9

Batchelder O. S. machinist, h 306 Main
Batchelder Mrs. Sarah A. h 63 Southbridge
Batchelor Silas H. carpenter, h 28 William
Bates Alfred, carpenter, h 73 Exchange
Bates H. W. clerk at Times office, bds Bay St. H.
Bates Jos. N physician, 7 Pearl, h 5 Pearl
Bates Moses, publisher of Daily Times, 179 Main
 bds Bay State House
Bates Mrs. Ruth. h 81 Main
BATTELLE GEO. L. & CO. (J.W.Battelle)man'rs
 of sewing machines, Union st. bds 12 Glen
Battelle Joseph W. (G. L. B. & Co.) bds 12 Glen
Battelle Geo. S. farmer, bds Belmont
Battelle Mrs. Mary, h 12 Glen
Bauer Charles, machinist. h 23 Grove
Bauer Paul, ornamental japaner, bds 23 Grove
Baylies Mrs. Adolphus, h 3 Trumbull   [Summer
Beach Lucius, broker, 2 Warren block, bds 79
Beal H. L. photographer, &c, 11 Piper's block, h
Beal Mrs. S. h 21 Crown   [6 William
Beals Edwin C. carpenter, bds 19 Carroll
Bean Caleb G. farmer, ladies Collegiate Institute
Bean E. J. watchman, at depot, bds 27 Grove
Bean Jacob. traveling stationer, h Abbott
Bean Otis, wire packer, h Auburn place   [chard
Bean Spencer D. Nashua freight depot, h 24 Or-
Beaumont Abraham W. boottreer, h Border, cor
 Mason
Beauvais Theo. F. machinist, bds 7 Winter
Beebe Orson W. heater, h 14 Temple   [ant
Belcher Chas. & Co. provisions, 246 Main, h Pleas-
Belser Wm. F. hostler, bds Farmer's hotel
Belveile Frank, machinist, h 2 Wilmot
Bell Mrs. Maria, h cor Union and Market
Bellilo Xavier, shoemaker, bds 32 Mechanic
Bellows Eph. H. machinist, h 16 Harvard
Bellows Horace, stitcher, 3½ Pleas't, h 32 Pleas't
Bellows Lyman, wire finisher, West Boylston st.
 Northville
Bellows Lyman O. farmer, W. Boylston, N'thville
Bemis Abel, mechanic, h 18 Elliot
Bemis A. J. blacksmith, 8 Laurel
Bemis Barna, clerk, h 4 Glen
Bemis Caroline A. matron at hospital
Bemis Daniel W. farmer at hospital
Bemis Edward, boot and shoe store, 2 Harring-
 ton cor. bds 302 Main
Bemis Elias T. foreman Spy office, h 4 Carroll
Bemis Geo. A. H. at hospital
Bemis Horace C. bootmaker, bds 33 Irving
Bemis J. Orlando, at E.A. Goodnow's, h 38 Austin
Bemis Merrick, sup't State Lunatic Hospital
Bemis Nathan T. livery stable, 34 Exchange, h
 20 Exchange
Bemis Samuel W. at N. T. Bemis', h 43 Exchange
Benchley Albert L. (J.A.Dorman & Co.)h 43 Salem
Benchley Mrs. A. P. h 16 Mulberry
Benchley Henry. machinist, bds 16 Mulberry
Benchley J. E. book keeper for J. A. Fay & Co. h
 10 Wellington   building, h 43 Salem
Benchley Jas. H. & Co. plow makers, Armsby's
Benlough Wm. laborer, bds Millbury
Bennett Ashel C. jobber & farmer, h Salisbury
Bennett Chas. F. manufacturer cloth-drying ma-
 chines, bds Central
Bennett J. C. clerk at V. A. Ladd's
Bennett Joseph, machinist. h 41 Main
Bennett Thomas, machinist, bds 5 High
Benson Alphonzo,mechanic,h rear 80 Southbridge
Benson Erastus O. bds 180 Pleasant
Bent Chas. M. book keeper Wor. Bank, bds 18
Bent John Q. blacksmith, h 7 Fulton   [Pleasant
Bentley Geo.W. sup't Nash. R. R. h Salisbury

Benton Calvin, truckman, bds 8 Edward
Benway Joseph, laborer, Jamesville
Benway Joseph, laborer, h 1 Elliot
Berkley R. H.(A. Wheelock & Co.) h 28 Thomas
Bernard Mrs. David A. h 2 Vine
Berrigan John, laborer, h E. Central
Berry Henry L. bds 6 State
Berry John, blacksmith, h Lovell
Berry Scotto, cashier Mechanics b'k, h 6 State
Berry Zebina E. janitor Mechanics Hall,h 8 Irv'g
Bessey Merritt E. engineer, bds 266 Main
Bessey M. H. clerk at G. Geer, bds 6 West
Betterly Edw. S. bread driver, h 73 Southbridge
Biall Nathaniel A. shoemaker, h Langdon
Bickford Chas. clerk at Pinkham's,bds 20 Pleas't
Bickford Wm. M. loom bld'r, Merrifield's build-
 ing, up stairs, Exchange, h 12 Main
Bigelow (Alex'r) & Barber(Geo.)manuf'rs, Hope-
 ville, h 15 Park   [Wellington
Bigelow Amos E.(G. C. & A. E.) carpenter, h 22
Bigelow Chas. P. at 2 Sargents block, h 6 Waln't
Bigelow David B. custom bootmaker, 233 Main,
 bds 1 Walnut
Bigelow Edward D. watchman at hospital
Bigelow Francis C. clerk P. O. h Mount Pleasant
Bigelow Francis E. bds 58 Front
Bigelow Mrs. Geo. C. bds Bay State House
Bigelow Geo. P. farmer. Vernon
Bigelow Geo. C. & A. E. carpenters, cor Central
 and Union, h Mount Pleasant
Bigelow Geo. F. wireworker, bds Farmer's Hotel
Bigelow G. P. clerk, bds 1 Portland
Bigelow Henry, moulder, bds 13 Mechanic
Bigelow Henry C. clerk 98 Main, h 11 Congress
Bigelow Henry E. cl'k Cent'l Bank, bds 41 Pleas't
Bigelow Horace W.(Freeland & Co.) h 300 Main
Bigelow John J. cutter for A. P.Ware, h 1 Hudson
Bigelow John W. wireworker, h 24 Newbury
BIGELOW JONAH H. wireworker, Sargent's
 block, h 15 Chatham
Bigelow L. H. clerk, bds 84 Southbridge
Bigelow Silas, boot finisher, h 84 Southbridge
Bigelow Solomon S. carpenter, h 5 Mason
Bigelow Walter, farmer, Burncoat
Bigelow Walter R. carpenter, h 8 Wash. Square
Billie Exivie, shoemaker, bds 32 Mechanic
Billing Mrs. Aaron, h 1 Orange
Billing Henry, h 1 Orange
Billings Hiram H. grocer, 48 Central, bds 80 Main
Billings James B. mach. ct. mill, h 44 Pleasant
Birnbaum Chas. wiredrawer, h 25 Grove
Birnbaum Frank, wiredrawer, bds 25 Grove
Bishop Henry F. dentist, h 14 Pearl
Bishop Joel H. machinist. bds 226 Main
Bishop Van Ornam, machinist, bds 32 Mechanic
Bishop Wm. H. h 314 Main   [Thomas
Bixby Austin W. pattern maker, Exchange, h 15
Bixby Geo. A. clk, 3 Bangs block. bds 15 Thomas
Bixby Geo. H. brass moulder, h Wall [h Webster
Bixby Jacob W. dresser tender, Trowbridgeville,
Bixby Montcalm, bootfinisher, bds 199 Pleasant
Black Amos R. farmer. h Salisbury
Black George, farmer, h 3 Salisbury
Black John, farmer, Salisbury
Black J. E. farmer, Cambridge
Black Mrs. Susan W. h 40 Grove
Blackmer Hiram M. carpenter, h 19 Carroll
Blair Mrs. Charles, Pleasant
Blair Robert H. farmer, Pleasant
Blaisdell Guilford C. machinist, bds 51 Austin
Blaisdell Parrit, machinist, h 51 Austin
Blake Barnum H. farmer, h Adams square
Blake D. D. (C. H. & D. D.) h 4 Newport

Blake Charles H. & D. D. machine jobbers, cor Union and Exchange, h 12 Arch
Blake Mrs. E. D. h 77 Summer
Blake Grenville, Quinsigamond
Blake H. G. O. teacher, h 3 Bowdoin
Blake James B. agt. Wor. Gas Co. Lincoln House
Blake R. E. machinist, bds 24 Central
Blake Simon, stone mason, h Suffolk
BLAKE S. E. & Co. manuf'rs hemmers, Armsby's building, h 6 Sudbury
Blake T. D. tinman, 24 Central
Blake Urial T. machinist, h 5 Prospect
Blakslee Mrs. Mary, h 3 Foundry
Blakeslee Wm. H. moulder, h 16 Washington
Blanchard Andrew J. bootfinisher, h Salisbury
Blanchard Chas. wheelmaker, bds 309 Main
Blanchard Geo. H. machinist, h Salisbury
Blanchard Jonathan G. artist, h 6 Maple
Blanchard Monroe, shoemaker, bds 17 Summer
Blanchard Wm. boarding, h 80 Main
Blanchard Wm. H. clerk, bds 80 Main
Blankenhorn Christopher, laborer, h 3 Millbury
Bliss C. A. h 13 Summer
Bliss Edward E. farmer, Woodland place
Bliss Edwin H. clerk, bds 1 Congress
Bliss Geo. L (Thurston & Bliss), 50 Central
Bliss Harrison, Central Exchange, h 2 Lincoln
Bliss Timothy S. road maker, h 26 Irving
Blodgett Calvin, lawyer, bds 9 Maple   [abeth
Blodget Nye P. machinist, cor Belmont and Eliz-
Blood Albert S. carriage maker, h 1 Green
BLOOD GEO. hatter, 125 Main, h John
Blood F. (O. Blood & Sons,)bds 19 Park
Blood J. L. painter, bds 36 Front   [Park
Blood Otis & Sons, carriage makers, Canal, h 19
Blood Otis H. (O. Blood & Sons,)h Chatham place
Blood Mrs. O. H. h 4 Wellington
BLOS WM. C. cabinet maker. Waldo, h 8 Central
Boardman Mrs. Teresa S. h 37 Salem
Bodwell Philander, truckman, h 13 Grafton
Boehmer P. (Zaeder & B.) 8 Foster
Bolce John F. farmer, Webster
Bolar Hermon, wiredrawer, h Langdon
Bolio Joseph, teamster, h 12 Lovell's court
Bolio King, stone cutter, h Belmont
Boland Tobias, railroad contractor, h 19 Temple
Bolster Geo. W. hostler, bds Webster
Bolster Leander, (Bolster & Son,) bds 24 Central
Bolster M. L. paper hanger, h 8 Green
Bolster Moses L. Jr., paper hanger, bds 8 Green
Bolster (Olney) & Son (L.) box-makers, Central, h 24 Central
Bolton Emery, laborer at Barber's, W. Boylston
Bond F. Alonzo, farmer, Benefit
Bond Jeremiah, agent, h 9 Portland
Bond Mrs. John B. h 1 Warren
Bond John S. butcher, h 58 Austin
Bond Joseph, farmer, Lincoln
Bond Joseph E. farmer, Lincoln
Bond S. F. machinist, h 12 Crown
Bonner Alexander, farmer, h Endicott   [Foster
Bonney Geo. F. & Co.(A. W. Wight)livery stable,
Bonzey Charles P. at N. Washburn's, h 5 Frank-
Booker Sanford, wire drawer at Goddards   [lin
Boomer Rev. Job B h 54 Austin
Boone Thomas, prof. Latin and Mathematics, College Holy Cross
Booth Charles, wire drawer, h 124 Southbridge
Booth James, reed maker, 14 Union, h N. Ashland
Booth Mason, painter, h 23 Orchard
Booth Wm. spinner, h Leicester, V. F.   [mer
Bootman Wm. O. at J. M. Goodell's, bds 95 Sum-
Borden John, stucco worker, h Edward cor Laurel

Boswell Charles H. machinist, bds 400 Main
Boswell F. W. wheel maker, bds 400 Main
Boswell Henry, machinist, h 400 Main   [Main
Boswell James S. watchmaker at Lamb's, bds 400
Bothwell E. G. wiredrawer, h 30 Grove
Bothwell Miss Mary E. teacher, bds Apricot
Bottomly Charles S. machinist,bds 19 Washington
Bottomly Charles L. wiredrawer, h Millbury
Bottomly Wm. boot crimper, h 32 Exchange
Botume George, clicker, bds 343 Main
Boulger Michael J. carpenter, h Leicester, V. F.
Bourne Franklin J. clerk at Tinkham's, bds 36
Bowen Charles, farmer, Plantation   [Front
Bowen Charles E. clerk, bds 343 Main
Bowen Mrs. Ebenezer H. h 343 Main
Bowen George, bds Lincoln house.
Bowen Smith, farmer, Plantation
Bowen Theodore, painter, h 14 Carrol
Bowen Truman, pastry cook, h 30 Hanover
Bowen Warren, painter, h 23 Summer
Bowers Lyman, at Wheeler's, h 18 Grove   [mer
Bowers Wm H. engineer Nashua R. R. b 81 Sum-
Bowker Chas. A. painter, 233 Main, h 77 South-bridge   [Clinton
Bowker George, clerk at S. R. Heywood's, bds 4
Bowker Sewall H. man'r hats & bonnets, Flagg's building, h 8 Harvard
Bowles Geo. T. shoemaker, Webster
Bowles Thomas, hatter, h 2 Central
Bowman Samuel M. machinist, bds 41 Summer
Boyce Rev. John, pastor St. John's church, h 20
Boyce Walter, laborer, 26 Temple   [Temple
Boyd Geo. bootmaker, h Apricot cor. Parsons
Boyd Henry, machinist, h Mill, N. W.
Boyd James, at Prov. Ft. house, bds 7 Winter
Boyd James, bootmaker, h 214 Pleasant
Boyden David, h 6 Irving   [14 Harvard
Boyden Elbridge, architect and civil engineer, h
Boyden Geo. Nashua R. R. shop, bds 83 Exchange
Boyden Geo E. bds 14 Harvard
Boyden H. W. painter, h 156 Main
Boyden John, machinist, h 13 Myrtle
Boyden John, broker, 2 Lin house b'lk, h Ashland
Boyden Joseph, h College   [cor. Pleasant
Boyden Joseph B. armorer, h 21 Myrtle
Boyden Jubal, farmer, bds College
Boyden Lewis, farmer, h Chelsea
Boyden Royal, blacksmith, h Barclay
Boylan Mrs. Sarah, h 99 Summer
Boyle James, laborer, h cor. Ward and Foyle
Boyle James, boottreer, h 49 Mechanic
Boyle John, moulder, h 3 Lamartine
Boyle Michael, painter, h Cypress
Boyle Patrick, moulder, bds Columbia
Boyle Patrick, woolwasher, bds 8 Millbury
Boyle Thomas, moulder, h 1 Lamartine
Boynton Edwin N. bds 8 Orange
Bracket Amos, veterinary surgeon, h 10 Shrews-
Bracket Calvin R. shoemaker, Tatnuck   [bury
Brackett Edwin A. millinery and fancy goods, 178 Main, h 2 Charlton
Brackett Gilbert, bds 10 Shrewsbury
Bradbury Edwin, machinist.ct. mill, h 4 Lexington
Bradbury Mrs. Susan, h 3 Blackstone
Bradbury Sam'l W. tinworker, bds Farmers Hotel
Bradford Edwin W. asst. at Telegraph office, bds 66 Austin
Bradford Geo. cigar maker, h 66 Austin
Bradford John, shoemaker, bds 63 Southbridge
Bradford Wm. B. wire finisher, bds 66 Austin
Bradish E. W. at Bowker's bonnet factory, bds 8 Harvard
Bradley Henry O. cl'k, h Elizabeth cor. Reservoir

Ayres Windsor, crimper, h rear 15 School
BABBITT HARRISON W. auctioneer, h 73 Pleasant
Babbitt Lewis daguerrean artist, 5 Piper block, h 6 Charlton
Babbitt Samuel F. carpenter, h John
Babcock Abraham, machinist, bds Elliott
Babcock Edward P. supt. of repairs W R R, h Grafton
Bacon Albert J. bootmaker at W. Bliss', h 13 Union
Bacon Charles H. machinist, bds Leicester st.
Bacon Mrs. Elizabeth, h Leicester
Bacon Julius E. clerk at W and Nashua R R ticket office
Bacon L. L. attendant at hospital
Bacon Martin, fireman B & W R R, bds 13 Mechanic
Bacon Peter C. counsellor, 1 Central Exchange, h 18 Elm
Bacon Samuel, h Oxford place
Back Arthur T. machinist, h 4 Winter
Back Wm. machinist, Wood, Light & Co. h N. Ashland
Bagnel Philip, moulder at Wheeler's
Bahan Michael, moulder, h 42 Mechanic
Bailey Benj. F. farmer, Bailey
Bailey Elisha K carpenter, h 9 Prospect
Bailey Francis A. carpenter, bds Edward
Bailey George. watchman, at B & W R R, h Grafton
Bailey Kendall, terracotta worker, bds 6 Pearl
Bailey Mrs. Adah, h Orchard
Bailey Samuel A. painter, Court mill, bds 4 Glen
Bailey Samuel A. painter, Court mill, h 11 Lincoln
Bailey S. H. clerk, bds 1 Portland
Bailey Silas, farmer, Bailey
Baird Mrs. Mary, h Grafton
Baird Thomas N. carpenter, Court mill, h 14 Grove
Baker Asa, carpenter, h 18 Winter
Baker Charles H. building mover, h 1 East Central
Baker Cyrus, carpenter, h 10 Green
Baker David, moulder, h Pine
Baker David J. livery stable, Webster
Baker Edward, agent and collector, h Newbury
Baker Francis, armorer, bds Exchange court
Baker Geo. F. bootmaker, bds Thomas
Baker Healy, (W, & H Baker) h 4 High
Baker Henry P. bds Clinton square
Baker James H. carpenter, h 40 Portland
Baker James S. moulder at Wheeler's, h Carroll
Baker John P. at H. Griffin & Co's. h Clinton
Baker Joseph C. coachman at Levi Lincoln's, Elm
Baker Lovell Jr. deputy sheriff and coroner, 3 Brinley hall
Baker Luther V. crimper, bds 71 Front
Baker Niles E mechanic at Court mill, bds 1 Concord
Baker Peter, laborer at Grove mill, h Grove
Baker Thomas J. boot bottomer, bds Cambridge
Baker Wm. J. (Waite, Chadsey & Co.) bds 1 Maple
Baker W. & H. furniture, 244 Main, h New Worcester

Balcom Madison A. clicker, h 59 Southbridge
Balcom Sumner W. daguerreau artist, 16 Harrington cor.
Baldwin Benj. hostler, bds Mrs. Wakefield's, Union
Baldwin Edward, laborer, h Madison
Baldwin George, cabinet maker, h 17 Salem
Ballard Chas. H. machinist at Ball & Rice, h 39 Summer
Ballard Salem L. machinist, h 36 Orange
Ballard Thomas E. cabinet maker, bds 4 Maple Court
Ball Mrs. C. A. R. 19 School
Ball Ebenezer, grocer, 48 Central, h 38 Summer
Ball Hollis, Grove mill, h Prescott
Ball Homer J. restorator, Har. cor. h Myrtle cor. So'bridge
Ball John G. clerk at American house
Ball Leander G. attendant at Hospital
Ball Lewis F. carpenter, bds 5 High
Ball Lyman E. armorer, bds 38 Summer
Ball Phineas, surveyor, 14 Cen. Exchange, h Grove
Ball, (Richard) & Rice (Thos. H.) manufacturers planing
    machines, Union mill, h Chestnut, corner Walnut
Ball Sawyer, architect, 14 Central Exchange, bds Grove
Ballord Marshal S. h 16 Portland
Ballou Amasa, painter, h 6 Southbridge
Ballou Darwin T. boot finisher, h Edward
Bancroft Chas P. auctioneer, h 17 Portland
Bancroft Chas. S. teamster, h Webster
Bancroft Henry L. carpenter, 9 Austin
Bancroft Joseph R. upholsterer at Bradley's h 13 Myrtle
Bancroft James H. acct.. 7 Cen. Exchange, bds 25 Thomas
Bancroft Nelson, farmer, h Lincoln
Bancroft Timothy, farmer, Lincoln
Bancroft Timothy W. auctioneer &c. 175 Main, h 23 Front
Bang Thomas, boot treer, Stone's, bds 1 Beach
Bangs Anson, carpenter, h Pleasant
Banister Emory, h Harvard
Banister Geo. C. machinist, h Lexington
Banister Jeremiah, machinist, h Lexington
Banister Julius K. clerk at Livermore's, bds 14 Park
Banister Samuel, clerk at Pratt's, 84 Main, h 14 Park
Banning Augustus, farmer, h Mill
Banning Erastus M. farmer, h Pleasant
Barber Almon A. engineer, Allen & Thurber's, h 18 Ex.
Barber Benjamin, stone cutter, h 15 Green .
Barber Geo. A. boot crimper, h Laurel
Barber James, 10 Winter
Barber John, farmer, Granite
Barber Josiah, car repairer, W. depot, h rear 3 Gold
Barber Levi, machinist, h Lafayette
Barber Silas, farmer, West Boylston
Barber Walter, armorer, bds Franklin House
Barber Wm. farmer, West Boylston
Barber (W. T.) & Stowell (F. P.) butchers, Ex. bds 45 Thos

Bradley John, tailor, bds 7 Maple
Bradley Osgood, car manu'r, Grafton, h 30 Front
Bradley Osgood Jr. car maker, bds 30 Front
Bradley Thomas H. machinist, bds 18 Lincoln
Bradshaw Thos.C. cutter at A. Davis', h 91 Pleas-
Brady Charles wiredrawer, Linwood place   [unt
Brady James. h 1 E. Central
Brady John, at Strong's coal yard. h Gold
Brady John G. engineer Nor. R. R. bds Burnside
Brady Martin, Prov. ft. depot, h Ludlow   [court
Brady Michael, tinman, bds 12 Thomas
Brady Mrs. Margaret, h 99 Summer
Brady Patrick, bootmaker, bds E Central
Brady Patrick, switchman, P. R. R. h Lamartine
Brady Patrick, flagman, Prov. R. R. h Gold
Bragg Dexter S. bootmaker, h King
Braman. Perham & Co. steam and gas fitting shop
    Warren block, Pearl
Braman Bradish, cobbler, h Main, N. Worcester
Braman Charles H. h Main N. W.
Braman Jason C. mechanic, bds Main N. W.
Bramfield Thomas, bootsider, bds 11 Charles
Bransuk John M. wiredrawer, h 43 Green
Brauckman August, wiredrawer, 7 Elliot
Braun Andrew, wiredrawer, h Columbian Court
Braun John, annealer, h 43 Green
Brautigam L. musical inst. maker, h 26 Exchange
BRATZ GOTTFRIED, cabinet maker, 12 Me-
    chanic, h cor Border & Mason
Brazil Michael, at N. Washburn's, h 7 Beach
Brazil Patrick, laborer, at J. Bonds
Brazil Patrick, currier, bds 31 Mechanic
Breck Moses T. carriage maker, School cor Union,
    h rear Court House   [rear Court House
Breck Osgood B. clerk at Kinnicutt & Co's, bds
Breckenridge Sam'l, shoemaker, h cor Edward &
Breen Andrew, at A. Mars, h Millbury [Belmont
Breen Andrew, wiredrawer, Columbian court
Brennan Michael, grocer, 3 Millbury
Brennan Michael, laborer, h Lovell court
Brennan Thomas, weaver, h 7 Millbury
Brewer Alfred, engineer at Armsby's, h 19 Central
Brewer Benjamin H. machinist, h 27 Summer
Brewer Elzaphan P. wood dealer, Front st, h 79
Brewer John, farmer, Mill,   [Pleasant
Brewer Thomas, carpenter, bds 12 Providence
Brewer Wm. M. grocer, 234 Main. h 2 Irving
Brewster Dwight T. clerk at A. Y. Thompson's,
    bds 20 Pleasant
Bricard W. A. harness maker, 68 Union
Brick Mrs. Mary, h 1 S. Irving
Brideu John, laborer, h Garden
Bridges Francis, machinist, bds 3 Belknap
Bridges Joseph E. asst. baker at Hospital
Bridges Sumner, truckman, h 3 Belknap
Brierly James, machinist, bds 12 Thomas
Briggs Chas. H. farmer, Mountain
Briggs David E. harness maker, h 1 Clinton
Briggs Frederick W. carpenter, ct mill, h 6 New-
Briggs Job H. farmer, Mountain   [port
Briggs Rufus, farmer at E. & O. Curtis's
Brigham Augustus A. engineer at T. K. Earle's,
    h 92 Summer   [bds 17 Chestnut
Brigham A. P. clerk at Barnard, Sumner & Co's,
Brigham Calvin, farmer, Grove, Northville
Brigham E. L. & Co, fancy goods. 160 Main, h 10
    Portland   [Mechanic, h 5 Laurel
Brigham Edmund R. custom boot manuf'r, 16
Brigham Frederick. reedmaker, h 3 Elliot
Brigham Hollis B.at Thompson & Co's, bds 6 Pond
Brigham J. M. farmer, Grove
Brigham Justin, farmer, h Grafton
Brigham L. E. bootmaker, h 63 Summer

Brigham Louis, blacksm
Brigham Lucius L. (Ultra
Brigham Luther, farmer
Brigham Mrs. Nahum, h
Brigham Samuel C. blac
Brigham Sherman, farm
Brigham Wm.A.general a
Brigham Wm. E. farmer
Brigham Mrs. Wm. R. h
Brimhall Alvin, plowma
Brimhall Caleb, plowma
Brimhall Hosea, mason,
Brimhall Joel J. h rear 8
Brimhall Silas J. plowma
Brinkworth Jeremiah, sh
Britt Richard, laborer, h
Britt Thomas, Quinsigar
Britt Thomas, blacksmit
Brittan Charles, bds Lin
Brittan Josiah, brick ma
Britton James D. mould
Broad Mrs. Elisha, h 7 F
Broad E. H. 1 Court hill
Broadbent James, bootn
Brobston Geo. H. bootfo
Broderick Martin, labore
Broderick Michael, wire
Broderick Mrs. Thomas,
Brodman Frederick, arr
Bronson Alfred R. mach
Bronson J. M at Bowke
Brooks Amos J. carpent
Brooks Chas. E. grocer,
Brooks Elijah F. clicker
Brooks John H. farmer,
Brooks Joseph B. truckı
Brooks Miss Julia P. tea
Brooks Lyman, conduct
Brooks Mrs. Mary, h Cli
Brooks Mrs. Rhoda, la
Brophy Mrs Ellen, h 18
Brophy Joseph, carpente
Brophy Wm. machinist.
Brothers Christopher, F
Brosnihan Mrs. Hannah
Brosnihan Jeremiah, m
Brosnihan John, machli
Brosnihan John J. groc
Brosnihan Michael, tail
Brosnihan Thomas, labc
Broten Henry, cabinet r
Brown Addison P. mach
Brown Mrs. Albert, h 10
Brown Albert S. crocke
Brown Alzirus, manuf'r
    ers, Merrifield's bui
Brown Mrs. Amos, h 26
Brown Archibald, mach
Brown Chauncey, h 5 W
Brown Daniel, harness i
Brown David, laborer. h
Brown David P. bds 17
Brown David W. engine
Brown Elbridge, baker :
Brown Ezra P. farmer,
Brown Frederick A. uph
Brown George, farmer, :
Brown George A. h 19 l
Brown Geo. P. farmer, I
Brown Henry A. bootm
Brown James C. machir
Brown James, peddler, I
Brown James H. blacks

Brown John, machinist, h 9 Washington
Brown John A. wheel maker, bds 61 Summer
Brown John, machinist, bds Exchange
Brown John C. machinist, h 124 Southbridge
Brown J.Stewart, house furnishing goods 96 Main, bds 10 Pearl
Brown Jonas F. baggage master, at Prov. R. R.
Brown Joseph L. machinist, h Cambridge, N. W.
Brown Jerome, machinist, bds 5 High
Brown Josiah W. clerk, 148 Main, bds 13 Main
Brown Louis T. clicker, h 3 Bridge
Brown Lyman, tinner, h 1 Columbian ct
Brown Nathaniel, tenements, h 6 Brown's block
Brown Phelix, farmer, Green's lane
Brown Phylonzo, carpenter, h 42 Orange
Brown Richard, laborer, h Gold
Brown Robert T. 3 Exchange, bds 93 Summer
Brown Samuel, armorer, h 79 Southbridge
Brown Mrs.S.A. clairvoyant physician, h 62 Front
Brown Seth, clicker, bds 63 Main
Brown Sylvanus, (Buttrick & B.) h 62 Front
Brown Theophilus, (W. & T. B.) h 14 Chestnut
Brown Thomas, soap and candle manuf'r, bds 17
Brown Thomas, laborer, h 52 Shrewsbury [Park
Brown Willard, 17 Park
Brown Willard jr, (Kenkrick & B.) bds 17 Park
BROWN WM. upholsterer, 236 Main, h Palmer
Brown Wm. laborer, h 21 Blackstone
Brown Wm. & T. tailors, 220 Main, h 17 Pearl
Brown Wm. E. shoemaker, 233 Main, h 1 Walnut
Brown Wm. H. machinist, Exch. cor Union, bds 1 Orange
Brownhill Charles, last maker, bds 2 Vine
Browning Alfred, farmer, h Holden
Browning Charles A. shoemaker. h 5 Orange
Browning Geo. R. clerk, bds 41 Pleasant
Browning James E. & Co. bonnets, &c., Mechanics Hall, bds Waldo house
Browning J. G. printer, bds 3 Maple
Bruce David L. moulder, bds Highland
Bruce Erastus W. armorer, h 7 Lagrange
Bruce Ezra T. carpenter, h Highland
Bruce John jr. foreman Nash. R. R. car repairs, h 47 Central
Brumley Silas, wiredrawer, bds 10 Grove
Bruso Charles, laborer, h 2 Webster
Bruso Charles jr. machinist, bds Webster
Bruso Edward, watchman at Curtis mill, h Webster [ster
Bruso Francis, laborer, Webster
Bruso Joseph, laborer, Leicester
Bryan Wm. blacksmith, 57 Salem
Bryant Geo. P. dry goods, 4 Mechanics hall. h 15
Bryant Ira, carpenter, h 10 Wellington [High
Bryant J. T. clerk, bds 13 Main
Bryant T. G. tinman, 3 Shelby
Bubser Joseph, bootmaker, h 14 Brown
Buchler Henry, painter, h 8 Mulberry
Buck Charles, (Buck Brothers,)h 35 Beacon
Buck Brothers, (John, Charles & Richard,) chisel manuf'rs at Junction shop, h 33 Beacon
Buck Joseph, bds 35 Beacon
Buck Mrs. Maria, cleaner, h Mason
Buck Richard T. (Buck Brothers,) h 56 Southbridge
Buck Spaulding, machinist, h Chatham place
Buckley Cornelius, porter at Pinkham's, h 33 Temple
Buckley Daniel, laborer, h 13 Blackstone [ple
Buckley Edmund, bds 6 Walnut
Buckley Jeremiah, at Strong's, h 20 Blackstone
Buckley Michael, h 9 Howard
Buckley Patrick, laborer, h Larkin [Arch
Buckley Wm. T. gardener at I. Washburn's, h 1
Budrow Nelson, shoemaker, h 60 Exchange
Budrow Peter, striker, h 11 Market

Buel S. K. constable, h Grafton
Buffum Geo. R. machinist, bds 8 Grafton
Bugbee Lyman, Intel. office, 236 Main, h 17 Salem
Bugbee Thos. L. stone cutter, h 6 Plymouth
Bugbee W. S. at Brinley hall, bds 17 Salem
Bugle Thomas, moulder, bds 3 Lamartine
Bulah Charles, (Johnson & B.) h Palmer
Bulinger Charles, gigger, h 1 Water
Bullard A. B. W. chemist, h Belmont, cor East
Bullard Augustus H. painter, bds Grove
Bullard Charles, carpenter, h 5 Chandler
Bullard Francis, painter, h 33 Grove
Bullard Francis R. melter, h 1 Newport
Bullard Hermon, coal dealer, h Grove
Bullard Hiram, machinist, h 5 Arch
Bullard Lyman D. painter, h 22 Union [Elm
Bullock Alex'r H. counsellor, Waldo block, h 26
Bullock Eugene, moulder, 104 Southbridge
Bullock John, shoemaker, h Pink
Bullock Richard, laborer, h N. Ashland
Bullock Sylvanus G. jobber, h 2 King
Bullock Thos. H. boottreer, h 44 Washington
Bundy Danford H. boot repairer, 2 Thomas, h 4
Bundy Julius A. lastmaker, h 56 Main [Carroll
Bunker Cromwell, sea captain, h 6 Southbridge
Burbank Asa L. & Co. (E. Dorr.) watches & jewelry, 205 Main, h 87 Summer [& Millbury
Burbank Charles W. machinist, bds cor Vernon
Burbank Mrs. David, h Vernon cor Millbury
Burbank David, machinist, h Greenwood
Burbank E. G. carriage painter, h 12 Salem
Burbank Geo. G. clerk at Jas. Green's, h 22 Lincoln [ison
Burbank James L. (M. B. Green & Co.) h 4 Madison
Burbank Nathan G. machinist, bds 1 Bartlet place
Burbank Samuel H. h Vernon
Burbank Silas D. machinist, h Greenwood
Burbank Timothy T. teamster, Quinsigamond
Burbank Wm. T. painter, Mechanic, h Franklin court
Burdick Theodore, plowmaker, at court mills
Burgess Alvin T. mason, h 11 Myrtle
Burgess Daniel S. mason, h 10 Providence
Burgess Joseph A. mason, bds 10 Providence
Burgess Tristam, clerk at Upton's, bds 2 Central
Burgin Lewis, at court mills, h 14 Main
Burke Mrs. Anne, h 2 S. Irving
Burke Edward, bootturner, bds 28 Winter
Burke James, laborer, h Summer st court
Burke James, laborer, h Goddard lane
Burke James, laborer, h 1 Tremont
Burke John, clicker, h rear Bangs block
Burke John, blacksmith, 25 Shrewsbury
Burke Martin, laborer, cor Vine & Foundry
Burke Michael J. mason, h 2 S. Irving
Burke Patrick, laborer, h 9 Spring
Burke Patrick, carpenter, h 72 Mechanic
Burke P. J. machinist, bds 8 Winter
Burke Mrs. Mary, h 10 Pond
Burke Richard, laborer, h rear 7 Charles
Burke Richard, laborer, h 11 Franklin
Burke Sylvester, bootfitter, h 11 Charles [st ct
Burke Thomas, at Arcade Foundry, bds Summer
Burke Thomas, carpenter, h 28 Winter
Burley John C. clerk at S. Pratt's, bds 5 Portland
Burley Wm. ropemaker, bds 2 Central
Burnett Mrs. Cynthia, h 32 Irving
Burnham Rev Geo. W. h 18 Wellington
Burnham Samuel A. machinist, bds 81 Exchange
Burnham Woodbridge, custom boot & shoemaker, 13 Pleasant, h 21 Orange
Burns Mrs. Betsey, h 15 Vine
Burns John, clerk at Barnard, Sumner & Co's

9*

Burns John, bootsider, bds 21 Winter
Burns Edward, moulder at Arcade Iron Co. h 15
Burns James, laborer, h 80 Exchange   [Vine
Burns John, laborer, h Canal
Burns Joseph, laborer, h cor Central & Union
Burns Martin, laborer, h 1 Brown
Burns Michael, bootbot:omer, bds 33 Mechanic
Burns Patrick, teamster, h Garden
Burns Patrick, engineer, h 28 Laurel
Burns Patrick, laborer, h 54 Shrewsbury
Burns Roger, bootbottomer, h 80 Mechanic
Burns Wm. liquor clerk, h 23 Winter
Burnside Mrs. Samuel M. h 5 Chestnut
Burr A. P. milkman, h 2 Dewey
Burr George, gilder, h 7 Gold
Burr George, at Spurr & Priest's
Burr John, painter, h 67 Exchange
Burrage John M. (B. F. Otis & Co.) h 3 Prospect
Burrington Rev. L. W. bds Waldo House
Burrill Frederick, painter, h 26 Washington
Burt Albro, machinist, bds 25 Mechanic
Burt Geo. P. prof. of music, 2J3 Main, bds 5 God-
Burt Nicholas, machinist, bds 5 Goddard   [dard
Burt Thomas, machinist, bds 3 Seaver
Burt Wm. S. h 5 Goddard
Burton Thomas, mechanic, h 2 Dix
Bush Wm. druggist, 34 Front, h 5 West [Charlton
Dushee James, ladies' school, Clark's block, h 4
Bushnell Geo. H. joiner, bds 4 Glen
Butler Berzalda, h 54 Chatham
Butler Charles A. soap maker, h Gold court
Butler Horace W. sash & blinds, shop Cypress, h
Butler John E. bds 54 Chatham   [8 Irving
Butler Mrs. Mary, h Northville
Butler Patrick, laborer, h 24 Chandler
Butler Richard, laborer, h 2 Beach
Butler Wm. armorer, h Salem cor Madison
Butman Benjamin, h May   [Newport
Butman Charles, machinist at court mill, h 3
Butman Moses, blacksmith, h 14 School
Butterfield Geo. V. printer, bds 12 Thomas
Butterfield Hiram, machinist, h 20 School
Butterfield Wm. H. at Grove Mills, bds Grove
Buttrick Albert C. civil engineer, h Bailey
Buttrick (Olvin) & Brown (S.) woodyard, 62 Front
Buxton C. H. painter, h Garden
Buxton C. Evander, machinist, bds 42 Portland
Buxton G. H. hackman, h 10 Cherry
Buxton H. W. pulmonist, h 42 Portland
Bynner Edwin, agt. Com. St. Co. 2 L. H. Block, h
Byrne Edward, painter, h 16 John   [3 Otis
Cahan James, carpenter, h 6 Howard
Cady Joseph W. laborer at W. F. Pond's
Cahill Dennis, laborer, h 19 Franklin
Caldwell Andrew, armorer, h 15 Plymouth
Caldwell J. F. bookkeeper, 1 Mechanics hall, bds
Caldwell Seth, h 21 High   [Lincoln House
Caldwell T. W. printer, 179 Main, h 2 Elliot
Callahan John, tailor, h 48 Southbridge
Callahan John, at College Holy Cross
Callahan Joseph, laborer, h 5 Winter
Callahan Martin, at Wellington's, bds 1 Tremont
Callahan Martin, grocer, 30 Shrewsbury
Callahan Michael, gas works, h Carbon
Callaghan James, tailor, h rear 23 Winter
Calligan Mrs. Sarah A. 2 Union
Calligan Simon, wiredrawer, h Prescott
Callighan Patrick, shoemaker, College Holy Cross,
Campbell Donald, tailor, 1 Leicester   [b. Ward
Campbell G. S. clerk at Hood's, bds 20 Pleasant
Campbell James, farmer, h 28 E. Worcester
Campbell James, farmer, Apricot
Campbell John, laborer, h 32 Shrewsbury

Campbell John, moulder, bds 11 Temple
Campbell Patrick, tailor, h 24 Exchange
Campbell Wm. A. shoemaker, h 5 Myrtle
Cann James, wiredrawer at Goddard's
Cannon Anthony, laborer, h 14 Bridge
Canley Daniel, laborer at M. M. Chaffin's
Cannally John, laborer, h 37 Madison
Cannovan Edward, blacksmith at Court Mills
Cannovan James, blacksmith, h rear 72 Mechanic
Cantwell Patrick, at C. mill, h rear Quinsig. Bank
Capron E. C. machinist, bds 76 Southbridge
Capron Geo. farmer, h 136 Southbridge
Capron Gilbert, shoemaker, h 76 Southbridge
Capron L. M. manufacturer, h 20 Trumbull
Carberry John, laborer, h 10 Spring
Carberry John, boottreer, h 73 Salem
Carberry Patrick, laborer, h 15 Vine
Carew Andrew G. forger, h 78 Southbridge
Carey Charles F. clicker, bds south end Benefit
Carey Mrs. Emily, h south end Benefit
Carey L. H. bds Farmers Hotel
Carey J. W. armorer, h 27 Portland
Carlisle Geo. carpenter, bds 70 Exchange
Carlisle Warren T. machinist, bds 26 Thomas
Carney Andrew, laborer, h 12 Brown
Carney James, laborer, h 64 Mechanic
Carney John, painter, h 6 Carlton
Carney Michael, h 12 Portland
Carney Patrick, laborer, h 13 Millbury
Carney Patrick, at rolling mill, h 64 Mechanic
Carney Simon, laborer, h 14 Brown
Carney Thomas, bootmaker, bds 76 Front
Carney Thomas, currier, h 35 Temple   [8 Grove
Carpenter Albion, carriage trimmer at Breck's, h
Carpenter Anthony A. carpenter, h Lamartine
Carpenter Anthony F. carpenter, h Barclay
Carpenter Charles H. clerk in Stowe's, bds 20 Park
Carpenter Edward M. h Newton
Carpenter Galen, machinist, h 7 Fountain
Carpenter H. F. boots and shoes, 93 Main, bds 5
    School
Carpenter Lafayette, court mill, h Sunnyside
Carpenter P. H. clerk at Div. 42, h 30 Portland
Carpenter Seba, shoemaker, 93 Main, h 5 School
Carr Geo. H. machinist, bds 369 Main
Carr John, shoemaker, bds Vine
Carr Michael, sawer, h 9 Blackstone
Carr Patrick, laborer, cor Liberty and Belmont
Carr Patrick, rag dealer, h E. Worcester place
Carrico Benjamin, shoemaker, bds 33 Thomas
Carrico J. W. shoe manuf'r, 22 Main, h 33 Thomas
Carrigan Simon, wire drawer, h Prescott place
Carroll Dennis, bootmaker, h 11 Vine
Carroll Henry, at L. Sprague & Co. h rear Sar-
Carroll James, laborer, h Canal   [gent's Block
Carroll James, carpenter, h 9 Charlton
Carroll John, shoemaker, bds 11 Vine
Carroll John, shoemaker, h 5 Charles
Carroll Lotty, machinist, bds 4 Water
Carroll Owen, laborer, h 21 Blackstone
Carroll Thomas, clerk, h 2 Goddard
Carter Daniel, laborer, h Larkin
Carter Mrs. Emma E. h 4 Sudbury
Carter Edw'd, machinist, h Pond st. court
Carter Eleazer W. stairbuilder and carpenter,
    shop 18 Mechanic, h 52 Chatham
Carter Ferdinand A. painter, bds 9 Highland
Carter Joseph, moulder, h Pond st. court
Carter Milton T. grainer, 231 Main, h 6 Congress
Carter Rufus, jailor, Summer
Carter Wm. shoemaker, h 52 Shrewsbury [block
Carter Wm. flagman, Nash. R. R. h rear Bangs
Cartright John, peddler, bds 1 Bloomingdale

Cary Alanson, Supt. Grove mill. h Harrington av.
Cary Jonathan, stoves &c. 231 Main, bds 5 Walnut
Case John S. h 212 Pleasant
Casey Dennis, laborer, h 32 Shrewsbury
Casey James, laborer at Court mills, h 9 Burt
Casey John, bootslder, bds 31 Union
Casey John, laborer, h Blossom
Casey Michael, laborer, h Lovell court
Casey Patrick, hostler, h Cypress
Casey Sylvester, machinist, bds Cypress
Casey Thomas J. blacksmith, bds 9 Burt
Caslew Edward, spinner, bds 1 Millbury
Cashel Mrs. Anne, h 16 Pond
Cashel Morris, shoemaker, h 2 Tremont
Cassady James, ct. mill, h 5 Howard
Cassady John, wiredrawer, h Ward
Cassady Patrick, wiredrawer, h 41 Green
Cassady Patrick, laborer, h Ward
Casson David, butcher, bds 6 Grove
Casson William, farmer, h cor Belmont and East
Caswell Lendall, painter, bds 41 Summer
Caswell Lowell, carriage painter, bds 41 Summer
Caulkins Edward M. master mechanic. Nash.R.R.
Cavanaugh John, tailor, h 9 Vine   [h 31 Laurel
Cawood John, boottreer, bds Towpath
Cawood Charles, boottreer, h 45 Exchange
Cawley Patrick, laborer, Millbury av.
Chadwick Stephen, farmer, Salisbury
Chaffee Alden D. h 42 Chatham
Chaffee Josiah H. conductor Norwich R. R. h 83
Chaffin Elisha, h 42 Central   [Southbridge
Chaffin Jones, carpenter, h 5 Cottage
Chaffin Moore M. farmer, Melrose
Chamberlain Calvin, varnisher, h 8 Jackson
Chamberlain Charles W. clerk, bds 44 Pleasant
Chamberlain Mrs. Cordelia, h 33 Main
Chamberlain Ephraim F. farmer, h Pleasant
Chamberlain Geo. A. farmer, Salisbury
Chamberlain Henry, wireworker, bds Pink
Chamberlain Henry C. clerk at Stowe's, bds 38
   Austin
Chamberlain Robert H.machinist, h cor Gold & As-
Chamberlain Salem, mail agent, Nashua R. R. h
   Irving, cor Chandler
Chamberlain Mrs. Thomas, h 41 Pleasant
Chamberlain Wm. T. machinist, bds 8 Jackson
Chamberlin Mrs. Arathusa, h 6 Portland
Chamberlin Augustus L. peddler, h Pink
Chamberlin Henry H. manufacturer, h Hammond
Chamberlin Lyman, farmer, Mill
Chamberlin L. B. farmer, Mill
Chamberlin M. A. cl'k at H. Griffin's, bds 24 High
Chamberlin T. D. (Miller & C.) bds 1 Harvard
Chambers Geo. F. wire coverer, h 23 Grove
Chambers Hiram E. machinist, h cor Gold & As-
Chancel Thomas, laborer, h Shrewsbury. [sonet
Champion Terry, Norwich R. R. bds 7 Myrtle
Champlin Robert H. brakeman, h 12 Goddard
Chandler Benjamin, h 9 Prescot
Chandler George, loomfixer, bds 12 Millbury
Chandler George, h 18 Pearl
Chandler John, machinist, bds 12 Millbury
Chandler Nathan, Nashua R. R. h Oak Avenue
Chandler Nathaniel, fuller, h 12 Millbury
Chandler Wm. E. bds Chatham place
Chant Charles R, machinist, h 9 Winter
Chapel Newel H. tin pedlar, h 78 Front
Chapin Edwin, h 165 Southbridge
Chapin (Henry) & Dadmun (A.) counsellors at
   law, 5 Bank block, h Linden
Chopin Jason, brassfoundry, 101 Sum'r,h 5 Laurel
Chapin Jonathan, moulder, h 55 Summer
Chapin Moses, bootbottomer, bds 25 Mechanic

Chapin Moses S. daguerreotypes, American house
   block, h 24 Salem   [and Mulberry
Chaplin Benjamin, blacksmith, h cor. Prospect
Chaplin John, carpenter, court mill, h 23 School
Chapman Elbridge, printer, Trans'pt, bds 7 Maple
Chapman I. S. shoe store. 67 Main, h 7 Thomas
Chapman James D. carpenter, h 2 William
Chapman Mrs. Dora, h 30 Grove
Chapman R. T. carpenter, h Sunny Side
Chapman Wm. R. wiredrawer, h 30 Grove
Chase B. D. & Co. Agents for Sloat's Sewing Ma-
   chines, 197 Main, bds Waldo house
Chase Mrs. A. H. bds 3 Trumbull
Chase Mrs. A. P. M. boarders, h 5 Maple
Chase Albert N. machinist, h 18 Summer   [Main
Chase Anthony, county treasurer, Ct. house, h 258
Chase Charles W. painter, bds 30 Thomas
Chase Mrs. Esther C. h 8 Grafton
Chase Henry A. pastry cook, Bay State house
Chase Miss L. board'ng, h 30 Thomas   · [Main
Chase Mrs. M. S. dress maker, 121 Main, bds 76
Chase Olney B. truckman, h 19 Orchard
Chase (Rufus H.) & Nichols (H. P.) painters, rear
   26 Front, h 99 Pleasant
Chase R. P. boot manu'r, 20 Main, h 59 Summer
Chase Wm. armorer, bds 90 Southbridge
Chase Wm. M. gardener, h West Boylston
Cheever Wm. D. civil engineer, 240 Main, h 14
   Oxford   [bds 17 Chestnut
Chenery John A. book-keeper at Geo. P. Bryant's,
Chenery Horace, (Rice, Co. & Co,) cotton manu-
   factory, h W. Boylston   [pect
Cheney Charles J. clerk at Grove Mill, bds 11 Pros-
Cheney Edson D. flour & grain, 14 Front, h 329
   Main cor. Charlton
Chency Mrs. Eunice, h cor Chandler and Mason
Chency John M. machinist, bds 14 Harvard
Cheney Leonard, foreman at H. S. Washburn's, h
   28 Providence
Cheney Mrs. R. children's clothing, 249 Main
Cheney Royal, engineer, Nash. R. R. h 249 Main
Cheney Wheelock A. foreman Fiske's printing
   office. h 32 Portland
Cheney Willard, carpenter, h 2 Chatham st. place
Cheney Wm. A. printer, h 104 Pleasant
Chickering Cyrus C. bds 47 Thomas
Chickering John, care of school houses, h Pied-
   mont near Chandler   [mont near Chandler
Chickering Mrs. Martha, boards children, h Pied-
Childs B. N. grocer, 77 Pleasant, h 2 West
Childs Charles S. car builder, h 7 Grafton
Childs Charles W. armorer, bds 26 William
Childs (E. N.) & Walker (A. G.) bootmanuf'rs, 1
   Bangs block, h 64 Pleasant
Childs Gardner, car builder, h 17 Shelby
Childs George, bds 2 West
CHILDS JACOB, dentist, 206 Main, bds 2 West
Childs Nelson H. confectioner, 82 Main, h 23½
   Thomas   [ers, 26 Front, h Home
CHILDS (Norman,) & HOWE (J. W.) wire work-
Childs Samuel, peddler, bds 1 Bloomingdale
Childs Wm. S. car builder, h 40 Pleasant
Chollar John, farmer, h 163 Southbridge
Chollar John B. (Taber & C.) bds 20 Pleasant
Christmas Joseph, mason, h 3 E. Worcester
Christmas Samuel, shoemaker, h Mason
Christopher Joseph N. B. barber, bds 13 Prospect
Church M. h 103 Pleasant
Church Pulaski M. mastic roofer, b ds Suffolk
Church Stephen, farmer, h 13 Winter
Church Stephen Jr. wiredrawer, bds 13 Winter
Church Wm. die rimmer, h 15 Winter   [Cross
Ciampi Rev. Anthony F. President College Holy

Claflin Charles R. B. daguerreotypes, sphereo-graphs & photographs. 188 Main, h 2 Charlton
Claflin John, machinist, h 47 Pleasant
Claflin Oliver W. machinist, h 2 Bartlett place
Claflin Wm. J. machinist, bds 2 Bartlett place
Clapp A. L. R. clerk at G. Spurr's, bds 5 Maple
Clapp Charles, carpenter, h Tatnuck [tain
Clapp Elizabeth, at Water cure, cor. Arch & Foun-
Clapp E. L. carpenter, 45 Elizabeth
CLAPP FREDERICK A. hats and furs, 223 Main, h 12 Washington
Clapp Henry E. (E. D. Wetherbee & Co.) h 33 Washington square
Clapp Harvey, stone cutter, h 7 Gold [dence
Clapp James, laborer, W. R R. Station, h 23 Prov-
Clapp John W. machinist, bds 43 Summer
Clapp Mrs. Levi, h 13 Park
Clapp Luther J. farmer, h 402 Main
Clapp Silas, h 402 Main [219 Main, h 3 Gold
CLAPP SIMEON & CO. (O. C. Haven) shoestore,
Clapperton Wm. h Pleasant, Tatnuck
Clark Mrs. B. R. physician & midwife, 309 Main
Clark Chas. A. B. R.R. freight house, h Mulberry
Clark Edward, tin pedler, h 3 Newton [court
Clark Ezra P. h 13 Grafton
Clark F. H. teamster, h Quinsigamond
Clark Geo. F. carpenter, h 4 Glen
Clark Geo. H. painter, Norwich, h 7 Trumbull
Clark George W. h Providence
Clark Harrison O. real estate broker, h rear Unit.
Clark Henry M. hackman, h 33 Green [Ch. Main
Clark Henry O. h 39 Summer
Clark Henry W. clerk, h 15 Laurel [cor. Summer
Clark Hiram, engineer Bay St. house, bds Charles
Clark J. H. dry goods, 148 Main, bds Bay State H.
Clark Joel C. pattern maker, h 309 Main
Clark John, laborer, bds 5 Spring
Clark John, bootfinisher, h 34 Southbridge
Clark John, umbrella man'r, h 1 Tremont
Clark John, bootfinisher, h Cypress
Clark John B. clerk, h 11 Winter
Clark John F. farmer, Burncoat
Clark John F. Jr. h Burncoat
Clark John S. B.&W. ft. house, bds 26 Southbridge
Clark John S. (Draper & Clark.) h 80 Front
Clark John W. carpenter, bds 42 Summer
Clark John W. baggage master, W. R. R. h 7 La-
Clark Mrs. Mary, h Ward [grange
Clark Merrifield, overseer, h Abbott
CLARK SAMUEL, tinworker, Foster, h 57 Front
Clark Sewell, (Putnam & C) h 52 Central
Clark Thomas A. book-keeper for John Firth. h
Clark Wm. farmer, bds 3 Salisbury [18 High
Clark Wm. C. h 9 High
Clark Wm L. grocer, 40 Main, h 5 Walnut
Clarke Henry, physician, office & h 3 Chestnut
Clarke Julius L. at State Auditors' office, 388 Main
Cleary John, laborer, W. Boylston
Cleary Michael, bootmaker, bds Hinds ct.
Cleary Peter, ice drawer, cor. Crescent & Nashua
Cleland James, letter cutter, bds 5 Maple
Cleland Thomas, clerk, bds 63 Main
Clemence Henry, bds 3 Lexington
Clemence Henry M. machinist, bds 309 Main
Clemence Wm. C. P. carpenter, h Newton
Clements Mrs. B. h 22 Irving
Clements Eli, shoemaker, bds 18½ Portland
Clements Mrs. Nancy P. h Beaver
Clements Nathan S. draftsman, bds Beaver
Clemmons Sam'l,cleaner, court mill, h 12 Liberty
Cleveland Cutler C. mason, h May
Cleveland Edwin C. woolen machinery, 12 Cen-tral, h 24 Orange

Clifford Ansou, moulding sticker, at Merrifield's,
Clifford Chas. W. h Abbott [h 2 Edward
Clifford Daniel, glazier, h 7 Blackstone
Clifford Jeremiah, glazier, bds 7 Blackstone
Clifford Jeremiah, laborer, h 7 Howard
Clifford Warner & Co. prop'rs of Bay State house
Clifford Young S. carpenter, h 7 Irving
Clinton John, shoefinisher, bds 30 Thomas
Clissold Mrs. C. h Tow path
Clissold Stephen, spinner, bds Tow path
Clissold Walter, machinist, bds Tow path
Clough Francis A. barber, 197 Main, Union block,
Clough J. L. h 2 King [h 109 Summer
Coats Elon, bootbottomer, bds 76 Front
Cobb Andrew S. boot and shoe finisher, bds 31 Portland
Cobb Chas. F. machinist, bds 4 Lynn
Cobb Henry E. grocer, 3 Bangs b'k, h 43 Summer
Cobb Leander M. machinist, bds 4 Lynn
Cobb Leander P. machinist, h 4 Lynn
Cobb Lewis A. machinist, h 26 Salem
Coburn Andros, machinist, bds 81 Summer
Coburn Henry, machinist, h 35 Green
Coburn Lemuel. clerk, h 25 Laurel
COBURN JESSE J. junk shop, 40 Union, bds 80
Coburn John B. clerk, h 41 Exchange [Main
Coburn N. S. clicker, h 26 Mechanic
Coburn Peter, machinist, h 5 Ash
Cochran Wm. machinist, bds 42 Summer
Codding W. W. pop corn dealer, h 12 Grove
Coe Edwin I. clerk, bds 63 Main
Coe John N. bds Mountain
Coe Stephen T. machinist, bds 25 Pleasant
Coe Wm. farmer, h Mountain
Coes Aury G.(L. & A.G.Coes.)h Main,N.Worcester
Coes John G. truckman, h 30 Washington
Coes J. H. merchant. cor Leicester and Webster, bds Main, New Worcester
Coes Loring & A. G. wrench manuf'rs, Main, N.W.
Coes Wm. machinist, bds 28 Southbridge
Coes Wm. W. bootmaker, h 28 Southbridge
Coffee Edmund, laborer, h 25 Shrewsbury
Coffee John, chair painter, h 68 Front
Coffee Michael, laborer, h 4 Tremont
Coffee Patrick, laborer, h 37 Madison
Coffee Patrick, laborer, h 10 Hibernia
Coffee Patrick, tailor, h Shrewsbury
Coffee Thomas. clothdryer, bds 1 Millbury
Coffin A. S. life insurance agent, 205 Main, h 15 William
Coffin Edmund, carpenter, Quinsigamond
Coffin Edwin A. machinist, bds 12 Glen
Coggins Bartley, laborer W. R. R. bds Winter ct.
Coggins Thomas, laborer, h 9 Burt
Coggins Thomas, jr.flagman,h Canal, near Winter
Coghlan Daniel, bootmaker, bds 25 Mechanic
Cogswell John C. hostler, bds Bloomingdale
College of the Holy Cross, College street
Colburn Mozart, refreshments, Western Depot, h
Coldin Henry, wiredrawer, h Ward [6 Grafton
Cole Henry, farmer, h Bailey
Cole Joseph, barber, 233 Main, bds 2 Mechanic
COLEMAN CHARLES C. jeweler, Am. house b'k, h 2 Oxford
Coleman Jacob, blacksmith, h Lamartine
Coleman James, coachman for G. W. Richardson, h rear 70 Mechanic
Coleman Timothy, wiretemperer, bds 4 Church
Coleman Mrs. Z. h 2 Oxford
Collan John, h rear 11 Market
Colleary Charles, boottreer, h 3 Brown
Collester Osgood, teacher of music, 121 Main, h
Collier Ebenezer, h 4 Maple [11 Laurel

Collier Francis A. machinist, h 183 Pleasant	Connelly John, laborer, h rear 7 Beach
Collier John A. blacksmith, bds 11 Lincoln	Connelly Mrs. James, h West Boylston, Northville
Collier Wm. F. wireworker, h Abbott	Connelly Patrick, candle maker, h 1 Temple
Collin Michael. shoemaker, bds 6 Millbury	Conner Mrs. Ann, h 3 Lamartine
Collins Cornelius, laborer, h 2 S. Irving	Conner Barney, laborer, h Cross
Collins Daniel, horseshoer, bds 24 Exchange	Conner Corn·lius, mason, 39 Shrewsbury
Collins Edward, clerk, bds 20 Pleasant	Conner Mrs. Cornelius, h 40 1-2 Shrewsbury
Collins John, laborer, h 8 E. Worcester	Conner Mis. Dennis, h rear of 16 Shrewsbury
Collins John, Nashua R. R. h 7 Bridge	Conner Dennis, laborer, h Larkin
Collins John, bootmaker, bds 2 Hinds ct.	Conner Edmurd, jobber, h 12 Shrewsbury
Collins M. A. S. lumber dealer, h 390 Main	Cunner James, laborer, h 51 Shrewsbury
Collins Mathew, Wellington's coal yard, h Cypress	Conner Jeremiah, laborer, h 91 Southbridge
Collins Michael, bootmaker, h 4 Goddard	Conner Jeremiah, mason, h rear of 72 Mechanic
Collins Stephen, grocer. 15 Millbury	Conner John, laborer, h 27 Union
Collins Thomas M. gardener, 22 Temple	Conner John, laborer, h 1 Hibernia
Collins Wm. tailor, 3 Columbia ct.	Conner John, peddler, h 17 E. Central
COLLINSON THOMAS, file maker, shop Armsby's building, h 7 Foundry	Conner Joseph, boot finisher, h 14 Madison
	Conner Mrs. Margaret, h 9 Hibernia
Colton Albert R. clerk, bds 13 Park	Conner Michael, laborer, h O'Rourke place
Colton Samuel H. nursery, Southbridge, h Queen	Conner Michael, laborer, h 2 Milk
Colvill James, card maker, bds 24 Grafton	Conner Patrick, wire sharpener, h Cross
Colvin Henry, wiredrawer, h 13 Millbury	Conner Thomas, shoemaker, h 4 Bridge
Combs Ezra, blacksmith, court mill, h 10 Lincoln	Conner Thomas, hostler, h 66 Front
Combs Royal, carpenter, h 23 Summer	Conner Timothy, bootmaker, h 12 Washington sq
Combs Samuel C. mechanic, h Russell	Connery John, laborer, h 9 Millbury
Combs Simon E. blacksmith, C. mill, h 18 Lincoln	Connor James, laborer, h 5 Shrewsbury
Comee Geo. W. crimper, h 16 Lincoln	Connor Stephen, carriage maker, h 11 Spring
Comer Michael, grinder, bds Mechanic	Connor Timothy, flask carrier at Wheeler's, h 16
Comins Danforth B. mechanic, h 44 Thomas	Connor Wm. bootmaker, bds Salem [Hibernia
Comirford Dennis, laborer, h Gold	Consen John, peddler, h E. Worcester place
Comrie James, boiler maker, bds 2 Lamartine	Converse Brigham, stone dealer, 1 Orchard
Comrie Mrs. Marion, h 2 Lamartine [21 Orchard	Converse Guilford, bootmaker, h 33 Mechanic
Comsett M. W. periodicals & library, 86 Main, h	Converse Harrison, Fuller's Express, h 300½ Main
Comstock Robert F. carpenter, h 1 Sycamore	Converse Luman D. truckman, h 1 Vine
Conant Albert S. clerk, 123 Main, bds 49 Main	Converse Merrick B. moulder at Wheeler's, h 1
Conant Mrs. Benj. K. h 6 Maple	Converse Wm. H. wiredrawer, h 2 Pink [Kendall
Conant Edwin, h 24 Lincoln	Conway Edward, laborer, bds Brown
Conant Harvey, bookkeeper, h 3 Webster	Conway Michael, book agent, h 16 Pond
Conant Mrs. J. dressmaker, h 49 Main	Conway Mrs. Patrick, h 15 Brown
Conant John, restaurant, 123 Main, h 49 Main	Cook George S. farmer, Fowler
Conant Marcus, shuttle maker, bds 24 Thomas	Cook Henry A. carriagesmith, h 8 Oxford
Cone Edward. shoemaker, Lafayette	Cook John R. book-keeper, at Pinkham's. bds 5
Cone John, spinner, Apricot	Cook Nath'l H. armorer, h 2 Jackson [Portland
Congdon Mrs. Fidella, h 2 Sudbury	Cook Norton L. machinist, h 4 High st. court
Congdon Samuel. bds Sunny Side	Cook Oliver K. farmer, Olcan
Congdon Sam'l B engraver & die cutter, Brinley hall, h Sunny Side	Cook Sumner, farmer, Fowler
	Cook Thomas, laborer, h 87 Front
Conkey John, loom builder, h 24 Grove	Cooke David W. mason, b 31 Austin
Conkey William, (T. Smith & Co.) machinists, h 15 Prescott	Cool James, moulder, bds 32 Thomas
	Cooley Henry, tinner, bds 2 Bartlett place
Conklin Geo. machinist, bds rear Court House	Coombs John, hostler, Bay State House
Conklin Henry W. (F. Willard & Co.) h Salisbury	Coonan John, laborer at S. H. Colton's, h King
Conlan Bernard, shoemaker, h 50 Southbridge	Coonan Martin, gardener, at I. Davis', h 33 Mechanic
Conlan Hugh, gas works. bds Linwood place	Coonan Thomas, laborer, h rear 31 Temple
Conlan Patrick, laborer, h Nashua	Coonan William, laborer, h Burt
Conlan Patrick J. laborer, bds Nashua	Cooney Martin, at Court Mills
Conley Mrs. Ann, h 7 Winter	Cooney Patrick, laborer, h 4 Bridge
Conley John, boot finisher, h 4 E. Central	Cooney Patrick, laborer, h 18 E. Worcester
Conlin James, painter, h 8 Charles	Cooney Wm. harness maker, at Tolman's, h 4
Conlin James, laborer, h Quinsigamond	Coonin Edmund, laborer, Quinsigamond [Temple
Conlin John, moulder, h 8 Charles	Coonin Patrick, laborer, Quinsigamond
Conlin Martin, Quinsigamond	Cooper Charles, h Cambridge
Conlin Patrick, laborer, h Nashua	Cooper Henry, weaver, h 2 Pond
Conlin Patrick, laborer, Quinsigamond	Cooper John, bootcrimper, h 28 Grove
Conlin Patrick, laborer, h Canal	Cooper John L. h 61 Front
Conlin Patrick C. moulder, bds 10 Pond	Cooper Mrs. Sarah, 4 Central court
Conlin Thomas, laborer, h Prescott place	Cooper Samuel G. machinist, h 51 Thomas
Conlin Timothy, laborer, h 10 Pond	Copeland James, machinist, h 24 Providence
Conlon Andrew, laborer, h 10 Pond	Copeland Salem, foreman at A. Brown's, h 27 Harvard
Connell Daniel, h 3 Tremont	
Connell Edward, h 53 Salem	Corbett Augustus, farmer, bds Leicester, N. W.
Connell Michael, armorer, h cor Salem & Madison	Corbett Henry M. carriage-smith, h 1 Carroll
Connelly John, bootfinisher, h 6 E. Central	

Corbett Otis, h Corbett
Corbin Abial, Norwich ft. house, bds 28 Portland
Corbin Simeon B. sash and blind manf'r, h Pleasant, Tatnick
Corcoran James, carpenter, h 24 Winter
Corcoran Michael, laborer, h 2 Canal
Corey Mrs. Eliza, h E. Worcester
Corey John, h 11 Chestnut
Corey Michael, bds E. Worcester
Corley John, laborer, h Burncoat   [Mechanic
Cormack Andrew, boot-finisher, h cor. Bridge and
Cornan Francis, wirethrasher, h 19 Liberty
Cornell Jacob, peddler, cor. Lafayette and Ludlow
Corrin James H. book-keeper, h 42 Portland
Corser H. C. P. boot-crimper, h 1 Lexington
Corson David, butcher, at 2 Bangs block, bds 6
Cosgrove Anthony, machinist, h 39 Green   [Grove
Cosgrove Francis, blacksmith, Water, h 7 Brown
Cosgrove James, Broad Meadow
Costello Stephen, tailor, bds 6 Lamartine
Cote Godfrey, R. R. agent, 13 Mechanic
Cotter Daniel, laborer, h Larkin
Cotting Edward P. att. at Hospital
Cotton James. painter. h 68 Mechanic
Coughlan Daniel, boot maker, 25 Mechanic
Coulahan Martin, at Ct. Mills, h rear Bangs block
Coulahan Patrick, painter and glazier, h 30 South-
Coulin Martin, Quinsigamond   [bridge
Courtney Thomas. picker, h Sutton's lane
Courtney Timothy, laborer, h 7 Tremont
Courtney Wm. brushmaker, bds 27 Mechanic
Cowen Miss S. M. dress-maker, 3 Piper's block,
Cowden Jonas, May   [bds 17 Chestnut
Cowden Silas, Nor. R. R. repairer, h Lafayette
Cowdrey Chas. H. machinist, h 20 Carroll
Cox Ebenezer, farmer, 361 Southbridge
Coxson William G. machinist, h 29 Grove
Cozzens Nelson P. machinist, h 15 Thomas
Cracken Geo. J. painter, h 42 Orange
Craft W. M. F. potter. h 22 Green
Crafts Eleazer, bookbinder, bds 5 Maple
Crane Emma. teacher Ladies Collegiate Institute
Crane Geo. E. baker, 86 Pleasant, bds 89 Pleasant
Crane Robert S. clerk, bds 89 Pleasant
Craggin Ebenezer, bds 20 Beacon
Cragin John, bootcrimper, h 21 Winter
Cratty John, laborer, h 76 Mechanic
Cratty John, laborer, h 8 S. Irving
Craven Mrs. Ellen, h E. Worcester
Craven John. laborer, h 5 E. W.   [h 26 Summer
Crawford O. T. book-keeper at Kinnicutt & Co.'s
Crawford Mrs. R., nurse, h 21 Prescot   [Pearl
Crawford Wm. H. book-keeper for S. Pratt, bds 3
Crimming Daniel, laborer, h 23 Franklin
Croake Dennis, laborer, h 13 Beach
Croake James, grocer, 26 Winter
Croake William, moulder at Arcade, h 28 Winter
Crocker H. A. melodeonmaker, 315 Main
Crockett James, gas fitter at Braman, Perham & Co.'s, bds 3 Carlton
Cromack Rev. J. C. h 9 Elliot
Cromack Joseph B. bootfinisher, bds 29 Portland
Crommead Charles, tailor, h Lafayette
Crompton Geo. loom builder. Green, h 11 Gold
Cromwell Oliver, laborer, h Bluff
Cronin Cornelius, laborer, h 1 E. Worcester
Cronin James, bootmaker, bds rear 21 Winter
Cronin James, carpenter, h 5 Tremont
Cron'n John, laborer, h Ward
Cronin John B. printer, bds 1 Eaton place
Cronin Marcus, carpenter, h 39 Shrewsbury
Cronin Michael, laborer, Dr. Snow's, Salisbury
Cronin Patrick, laborer, h 3 E. Worcester

Cronin Timothy, laborer, h 5 Cross
Croning Daniel, laborer, h rear 3 E. Central
Crosby Benjamin, bootmaker, h cor. Gold and Ashland
Crosby David, wire finisher, h 27 Grove   [sonet
Crosby Henry S. wiredrawer, h N. Ashland
Crosby Mrs. Mary, nurse, bds 16 Grove
Crosby Samuel B. grocer, h 8 Myrtle
Crosby Thomas S. wiredrawer, bds 16 Central
Crosson Patrick, moulder, h 73 Salem
Cross Benj. C. polisher. h Portland place
Cross C. H. carpenter, N. Ashland cor. Bowdoin
Cross Nelson A. wheelwright, h 3 Newport
Cross Wm. cashier Wor. Bank, bds Bay St. House
Crowe Andrew, bootmaker, h 4 Tremont
Crowe Mrs. Bridget, h 25 E. Central
Crowfoot Joseph. machinist, h N. Ashland
Crowley Jeremiah, laborer. h 11 Brown's Block
Crowley Thomas, blacksmith, h 31 Temple
Cuddy David. printer, h 3 E. Worcester
Cuddy Mrs. Mary, h 16 E. Worcester
Cullen Mrs. Dominick, h Canal
Cullen Martin, bootsider, bds 8 Howard
Cullen Michael, shoemaker, bds 8 Millbury
Cullin Francis, at Wellington's, h 8 Howard
Culver Austin L. machinist. h 34 Mulberry
Culver Geo. E. forger, h 1 Allen
Culver Joshua. h Jefferson
Cummings Chester, gilder and picture-framer, 172 1-2 Main, h 1 Chandler
Cummings Charles, carpenter, h 25 School
CUMMINGS CHAS. A cutler & gunsmith, over 205 Main, h 21 Orange
Cummings Mrs. Drusilla, h 102 Southbridge
Cummings (David) & Hudson (Wm.) ladies boot and shoe manuf'rs, Foster, h 13 1-2 Myrtle
Cummings E. A. financial Sec'y Ladies Coll. Inst.
Cummings Estes, at malleable Iron foundry, h 22
Cummings Frank, waiter at Lin. House   [Park
Cummings James, laborer, h Lovell's Court
Cummings James W. moulder, h 30 Hanover
Cummings J. A. varnisher, bds 25 Mechanic
Cummings Joel D. boxmaker, bds 42 Central
Cummings John, machinist, h 34 Grove
Cummings Michael, laborer. h Grove
Cummings M. W. carpenter, h 20 Chatham
Cummings Patrick, laborer, h 62 Salem
Cummings Richard M. at Shepard, Lathe & Co's
Cummings S. B. farmer, bds Jefferson
Cummings S. L. boxmaker, bds 42 Central
Cummings Timothy, moulder, E. Wor. place
Cummings Willard, moulder, h 32 Thomas
Cunliffe John, boottreer, h 55 Shrewsbury
Cunningham Elliot E. carpenter, h 1 Eden
Cunningham Edward, watchman at Bradley's, h
Cunningham James, helper, h 12 Pond   [Larkin
Cunningham John, laborer, h Salem cor. Madison
Cunningham J. E. carpenter, h 7 Clinton
Cunningham Lorenzo, cloth drier, bds 1 Millbury
Cunningham Roger, laborer at Isaac Mills'
Cunningham Thomas, laborer, h 7 E. Central
Cunningham Wm. laborer, h Gold
Curby Francis A. hackman, h 17 Thomas
Curran John, wiredrawer, h 70 Mechanic
Curran Patrick, laborer, h 50 Southbridge
Curran Patrick, bootcrimper, bds 49 Mechanic
Currier Aug. N. Sec'y People's Ins Co. h4 Harvard
Currier Barney M. wood-worker, h 9 Summer
Curtain Christopher, baggage master, Nor. R. R.
Curtain Mary, h 39 Mechanic   [h 4 Church
Curtain Patrick, grocer, h 60 Mechanic
Curtis Albert, manufacturer. N. W. h Webster
Curtis Albert W. merchant. N. W. Wor. h Tirrell
Curtis Austin, farmer, 104 Pleasant

Curtis Boriah, bank messenger. h Carroll
Curtis C. W. laborer, W. R. R. bds 77 Summer
Curtis Edward and Oliver. farmers, Stafford
Curtis Geo. blacksmith, bds 32 Thomas
Curtis James, laborer. h 24 Elliot
Curtis Jared, laborer, h 7 Union
Curtis Joseph, (E. B. Lamson & Co.) h 4 George
Curtis Joseph, farmer, Leicester, N. W.
Curtis Marcus, farmer, h Stafford
Curtis Randall, cabinet maker, h 2 West
Curtis Salem N. painter, shop 18 Mechanic, h 11
Curtis Sam'l G. farmer, Plantation   [Seaver
Curtis Tyler P. farmer, Lincoln
Cushin John, wiredrawer, h 5 Charles
Cushing Geo. W. millwright, h 5 Queen
Cushing Isaac, carpenter, h 8 Chandler   [gress
Cushman Chas. A. clerk 230 Main, bds 12 Con-
Cushman Hiram, shoe findings &c., 89 Main, h 20
   Washington
Cutler Charles B. clerk. bds 12 Thomas
Cutler Ebenezer, machinist, h 2 Summit [Pleas't
Cutler Rev. Ebenezer, pastor Union church, h 73
Cutter Chas. N. pistol-maker, bds rear 11 Lincoln
Cutter Nath'l F. plowmaker, h rear 11 Lincoln
Cutting Caleb (J. Barrett & Co.) h Jefferson
Cutting Charles H. cl'k 218 Main, bds 21 Thomas
Cutting Elmer, butcher, bds 266 Main
Cutting Frederic, book-keeper at L. & A. G. Coes,
   h Main, New Worcester
Cutting Joshua, machinist, h Jefferson   [Court
Cutting Mrs. Sophia J. tailoress, h 2 High St.
Cutting W. H. cabinet-maker, h 21 Thomas
Cutting Wm. at Court Mills, h 23 Prescott
Dadmun Appleton, (Chapin & D.) bds 44 Front
Dady Patrick, laborer, h S. Irving
Dahlman Henry, bootmaker. bds 49 Front
Dailey Michael, grocer, h Grafton
Dailey John, at Wellington's, bds Winter Court
Dailey John, machinist, h 13 Winter
Daily James, tailor, h 68 Mechanic
Daily John, gardener, h 57 Salem
Daily Owen, painter, h 4 Brown's Block
Dakin Levi, farmer, Chester
Dakin Luther, farmer, Chester
Daley John, laborer, h 7 Hibernia
Daley Michael, boot sider, h E. Central
Daley William, moulder, bds cor. Spring & Front
Dainty Thomas, wiredrawer, bds Columbia Ct.
Dallagan Mrs. Bridget, h Northville
Dallagon Patrick, lapper-tender, h Northville
Dalton Walter, laborer, h 4 Charles
Daly Daniel, hostler, h 1 Shrewsbury
Damon A. P. clerk at Vaill's, bds 80 Main
Dana Caleb, 141 Main, h 63 Pleasant
Dana DeLoss T. porter at Waldo House
Dana Ebenezer, farmer, h Plantation
Dana E. Beaman, brickmaker, h Plantation
Dana Geo. B. Plantation
Dana Henry, student, bds 8 Hanover
Dana Jesse, bds Plantation
Dana John A. attorney, 8 Cen. Ex. h Hammond
Dandurand Jacob, engineer W. R. R. h Providence
Danforth Joseph, cabinet maker, h 30 Irving
Danforth Patrick, laborer, h rear Bangs' Block
Danahy Edmund, tailor, h 5 Tremont
Daniels Adolphus, h 201 Pleasant   [11 Irving
Daniels Austin F. photographer, opp. City Hall, h
Daniels Byron, moulder, h 3 Piedmont
Daniels Charles H. stove dealer, Chelsea
Daniels Ezekiel, h 201 Pleasant
Daniels Ezekiel F. clerk, bds 201 Pleasant
Daniels E. D. carpenter, h 14 Fruit
Daniels Henry W. carpenter, bds 2 Congress

Daniels James, machinist, bds 30 Thomas
Daniels Joseph, machinist, bds 80 Southbridge
Daniels J. D. carriage trimmer, h 18 Harvard
Daniels John M. h 3 Piedmont
Daniels Sabin A. agent for A. Brown, h 325 Main
Daniels Thomas, machinist, bds 11 Temple
Daniels Wm. P. lumber, Grove St. near W. & N.
   freight depot, h 2 Congress   [11 Orange
Darling Alex. C. brass moulder at Wheeler's, h
Darling Cyrus, manufacturer. h Leicester, N. W.
Darling Darius, watchman, bds Taft's Hotel
Darling Francis, finisher, h Apricot
Darling Mrs. Sylvia, h Valley Falls
Darney Daniel, mason tender, h 25 Temple
Dart Chas. E. carder, h Leicester, Valley Falls
Daucet Louis, carriagesmith, h 60 Exchange
Daugherty Michael, gigger, bds 1 Millbury
Davenport J. wiredrawer at Goddard's
Davidson John C. carpenter, h 24 Irving
Davie Joseph, machinist, h 43 Washington
DAVIS ADDISON H. cabinet & desk maker, 51
   Front, h 18 1-2 Portland
Davis A. & Co. (L. D. D. & J. F. Fetey) melodeon
   reed manuf'rs, Junction, h 13 Beacon [Arch
Davis Alba C. machinist at Ball & Williams, h 5
DAVIS AVERY, clothing, 3 Flagg's Block, h 10
   Crown
Davis A. C. switchman B. R. R. bds 52 Mechanic
Davis A. E. baggage master, Nor. R. R. h 24 Port-
   land
Davis A. McF. counsellor, 188 Main, bds 25 Lincoln
Davis Benjamin, brakeman Nor. R. R. h Burnside
Davis Charles, tailor, bds 17 Providence   [ct
Davis Charles, clerk at Grove mill, h 11 Prescott
Davis Charles, teamster for Tabor & Chollar, h 4
   Central ct
Davis Danforth, farmer, h Granite   [Elm
Davis Edward L. at Washburn Iron Works, h 40
Davis Edwin T. clerk, bds 20 Pleasant
Davis Mrs. E. boarders, h 36 Front
Davis Francis A. farmer, h Holden
Davis Geo. A. att. at Hospital
Davis Geo. D. machinist, bds Hermon cor Beacon
Davis Henry A. mechanic at A. M. Howe's, h 4
Davis Isaac, painter at Court Mills   [Wilmot
Davis Isaac, counsellor, 141 Main, h 252 Main
Davis James, eating saloon, 1 Temple
Davis J. Edgar, clerk, bds 76 Main
Davis Joel & Co., (E. R. Estabrook,) granular fuel,
   foot of Foster, h 8 Charlton
Davis John B. clerk, bds 9 Maple
Davis Mrs. John, h 25 Lincoln
Davis John, carpenter, h Grove
Davis (John W.) & Jewett, (E.) refrigerator ma-
   kers. 53 Front, h Holden
Davis John W. painter, h 21 Austin
Davis John W. tin plate worker, h 37 Millbury
Davis Joseph, farmer, h Holden
Davis Leander, hostler, Bay State House
Davis L D. (A. Davis & Co.) h 50 Austin
Davis Mrs. M. A. h 1 Plymouth
Davis Porter, Warren's roofing, bds 8 Hanover
Davis Samuel, (Nourse, Mason & Co.) h Belmont
Davis Samuel E. bds Belmont place   [place
Davis Samuel N. blacksmith, 1 Pond   [Elm
Davis Solomon W. shoemaker, h cor. Hudson and
Davis Thomas W. (A. Peaslee & Co) h 61 Pleas-
Davis Walter H. farmer, Holden   [ant
Davis Wm. S. (Mellen & D.) 188 Main, rooms 7
   Pearl
Davis Wm. bag. master B. R. R. h 23 Mechanic
Davlin Felix, box maker, h 17 Blackstone
Dawson Adam, contractor, bds 44 Front

Dawson John, machinist, h 30 Green
Dawson Moses, mule spinner, b Webster
Dawson Thomas, wiredrawer, bds 12 Grove
Day Frederick, wheelwright, h 16 Liberty
Day George, carpenter, h 32 Temple
Day Hiram J. bootcrimper, bds rear 48 Front
Day John L. machinist, h 9 Jackson
Day Jonathan, dep.sheriff 3 Cen. Exchange, h 298
Day Joseph M. wiredrawer, bds Grove   [Main
Day Michael, blacksmith. h 3 Burt
Day Michael, wiretemperer, 13 Summer
Day Michael, laborer, Webster
Day Patrick, laborer, h 21 Blackstone
Day Samuel, bootcrimper, h rear 46 Front
Day Thomas, at Chas. Washburn's, h 15 Summer
Day William, laborer. h 8 Central
Dayton H. H. fancy goods, 124 Main, h 10 Crown
Dean A. B. attendant at hospital   [Pleasant
Dean Alex'r H. shoe manufacturer. 305 Main, h 74
Dean Geo. W. farmer at hospital, h 6 Fulton
Dean H. H. shoemaker, h 8½ Maple
Dean James, at Goddard & Rice's, h 2 Tremont
Dean (John) & Emerson, (S. P.) daguerreotype
    mat manufacturers, &c., N. W. h Leicester
Dean Paul J. hostler, bds 23 Exchange
Dean Z. H. stage hostler, bds 19 Thomas[Central
Dearborn W. F. bread driver, 86 Pleasant, h 44
Dearing Henry L. clerk at Goulding's. bds 20
Deedy Richard, farmer, h Taylor   [Pleasant
Deery James, assistant cook Bay State house, h 2
Deets Mrs. Harriet, h 16 Brown   [Charles
Defose Francis, wire finisher, h 10 Belmont
Degan Jeremiah, laborer, bds 39 Mechanic
DeLacy Peter, bricklayer, h 17 Orchard [Vernon
Delahanty Chas. J. book-keeper for Fox & Rice, h
Delahanty James F. moulder. bds Goddard
DeLand A. B. physician, New Worcester
DeLand Ebenezer H. physician, Main st. N. W.
Delano Isaiah, at Ellis & Flagg's, bds 12Trumbull
Delano John, mason, h 12 Trumbull
Delanty Michael, wiredrawer, h School
Delanty Thomas, wire drawer, bds Summer
Delany James, grocer. 19 Franklin   [29 Temple
Delany James, watchman at Rice & Goddard's, h
Delany James, carriage-smith. bds 7 Blackstone
Delany Michael, laborer, h rear Waldo
Delany Mrs. Sarah, h 10 Prospect
Delany William, laborer, h 7 Blackstone
Demond Joseph, carpenter, h Jefferson
Denin John, laborer, h Cypress
Dennis Henry, machinist, h N. Ashland
Dennis John B. tinner, bds 12 Thomas
Dennis John, wirepacker, bds Grove
Dennis (Joseph D.) & Houghton (Lemuel,) meat
    market, 207 Main, h 12 Myrtle   [h 6) Pleas't
Dennis,(Sam'l B.) & Lee (H.A.) carpenters, Union,
Denny E. A. local editor Times, h Clinton
Denny Ed. W. woodworker, ct mill, h 9 Highland
Denny Henry A. am. steam music co., Clark's
    block, h 12 High cor. Chatham
Denny H. W. supt. steam music co. h 250 Main
Denny J. Waldo, cook at hospital   [oming site
DENNY WM. S. ins. agent. Clark's block, h Wy-
Depot Jeremiah, blacksmith. h 22 Carrol
Derby Augustus, hackman, bds Lincoln house
Derby Geo. A. currier, h 4 Fulton
Desoe Joseph, engineer W. R. R. h 20 Shelby
Desper Wm. E. machinist, h 25 Shelby
Devens Chas. jr. counsellor. 2 Bank bl'k, h7 Pearl
Devereaux Anthony, laborer, h 45 Mechanic
Devereaux John B. tailor at Lewisson's, h 15 Coh-
Devereaux Wm. laborer. h 26 Madison   [gress
Devlin Aaron, laborer, Westboro'

Devlin John, laborer, h 3 Howard
Dewar Alexander, machinist at court mills
Dewar Alexander, machinist, bds 30 Chandler
DEWEY (Francis H.) & WILLIAMS, (Hartley,)
    counsellors, 318 Main, h 9 Chestnut
Dewey Geo. C. forger, bds 15 Charlton
Dewing Chas. P. pistol maker, bds 90 Southbridge
Dexter John B. carpenter, h 27 Southbridge
Dexter John B. jr. h 27 Southbridge
Dexter Richard R. carpenter, h 27 Southbridge
Dexter Wm. H. & Co. (Wm. D. Holbrook) flour &
    grain, 307 Main, h 3 Charlton
Dickerman S. E. American telegraph, bds 59 Main
Dickinson Henry B. stone cutter, h 24 Providence
Dickinson H. W. clerk, bds 24 Providence
Dickinson James S. clerk at C. A. Harrington's,
    bds 15 Main   [Main
Dickinson William, notary public, 98 Main, h 118
Diemar Frank, armorer, bds 21 Madison
Digelow Joseph, moulder, h 29 Summer
Dignon John, Quinsigamond
Dillon James, moulder, bds 3 Lafayette
Dinnan Terry, wire temperer, h Garden
Dinskelmeier Michael, wiredrawer, bds 25 Grove
Dinsmore Everett S. clerk, bds 5 Thomas
Dinsmore Silas, druggist, 59 Main, h 5 Thomas
Dippolt Andrew, gigger at Fox's, h 6 Millbury
Dippolt John, machinist, bds 1 Millbury
Divol John H. soap maker, Mill, h Stafford
Dixon George, machinist, h 3 Fulton
Doane Amos L. moulder, h 14 Fruit
Doane Wm. F. jr. boottrimmer, h 73 Southbridge
Dodd Alonzo, saloon, h 2 Lynn
Dodd Joseph H. (Towne & Co.) h 2 Oxford place
Dodd Simon, weaver, h 1 Water
Dodge A. H. machinist, h 43 Washington
DODGE (Andrew) & AMMIDON, (John,) livery
    stable, Foster, h 20 Washington
Dodge Benj. J. foreman Palladium office, h 18 Con-
Dodge Charles. bootcrimper, at 1 Park   [gress
Dodge Edwin L. carriage painter at Tolman's, h
    Grafton
Dodge George W. painter, h 14 Grafton
Dodge Henry T. carpenter, h Leicester
Dodge John A. hackman, h 11 Grafton
Dodge Pickering, manufacturer, h 62 Pleasant
Doherty Charles B. machinist, h rear 23 Winter
Doherty Frank, moulder, bds 59 Laurel
Doherty Hugh, merch. tailor, 119 Main, h 4 God-
Doherty James, hostler, h 14 Bridge   [dard
Doherty Stephen, boottreer, h 8 Brown
Doherty Thomas, printer, bds 29 Laurel
Dolan John, laborer, h 97 Summer
Dolan L. teamster, h Oak Avenue
Dolan Michael, laborer, h 5 Cross
Dolan Michael, coachman at D. Foster's, bds 31
Dolon Michael, h 4 Bridge   [Union
Dolan Neil, wire drawer, Oak Avenue
Doliver Mrs. John B. h 6 Pond
Dollen Archibald, baker, bds College
Dollen John M. farmer, h College
Dollen John M. jr. machinist, h Southgate
Donahue Barney, bootmaker, h Tremont
Donahue Jeremiah, pressman at Freeland's
Donahue John, wiredrawer, bds 1 Tremont
Donahue John, tailor, h Cross
Donahue Michael, wiredrawer, h 14 Pond
Donahue Michael, boottreer, bds 9 Fulton
Donahue Michael, laborer, h Oak avenue
Donahue Patrick, laborer, h 72 Salem
Donahue Thomas, laborer, h 13 Blackstone
Donahue Thomas, laborer, h 32 Shrewsbury
Donahue Thos. D. wheel maker, h 39 Shrewsbury

Donahue Timothy. moulder, h 30 Temple
Donanvan Mrs. Catharine, h 8 Spring
Donavan Dennis, laborer, h 27 Temple
Donavan Dennis, laborer, h 2 Milk
Donavan Michael, laborer at John Barnard's
Donavin Jeremiah, laborer, h 14 Vine
Donnaho Jeremiah, tailor, h 9 Tremont
Donnelly James, laborer, h 50 Southbridge
Donnelly John, laborer, h 26 Madison
Donnelly Owen, bootmaker, bds 50 Southbridge
Donohoo Hugh, heatler, bds 2 Milk
Donohue Cornelius, laborer. h 2 Milk
Donohue Daniel, laborer, h 3 Milk
Donohue John, laborer, h 19 Blackstone [Temple
Donohue John, moulder at Arcade Iron Co. h 7
Donohue Michael, wiredrawer, h 14 Pond
Donovan John Jr. machinist, h Charlton cor.
Doody Wm. laborer, h 26 Shrewsbury [Beacon
Dooly Richard, helper, h 4 Charles
Doran Michael, at Grove Mill, bds Liberty
Doran Neal, wiredrawer, Oak avenue
Dorchester Rev. Daniel, h Leicester
Dorfer John, laborer, h 24 Temple
Dorman A. E. at Exchange eating house, h 7 John
Dorman Charles K. (H. E. & C. K.) h 61 Summer
Dorman Henry E & C. K. Exchange eating house,
    h 5 Washington
DORMAN JAS. A. & Co. (A. L. Benchley,) music
    store, 203 Main, bds 1 Walnut
Dorman Lathrop, h 19 Bowdoin
Dorn Mal. wiredrawer, Oak Avenue
Dorn Michael, wiredrawer. bds Liberty
Dorr Enos & Co. (A. L. Burbank,) booksellers, 205
    Main, h 18 Summer
Dorsay Mrs. Martha, h 1 Tremont
Dorsay Mathew, laborer, h 1 Tremont
Dort Charles, cor. Cambridge and Southbridge
Dougherty Patrick, laborer at D. Harrington's
Douglas Francis, carpenter, 59 Chandler
Douglas John E. engineer at F. Willard & Co.'s, h
    18 Carroll
Dover Pierre W. machinist, bds 32 Mechanic
Dowd Charles, machinist, h 21 Summer
Dowd Michael, tailor, h 9 Spring
Dowd Timothy, at rolling mill, h 23 Franklin
Dowd William, laborer, h 9 Hibernia
Dower John, bootfitter, h 18 Park
Dower Patrick, boottreer, h 34 Southbridge
Downes Andrew, harness maker, h 4 Columbia ct.
Downes Luther, machinist, Cambridge
Downes Newton, carpenter, bds 37 Summer
Downey Dennis, clerk, bds 44 Front
Doyle Dennis, moulder, h 9 Burt
Doyle Dennis, hostler, h Cypress
Doyle James, laborer, bds Grove
Doyle James, laborer, h 18 Blackstone
Doyle James E. wiredrawer, h 30 Winter
Doyle John, at city coal yard, h Madison
Doyle John, laborer, h Grove
Doyle Michael, laborer, h 2 Howard
Doyle Patrick, hostler, h 20 John
Doyle Wm. bootsider. h Brown
Drake Mrs. Samuel, 84 Pleasant
Draper James. bds Plantation
Draper Mrs. Wm. A. h Plantation
DRAPER (Edwin) & CLARK (J. S.) flour & grain
    store, 95 and 97 Front, h 8 Portland
DRASSER CHARLES, ornamental japanner, 30
    Exchange, h 26 Exchange
Drennan J. M. at Crompton's, bds 11 Exchange
Drennan Martin. at H. S. Washburn's wire works,
    h 3 Bartlett place
Dresser Samuel, machinist, 3 Prospect

Drew Josiah R. printer, bds 2 Sudbury
Driscoll Alonzo M. Nash. R. R. repair shop, h 50
Driscoll Dennis, laborer, h 14 Blackstone [Front
Driscoll Dennis, at G. T. Rice's, h 37 Mechanic
Driscoll John, court mill, h 11 Spring
Driscoll Michael, laborer at C. Paine's, h 2 Milk
Driscoll Michael O. grocer, h 13 Spring
Drohan Nicholas, laborer at S. H. Colton's. h 13
Drohan Robert, moulder, h 1 Tremont [Beech
Drury Enoch P. printer, bds 18 Salem
Drury Ephraim, farmer, rear 93 Summer
Drury Ephraim L. watchman, bds at almshouse
Drury E. P. box maker, h 28 Crown
Drury L. B. supt. at Alms house, Lincoln
Drury Lyman, h 4 Sycamore
Drury Marshal L. painter, 13 Mechanic, h 36
Drury Mrs. Mary, h 18 Salem [Newbury
Drury Thomas A. machinist, bds 18 Salem
Drury Mrs. Wm. E. h 26 Grove [nut
Drury Wm. H. cl'k at H. W. Miller's, bds 14 Wal-
Dryden Geo. machinist, h 10 Glen
Dryden John, bread peddler, h 20 Lincoln
Dryden John P. machinist, h 15 Lincoln
Dryden Martin F. machinist, h 27 Shelby
Ducet Louis, blacksmith, 60 Exchange
Ducklow Joseph, moulder, h 29 Summer
Duckworth Geo. S. last maker, bds 2 Vine
Dudley Edwin R bootcrimper, bds 29 Portland
Dudley Geo. A. clicker, h 22 Main
Dudley James, farmer, Burncoat
Dudley Marcus, laborer, h Plantation
Dudley Sidney B. farmer, West Boylston
Dudley Wm. teamster, h 16 Seaver
Duffee Mrs. Thomas, h cor Mechanic & Bridge
Duffy James, laborer. h 10 Spring
Dufty John, laborer, h Cross
Duffy Michael, blacksmith, h 10 Spring
Duffy Michael, rolling mill, h 12 Bridge
Duggan Walter, machinist, h 87 Southbridge
Duncan Andrew J. farmer, h Lincoln
Duncan Harlan P. clerk at C. Foster & Co's. bds
Duncan Wm. engineer, h 17 Mechanic [44 Front
Dunlap Richard C. blacksmith, bds 12 Thomas
Dunlap Mrs. R.C. ladies' furnishing store 120 Main
Dunn James, at Dr. Sargent's, 256 Main
Dunn James, watchman, h 31 Temple
Dunn James 2d, tailor, h 9 Vine
Dunn John, tailor, h 33 Madison
Dunn John, bootbottomer, bds rear 21 Winter
Dunn Matthew, laborer, h Cambridge
Dunn Nicholas, laborer, h 14 E. Worcester
Dunn Wm. moulder, h 21 Franklin
Dunn Wm. C. clerk, bds 31 Temple [Chandler
Dunnels Horace L. shoemaker, h cor. Mason and
Dunster Wm. laborer, h Lovell court
Durfee Peter, Valley Falls [Austin
Durkins J. A. whitewasher & paper hanger, h 11
Durning Wm. moulder, h rear 19 Winter
Dusenbury Joseph, machinist, h 25 Portland
Dutton Geo. H. grocer, 41 Main, h 67 Main
Dutch J. C. (Knowlton & Dutch) h 35 Pleasant
Dwinnell Benj. D. clerk, bds 1 Congress
Dwight Josiah E. clerk for E. H. Sanford, bds 1
Dwye Philip, laborer, h 35 Mechanic [Portland
Dwyer Edmund, helper, h rear 12 Grafton
Dwyer John, laborer, h 23½ Winter
Dwyer Patrick, bootbottomer, h 10 Charles
Dwyer Patrick, waiter at Lin. house, h 13 Brown
Dwyer Thomas, bootmaker, h 20 Chandler
Dwyre Mrs. Bridget, h 6 Brown
Dyer Calvin, ticket master Bost. R. R. h 4 Cottage
Dyer Geo. H. plate printer,197 Main, h 20 Bowd'n
Dyer Joseph, fireman W. R. R. h 24 Mulberry

Dyer Thomas, stone mason, h Grafton
Dyson Robert, finisher, at Fox & Rice, h 3 Towpath
Eager Charles, carriage maker, h 32 Summer
Eager Charles D. supervisor at hospital
Eager Geo. L. at court mill, bds 2 Maple place
Eahort Joseph, cabinet-maker, bds Mechanic, cor Foster
Eames Edwin A. wheelmaker, bds 23 Portland
Eames D. H. clothing, Har.cor, h east of Common
Eames Geo. P. carpenter, bds Farmer's Hotel
Eames Levi, farmer, Rice's court
Eames Levi Lincoln, farmer, Burncoat
Eames Luther R. farmer, Rice's court
Eames Wm. farmer, West Boylston
Eary James W. blacksmith, bds 59 Salem
Earl Anthony, stairbuilder, bds 7 School
Earl Mrs. Henry, h 7 School
Earle Chas. G. machinist, bds 46 Central
Earle Clark, woodworker, bds 7 School
Earle Edward, (T. K. Earle & Co.) h 10 Summer
Earle Elmer, bootbottomer, h 46 Central
Earle Mrs. Enoch, h 14 School
Earle Geo. clicker, h 60 Austin
Earle James C. clicker, h 46 Newbury
Earle Joel, wiredrawer, bds Round Hill
Earle John M. bds cor. Fountain & Arch
Earle (Oliver K.) & Jones (W.) iron foundry, Union & Southbridge sts., office Union, h Edward
Earle Mrs. Ralph, h 24 Thomas   [ward
Earle Stephen C. bookkeeper at T. K. Earle's, bds 10 Summer   [dealers, Wash. sq, h 52 Pleas't
Earle (Thos.) Tenney (Chas. A.) & Co. lumber
Earle Timothy K. &Co. (E. Earle) card manuf'rs, Grafton, h Edward
Earle Wm. H. at J. K. L. Pickford's
Earley Michael, currier, bds 10 Charles
Eastman Moses L. farmer, Mill
Eaton Mrs. Amherst, h 19 Mechanic
Eaton A. J. real estate agent, 207 Main, h cor. Chatham and Quincy
Eaton Amos M. grocer, 19 School, h 15 Arch
Eaton Charles B. (E. H. Sanford & Co.) h Main cor Charlton   [h 5 Chatham
Eaton Frederick, boot and shoe repairer,233 Main,
Eaton Hollis, farmer, Bloomingdale road
Eaton Rev. Henry A. grocer, cor Pleas't & Mason
Eaton J. Fiske, cl'k at Freeland's, bds 5 Portland
Eaton Leander, watchmaker, 89 Main, h 5 High-
Eaton Mrs. Mary, h 49 Summer   [land
Eaton Marson M. printer, h 12 Lincoln
Eaton Marson, blacksmith, h 1 Dewey
Eaton Mrs. Nancy, h 14 Salem
Eaton Mrs. Russel, h 9 Mulberry
Eaton Mrs. Sally F. boarders, h 5 Portland
Eaton Miss Sarah, 56 Main   [Portland
Eaton Thomas B. acct. at J. H. Clarke's, bds 5
Eaton Mrs. Wm. Bloomingdale road
Eaton Wm. jr. farmer, h Bloomingdale
Eaton Wm. H. commercial institute, Bank bl'k, h West Boylston
Eddy Albert M. bds 77 Southbridge
Eddy Henry W. carpenter, Norwich, h 5 Oxford
Eddy L. A. jeweller, bds Waldo House
Eddy Lewis, carpenter, bds 77 Southbridge
Eddy Lorin, carpenter, h 43 Chandler
Eddy Milton L. clerk, bds 77 Southbridge
Eddy Samuel S. paper hanger, h 19 Oxford
Eddy Samuel jr. bookkeeper at Draper & Clark's, h 18 Oxford
Edgarton Jay, brakeman, bds 11 Temple
Edge Joseph, engineer at Crompton, h 10 Vine
Edgecomb Joseph, pattern-maker, 11 Cypress, h
Edwards John, engineer, h 22 Grove   [23 Shelby

Edwards R. C. h 17 Pleasant   [Main
Edwards Thomas, artist, 20 Flagg's block, h 294
Edwards Thomas W. at H. W. Miller's, bds 19
Egan James, painter, h 7 Temple   [Mechanic
Egleson John, laborer, h rear 32 Winter
Eidt Henry, French boot & shoemaker, 6 Mechanic, h 18 Mulberry   [Bartlett place
Eidt Jacob, upholsterer for J. B. Lawrence, h
Eisentrout Henry, wire drawer, h 31 Grove
Ekins John, bootfinisher, h 13 Millbury
Elder Ansel, Norwich R. R.
Eldred Edwin A. carpenter, bds 5 Clinton
E'dred F. A. hat store, 247 Main, h 17 Chatham
Eldred Wm. H. carpenter, h 10 High   [Orange
Eldredge Julius A. at Taber & Chollar's, h 42
Eldridge Abner F. machinist, h 15 Plymouth
Eldridge Mrs. Sarah, h 27 Grove
Elkins Geo. W. pattern maker, h 20 Providence
Ellinwood Chas. A. painter, ct mill, h 54 Pleasant
Elliot Alex'r, soap manuf'r, Lafayette
Elliot F. G. clicker, bds 27 Chatham
Elliot Gustavus, real estate broker, h Highland ct
Elliot Henry, cabinet maker, bds 2 Central
Elliott Fred. W. dentist, with Dr. Harris, bds 39
Main   [Summer
Ellis Mrs. Betsy, h 309 Main
Ellis George W. B. at Grove Mills, h Grove
Ellis Geo. boottreer, h Mason
Ellis Hartwell, bootcrimper, h 32 Thomas
Ellis James, moulder, h Benefit
Ellis Nathan B. (Scott & Ellis) h 29 Portland
Ellis Reuben A. tinsmith, h 57 Front
Ellis (Sylvester) & Flagg (Henry) butchers, 18
Ellis Wm. moulder, bds Benefit [Park, h 78 Front
Ellis Wm. F. civil engineer, 249 Main
Elvard James, blacksmith, Quinsigamond
Elwell Mrs. Jonathan F. h 3 Hanover
Elwell L. J. machinist, bds 3 Hanover
Emerson Benj. clicker, 12 Foster, h 8 Quincy
Emerson Mrs. E. K. boarders, h 17 Chestnut
Emerson Lowe (D. D. Allen & Co.) bds Bay State House
Emerson Sam'l J. whipmaker, Foster, h 26 High
Emerson Sam'l P. (Dean & E.) h Leicester, N. W.
Engley Davis B. carder, h Northville
Engley James N. real estate broker, h 4 Vine
English Phillip, upholsterer, cor. Exchange and Waldo, h 23½ Thomas
Eno Wm. F. spinner, bds Webster
Enright Michael, teamster, h 18 Winter
Enright Thomas, blacksmith, h 14 Winter
Erler Louis, armorer, h 7 Charlton
Ervin Edward, machinist, bds 28 Winter
Estabrook A. E. bds 51 Southbridge
Estabrook Daniel F. (Freeland & Co.) h 1 Crown
Estabrook Dennis F. paper box maker, 245 Main,
Estabrook Mrs. Eliza R. bds Pratt [bds 318 Main
Estabrook E. R. (Davis & Co.) h 54 Pleasant
Estabrook Geo. H. clerk of clerk of courts, h Pratt
Estabrook James, h 51 Southbridge [Southbridge
Estabrook James E. counsellor, 5 Cen. Ex. bds 51
Estey James F. (A. Davis & Co.) h 41 Chandler
Estey James L. printer, h William
Estey Nelson, farmer at Salisbury's, h Salisbury
Estey Wm. H. printer, bds 13 Thomas
Ethey Andrew, bootmaker, h 64 Mechanic
Eusebe Roy, blacksmith, h Mechanic
Everett Edward S butcher, bds 5 High
Ewell Jackson, blacksmith, bds 59 Main
Ewins Ralph, bootcrimper, h Franklin ct.
Exley Joseph, grinder, bds 59 Salem
Fagan Lawrence, shoemaker, bds 1 Water
Fagan Michael, h 1 Water
Fagerty Alexander, wire drawer, h Millbury

Fahey John. wire drawer, h Belmont
Fairbanks Asahel, shoemaker, h 63 Main
Fairbanks Charles F. boot forms, bds 2 Clinton
Fairbanks D. F. spoke maker, bds 2 Clinton
Fairbanks Eli B. carpenter, 103 Pleasant [nut
Fairbanks Geo. E. clerk, 242 Main. bds 17 Chest-
Fairbanks Geo. H. clicker, bds 63 Main
Fairbanks Henry M. blacksmith, cor School and Union, h W. Boylston
Fairbanks James, machinist, h 7 Fulton
Fairbanks Lewis T. machinist, h 43 Washington
Fairfield Geo. W. bookkeeper for Allen & Whee-lock. bds 296 Main
Fairchild Lewis, wood engraver, 24 Central, Ex.
Fairons Michael, tailor, bds 6 Lamartine
Fairweather Thomas S.dresser at Curtis' mill,h 17
Fales Andrew, machinist.bds 18 Irving [Webster
Fales Joseph, truckman, bds 5 Cherry
Fales Joseph E. pattern maker, h 18 Irving
Fallan Edward, laborer, h 8 E. Worcester
Fallon James, boottreer, h 21 Winter
Fallon John, gardener and grocer, h Lamartine
Fanning David H. clerk, h 44 Elm
Fanning Elihu H. engineer Nash. R. R. h 20 Wil-
Farley Geo. F. milk dealer, h 19 Austin [mot
Farley J. A. (Taylor & F.) h 55 Austin
Farmer John, wire cleaner, h cor Ward & Mill-
Farnham E. G. wiredrawer, h Grove [bury
Farnsworth Calvin, h 3 Maple place [Exchange
Farnswo.th Wm. A. travelling stationer, bds 22
Farnum Geo. S. & Co. (D. Arnold) boot manuf rs, 24 Front. h 4 Sudbury [West
Farnum Joseph S. cashier Quinsig. bank, h 1
Farr Geo. W. clerk at Burk's, bds 69 Southbridge
Farr Wm T. clicker at Stone's, h 69 Southbridge
Farrell Francis, teamster, h Bloomingdale
Farrell Mrs. Patrick, h 20 Shrewsbury
Farrell Wm. fireman, bds 2.) Shrewsbury
Favor John, tailor, h 59 Salem [h 33 Wash. sq
Fay Appleton, pattern maker at W. A. Wheeler's,
Fay Geo. W. wrench maker, bds 27 Hanover
Fay H. B. boot & shoe manuf'r, 6 White's block, h 26 Irving
Fay J. A. & Co. (E.C. Tainter. H. A. Richardson) manuf'rs of wood working machines, Junct'n
Fay Jerome, machinist, h 3 Plymouth
Fay John, at Grove mill, h 7 Belmont
Fay John, cook at Bay State House, h 6 Winter
Fay John, h rear 5 Howard
Fay John, laborer, bds 7 Howard
Fay J. R. shoe manuf'r, 6 Southbridge, h 5 Con-
Fay Lyman, bds 3 Mason [gress
Fay Mrs. Martha C. h 3 Mason
Fay Russell, carpenter, h 5 Fountain
Fay Thomas, moulder, h 7 Howard
Fay Wm. J. machinist, bds 6 Winter
Fay Wyman, shoe manuf'r, h 180 Pleasant
Fawcett (Edwin A.) & Warfield, (A.J.) fruit store, 250 Main, h 250 Main
Fawcett Jonathan, farmer, h 13 Chatham
Fellows D. F. blacksmith, Central, h 24 Thomas
Felton Mrs. R. millinery & fancy goods, 35 Main
FEMALE COLLEGE, on Providence st
Female Employment Society, office 100 Main
Fenner Benj. S. truckman. h Southgate [Assonet
Fenner H. W. engineer, W. R. R. h 18 Gold, cor.
Fenner Wm.G.machinist.bds 18 Gold cor Assonet
Fenno Chas. W. (Wm. D. F. & Son) bds 9 School
Fenno Mrs. Sarah, h 9 School [Main, h 9 School
FENNO WM. D. & SON, (C. W.) jewellers, 166
Fenton Jacob, armorer, h 4 Jackson
Fernald Henry W. clerk, bds 5 Portland
Ferris John, Quinsigamond

Ferrin Gilman, car maker, h 1 Warren
Ferritor Nicholas, laborer, h 47 Shrewsbury
Field Daniel W. ambrotypist, h 12 Charlton
Field H. T. machinist, h 17 Shelby
Field John H. clerk, bds 15 Main
Field Peter, laborer, h E. Worcester
Fillegan Patrick, laborer, h Foyle
Finley Thomas, weaver, h Langdon
Finn James, laborer, h rear 16 Shrewsbury
Finn James, bootbottomer, h 1 Hibernia
Finn Thomas, hostler, h rear of Waldo
Finnegan Charles, laborer, Northville
Finnegan Cornelius, brakeman. h 20 Blackstone
Finnegan Dennis, wiredrawer, h Belmont
Finnegan James; laborer, h E. Worcester place
Finnegan Jeremiah M. grocer, h 30 Temple
Finneran James, laborer, h E. Central
Finneran Matthew, laborer, h Cross
Finneran Michael. laborer, h 13 E. Worcester
Finneran Patrick, h 12 E. Worcester
Finneran Thomas, laborer, h 10 E. Worcester
Finneran Wm. wiredrawer, bds Cross
Finney Ralph, at Nashua R. R. bds 95 Main
Firth Abraham, agent B. & W. R. R. h 8 Walnut
FIRTH JOHN, crockery, &c. 130 Main, bds B. St. [House
Fish David, h 1 Dix
Fish David A. blacksmith, h Forest, cor Holden
Fish Henry C. iron railing, Union cor Exchange, h 2 Church [Block, bds 1 Dix
FISH ISAAC, jewelry & fancy goods, 2 Bay State
Fish Jonathan, grocer, cor Prospect & Summer, h 3 Arch [h Holden
Fish Rufus A. hammer manufacturer, Northville,
Fisher Andrew, machinist, bds 1 Millbury
Fisher Charles F. city hand, bds 4 Newbury
Fisher Mrs. Emily R. h 4 Newbury
Fisher Erastus, cotton manuf'r, h 26 Pleasant
Fisher D. W. court mills, h 37 Summer
Fisher Geo. (Seagraves & Co.) cor Cambridge & Fisher Geo. shear grinder, h Lovell [Southbridge
Fisher Harris W. clerk, bds 296 Main
Fisher James B. machinist, h Benefit ct
Fisher James T. coffins, bds 4 Bartlett place
Fisher John W. truckman, h 6 Mulberry
Fisher Judson, bootmaker, h 59 Front
Fisher Robert D. millwright, h 29 John
Fisher Russell D. coffins, h 4 Bartlett place
Fisher Waterman A. cotton manuf'r, office 2 Warren Hall. h 8 Oxford
Fisher Wm. R.phonographic reporter,bds 29 John
Fisk Alexander, carpenter, h Shrewsbury
Fiske Alonzo H. clerk at Exchange hotel
Fiske Calvin J. clerk at Scott's, bds 44 Front
Fiske Edw'd R. printer,Foster bl'k,Foster,h 1 Dix
Fiske Isaac, musical inst. maker. Foster, h 0 Pied-mont [ellers, 195 Main, h 13 Clinton
FISKE (Richard) & GODDARD, (Chas. A) jew-
Fiske Samuel, coal weigher at Wellington's, bds
Fiske Walter B. printer, h 1 Seaver [83 Summer
Fisk Wm. R. cabinet maker, h 83 Salem [High
Fitch Charles H. boot manf'r, Sargent's block, h 3
Fitch (Dana H.) & Winn (Jeremiah,) spoke man-ufacturers. Cypress, h 10 Park
Fitch Ezra, h 11 Maple
Fitch Geo. H. pattern maker, bds 7 Elliot
Fitch Geo. H. pattern maker, Cypress, h 7 Elliot
Fitch James H. clicker, h Plantation
Fitch Jeremiah C. carpenter, h 8 Orange
Fitman John, laborer, h 12 Charles
Fitton Alfred, wiredrawer, h Millbury avenue
Fitton Joseph W. watchman at W R. R. depot, h
Fitton Edward, machinist, h 21 Grove [50 Salem
Fitts Abraham, machinist, h Piedmont

Fitts Benaiah, machinist at J. A. Fay & Co.'s h 6
Fitzgerald Daniel, laborer, h Cross [Jackson
Fitzgerald Edward, hod carrier, h 10 Hibernia
Fitzgerald Frank, R.R. repairer, h 47 Shrewsbury
Fitzgerald James, at T. Ward & Co.'s, bds 5 Fruit
Fitzgerald James, bootmaker, bds 64 Front
Fitzgerald James, laborer, h Benefit
Fitzgerald Michael, blacksmith, h Garden
Fitzgerald Patrick, laborer, h 24 Millbury
Fitzgerald Thomas, bootcrimper, h 33 Shrewsbury
Fitzgerald W. (T. Ward & Co.) h 5 Fruit
Fitzgerald Wm. laborer, h 81 Front
Fitzgerald Wm. printer, h rear 58 Exchange
Fitzpatrick Christopher, laborer, h Hill [lett place
Fitzpatrick Dennis B. carriage trimmer, h 3 Bart-
Fitzpatrick John, machinist, h rear 21 Winter
Fitzpatrick Michael, trunk maker. 95 Main
Fitzpatrick Richard, moulder, 64 Front
Fitzpatrick Wm. helper, b 35 Temple
Fix Peter P. pistol maker, h Lamartine
Flagg Abel, farmer, Millbury av.
Flagg Benjamin, farmer, Pleasant, Tatnuck
Flagg Calvin, h 43 Washington
Flagg Charles, h 1 Bowdoin
Flagg Chas. engineer R. R. R. bds Waldo house
Flagg Mrs. Cynthia, h Burnside court
Flagg Daniel, farmer, Millbury av.
Flagg Dexter, machinist. h 4 Garden
Flagg Ebenezer, farmer, Millbury av.
Flagg Edwin B. student, bds 10 Trumbull
Flagg Elijah, farmer, Burncoat,
Flagg Francis A. bds 2 Sudbury
Flagg Henry C. clk. bds 15 Newbury
Flagg Henry, (Ellis & F.) h 7 Trumbull
Flagg H. K. prop'r Balm of Excellence, 20 Elliot
Flagg James, farmer, h Clark
Flagg John, farmer, h Millbury av.
Flagg John, farmer, Salisbury
Flagg John jr. farmer, Salisbury
Flagg Jonathan, farmer, at R. Wesson's
Flagg J. W. carpenter, h 32 Summer
Flagg Levi, carpenter, h Leicester, Valley Falls
Flagg Marshall, farmer, Flagg st., office Flagg's
Flagg Nahum, farmer, Grafton [building
Flagg Nahum, farmer, h Flagg
Flagg N. H. carpenter, h 7 Cherry
Flagg Oliver, laborer, Northville
Flagg Robert W. carpenter, Newton
Flagg Samuel, machinist, h 14 Trumbull
Flagg Samuel, physician, office 157 Main
Flagg Samuel H. machinist, h Mill, Tatnuck
Flagg Sam'l H. 2d, blacksmith, Canal, h Trumbull
Flagg Tyler C. tinman at Oliver's, h 2 Sudbury
Flagg Waldo, machinist, h 7 Highland
Flagg Wm. horse shoer, h 30 Exchange [6 Carroll
Flagg Wm. H. carriage maker at M. T. Breck's, h
Flaherty Edward, Prov. R. R. repairs, h Benefit
Flaherty James, carpenter, h 13 South Irving
Flaherty John, bootfinisher,Stone's, h 11 S. Irving
Flaherty Martin, Prov. R. R. repairs, h Benefit ct.
Flannegan Francis, bootbottomer, h 33 Shrews-
Flannegan John, laborer, h 12 Charles [bury
Fleming Garrett, bootmaker, bds 10 Hibernia
Fleming Patrick, laborer, h 21 Franklin
Fleming Thomas, stone cutter, bds 81 Front
Fleming William, laborer, h 30 Temple
Fletcher Benj. W. carpenter, h 27 Green
Fletcher David E. watchmaker at Fisk & God-
dard's, bds 300 Main
Fletcher Mrs. Eliza, h 3 Sudbury
Fletcher H. L. hackman, h Kendall hill
Fletcher Joel, h 7 Orchard
Flint Mrs. Austin, h 106 Main

Flint C. C. machinist, 5 Trumbull
Flint J. H. city watchman, h East
Flood James, brakeman, h 39 Mechanic
Flood Owen, brakeman, Nor. R. R. h 58 Mechanic
Floody Patrick, laborer, h E. Worcester place
Flynn James W. painter, 3 Howard
Flynn John, laborer, h rear Bangs' block
Flynn John, laborer, h Lynde
Flynn John, laborer, h 8 S. Irving
Flynn Owen, laborer. h Margin
Flynn Patrick, blacksmith, Hibernia
Flynn Patrick, laborer, h rear 87 Beach
Flynn Patrick, laborer, h 46 Shrewsbury
Flynn Richard, moulder, bds rear Sargent's block
Flynn Robert, boottreer, h 50 Southbridge
Flynn Terence, at rolling mill, bds 9 Fulton
Flynn Thomas, machinist, bds 32 Thomas
Flynn Timothy, laborer. h Millbury
Flynn Wm. machinist, h 18 Chandler
Fobes Hiram & Co. (L. L. Brigham) butchers, 84
Front. bds 25 Mechanic
Foell Adolf, bologna sausages, h Bloomingdale
Fogg N. G. at Grove mill, bds 18 Lincoln
Fogherty John, laborer, h rear Temple cor. Canal
Fogherty John, tailor, 24 John
Fogherty Michael, laborer, h 1 Apricot
Foley Daniel, grocer, h 16 Blackstone
Foley Daniel, roller, h Quinsigamond
Foley Jeremiah, laborer, h Eaton place
Foley Jeremiah, grocer, 11 Wash. sq. h Eaton
Foley John, heater, h 9 Vine [place
Foley John, book agent. h 32 Southbridge
Foley John, laborer, h Foyle
Foley Michael, laborer, h 13 Beach
Foley Morris, tailor, h Eaton place
Foley Patrick, at Grove mills, h Belmont
Foley Patrick,Wellington's coal yard, h 3 Belmont
Foley Thomas, furnace man at N. Washburn's, h
Foley Wm. H. grocer, h 70 Mechanic [13 Pond
Folger Orestes B. machinist, bds 5 High
Folger T. P. machinist, bds 16 Congress
Folger W. H. last maker, bds 23 Hanover
Follansbee Jas. M. wool dealer, 3 Wash. sq. h 264
Follen Albert machinist, bds 103 Summer [Main
Follen Mrs. Anna, h 16 Pond
Follen Henry, laborer at Dana's, Plantation
Follet John, laborer. h 12 E. Worcester
Fo'som Mrs. Eliza, talloress, h 13 Thomas
Folsom Wm. H. printer, Spy office, bds 13 Thomas
Forbes A. P. at Kinnicutt & Co.'s, bds 5 Portland
Forbes Chas. clicker, h 96 Chandler
Forbes Mrs. E. L. h 5 Portland
Forbes John, farmer, h Highland
Forbes Walter E. clerk, bds 12 Park
Forbush Curtis, restaurant, Piper's bl'k, h 6 Park
Ford Augustus, machinist, h 1 Church
Ford James, laborer, h 19 Franklin
Ford Miles, tailor, h 14 Bridge [30 Chatham
Forehand Sullivan, acct. at H. S. Washburn's, h
Forrest Thomas, machinist, h 29 Union
Fosgate Oliver, h 79 Exchange
Fosket Albert O. moulder, bds rear 10 Prospect
Fosket Orrin, moulder, Wheeler's, h rear 10 Pros-
Foster Albert H. bds 4 Belknap [pect
Foster Mrs. Alfred D. h 7 Chestnut
Foster Benjamin F. engineer at Junction Shop, h
Beacon cor Charlton
Foster Calvin & Co. (D. Whitcomb) hardware,
&c. 222 Main, h Chestnut
Foster Charles H. bds 5 Oxford
Foster C. M. clicker, h 21 Prescott
Foster DeMarcus, carpenter, h Harrison
Foster Geo. T. farmer, h Salisbury

Foster (Dwight) & Baldwin (G. W.) counsellors, 1 Brinley hall, h Oak cor Cedar
Foster Henry C. silver smith, 15 Central, bds 18
Foster James, at rolling mill, h 8 Burt [Pleasant
Foster John J. marble cutter, bds 20 Temple
Foster Loring, carpenter, h 1 Green
Foster Mrs. Lucy H. h 82 Pleasant
Foster Reuben R. machinist, 13 Market
Foster Stephen S. farmer, Mower
Foster T. R. jobber, h 24 Green
Fowler Austin, manufacturer, bds Bay St. House
Fowler Edwin, farmer, Newton's, Pleasant
Fox Charles, at Fox & Rice's, h 6 Millbury
Fox Henry, clothing store, 101 Main, h 2 William
Fox Jeremiah, switchman B. R. R. h 14 Cherry
Fox John L. clerk, 101 Main, bds 2 William
Fox Thomas W. counsellor, 3 Brinley hall, bds Vernon [ufacturers, Green, h Vernon
Fox (Wm. B.) & Rice (Geo. T. jr.) woolen man-
Foye Moses, machinist, bds Trowbridgeville
Foye Solomon, picker, Trowbridgeville
Francis Converse, mason, h 28 Myrtle
Fraser John, currier, bds Front
Freeland Chas. W. & Co. (J. H. Freeland, H. W. Bigelow, D. F. Estabrook, D. W. Knowlton, Geo. Paul) clothing, 193 Main
Freeland James H. (Freeland & Co.) bds Bay St.
Freeman Charles, clerk, bds 19 Portland [House
Freeman Edwin, agent, h 19 Portland, cor Myrtle
Freeman Elisha & Co. (C. Wilder) lightning rod & rare manufacturers, Merrifield's building, h 40 Chandler
Freeman Elias H. painter. bds cor Coral & Ward
Freeman Geo. E. machinist, h cor Portland and Myrtle
Freeman Josiah G. carder at Fox's, h Vernon
Freeman Lindal. painter. shop cor Mechanic and Norwich, h Coral cor Ward
French Cornelius, tire welder, h 11 Grafton
French Frederic L. harness maker, 45½ Ex-change, h 33 Salem [Main, h 11 Portland
French Hiram, boot manuf'r, Sargent's block,
French Jona. C. carpenter, h 74 Southbridge
Frerich John, clerk, bds 11 Maple
Frost Edward H. lastmaker, h 20 Wellington
Frost Geo. F. h 3 Chandler
Frost Geo. M. at ct mills, h 28 Laurel
Frost Henry A. machinist. h 104 Pleasant
Frost Wm. painter, h Mason
Fuchs Charles, confectioner, h 100 Southbridge
Fuller Amos W. blacksmith, bds 8 Grafton
Fuller Barnard, machinist, h 2 Elizabeth
Fuller Mrs. Caleb S. h 301 Main
Fuller Chas. A. shoemaker, Blithewood av.
Fuller E. S. milk dealer, h Brattle
Fuller James, machinist, h 13 Chandler
Fuller James A. machinist. h rear 13 Chandler
Fuller Jerome H. clerk, bds 17 Chestnut
Fuller Joel B. h 19 Hanover
Fuller Manson, farmer, Ararat
Fuller Mariner, Holden [bds 304 Main
Fuller Theo. S. Norwich express, I L. H. Block,
Fuller Warren A. clerk, bds 11 Congress
Furnel Henry, clerk. bds 5 Portland
Furness John, machinist, h 5 Highland
Gaffee Michael, laborer, h rear 72 Mechanic
Gaffney, Rev. J. B. Prof. of Latin, disciplinarian, College Holy Cross
Gagan Michael, laborer, h E. Central
Gage Thos. H. physician, 4 Elm
Gagnon Marimo. cook, h 31 Shrewsbury
Golaher Peter, shoemaker, h 13 Pond
Gale Mrs. Amory, bds 14 High

Gale Elisha, carpenter, h 69 Southbridge
Gale Geo. W. paper maker, h 10 Elizabeth
Gale Henry M. moulder, h 1 Salem
Galeghan John, fireman, bds 2 Central
Galvin Michael, boottreer, h 6 Spring
Gardner Ann, laundress, rear 27 Central
Gardner David S. machinist, h Millbury ct.
Gardner Eliza, laundress, h 9 E. Worcester
Gardner Miss E. J. English, French, and Classical Institute, Clark's block, 257 Main
Gardner Gilbert, shoemaker, h 12 Chandler
Gardner James, fireman Nash R. R. bds 7 Myrtle
Gardner John, shoemaker, h 13 Summer
Gardner Wm. shoemaker, h 12 Chandler
Gardner Wm. shoemaker, h 27 Central
Garfield Hiram B. farmer, W. Boylston
Garfield John, machinist at Goddard & Rice's, bds
Garfield Silas, wiredrawer. h 32 Grove [3 Maple
Garland Charles A. att. at hospital
Garland Frank, shoemaker, bds 58 Front
Garland Frank A. shoemaker, bds 70 Front
Garland Horace L. shoemaker, h 70 Front
Garner David, repairer W. R. R. h 7 E. Central
Garner H. G. barber, 23 Washington square
Garrity James, tailor, bds rear 70 Mechanic
Garrity John, tailor, h 16 Bridge
Garrity Thomas, machinist, bds 64 Front
Garvey Daniel, currier, h 14 Temple
Garvey Michael, laborer, 3 E. Worcester
Garvey Wm. wheelmaker, bds Cypress
Garvin James, machinist, bds 3 Goddard
Garvin Michael, laborer, h 66 Front
Garvin Patrick, teamster, h Endicot
Garvin Richard, engineer for Thayer, Houghton & Co. h 3 Goddard
Gates Andrew, bootmaker, Vernon
Gates Asa, farmer, Mill
Gates Charles A. grocer, h Quinsigamond
Gates Charles E. grocer, Exchange cor. Union, h 44 Central [mer, bds 3 Maple
Gates Charles, provisions, cor. Central & Sum-
Gates Daniel C. fruit stall, Harrington corner, h cor Prospect and Carroll
Gates David R. farmer, Gates' lane
Gates E. L. machinist, bds Quinsigamond
Gates Mrs. Elizabeth, h 74 Front [tral
Gates Frank W. at Tolman & Russel's, bds 4 Cen-
Gates Geo. A. at Gates' lumber yard, h 29 Thomas
Gates Harvlin T. farmer, Gates' lane
Gates Henry B. farmer, h Greenwood
Gates Mrs. Henry, h N. Ashland [Pleasant
Gates Janlam, carrier for Leonard's express, h 173
Gates John, lumber dealer, Union, h 51 Central
Gates John B. clerk, bds 23 Exchange
Gates Joseph, bootmaker, bds Quinsigamond
Gates Larkin N. carpenter, h 5 Clinton
Gates Mrs. Latitia, h 9 Summer
Gates Leonard, butcher and farmer. h Pleasant
Gates Levi, farmer, Pleasant, Tatnick
Gates Lewis, farmer, Pleasant
Gates Nathan, farmer, bds Pleasant
Gates Nathan B. farmer, Gates' lane
Gates Nathaniel P. farmer, Pleasant. Tatnick
Gates Samuel F. butcher, bds 3 Maple
Gates Samuel F. farmer, Plantation
Gates Samuel W. machinist, h 1 Bartlett place
Gates Simon D. wiredrawer, bds 9 Summer
Gates Thos. Bay st. market. 177 Main, h 74 Front
Gates Walter, butcher, bds 309 Main
Gassett Curtis W. bootfitter, h 35 Millbury
Gavin Anthony, machinist, h 24 Millbury
Gay Geo. truckman, h 36 Thomas
Gay N. D. flour and grain, 3 Foster, h 64 Pleasant

Geary John, at Hacker's, h 22 Madison
Geary John, bootmaker, h 30 Oxford
Geary Patrick, at Wellington's, bds 12 Charles
Geary Thomas, at Wellington's, bds 12 Charles
Geary Wm. bds 30 Oxford
Gee James S. W. shuttle maker, h 24 Thomas
Geer Edward D. cardmaker, bds 73 Exchange
Geer Geo. hats,caps & findings, 219 Main, h 6 West
Geer Henry F. coat maker, h 71 Exchange
Geer Mrs. Sarah A. talloress. h 73 Exchange
Geery Pa'rick. helper, et. mills, bds 12 Bridge
Gegnum Maxum, cook for Spurr & Priest, h 31 Shrewsbury
Gehan Michael, teamstor, bds 39 Mechanic
Geiger Geo. butcher. bds 74 Front
Gelineau Alex. blacksmith, bds 13 Mechanic
George Andrew, clerk at W. L. Clark's, bds 5
Gerald Vincent, gilder, h East   [Walnut
GERELDS Mrs. M. W. physician, h 43 Exchange
Gerelds S. W. blacksmith, h 43 Exchange
Gericks John, wiredrawer, h 10 Washington sqr.
Gernhardt Adam J. machinist, h 35 Pink
Gernhardt Joseph, machinist, h 33 Pink
Gernhardt Michael, tailor, h 47 Front
Gerould James H. h 31 Lincoln
Gibbons John, rolling mill, h 3 Foyle
Gibbons John, laborer, h 4 Tremont
Gibbs Francis, h Cliff   [h 24 Union
Gibbs Ivers, pattern maker and carver, Cypress,
Gibson A. J. patent rights, h 24 Mechanic
Gibson Wm. brakeman B. R. R. h 42 Washington
Gibson L. R. tin plate worker, bds 24 Thomas
Gibson J. S machinist, h 4 Grove
Giddings J. S machinist, h 4 Grove
Giffin Wm. moulder, h under Zion's church
Gifford Wm. P. shoemaker, Canterbury
Gilbert Chas. W. acct. at Daniel Tainter's, bds 13
Gilbert Geo. H. jr. clerk, bds 1 Portland   [Main
Gilbert H. G. O. at W. R. R. freight house, h 4
Gilbert Jos. A. machinist, h 13 Green   [Franklin
Gilbert Mrs. Orrin P. h 15 Main
Gilbert P. B. machinist, h 15 Chatham
Gilchrist Owen, wiredrawer. h Goddard's lane
Gill Geo. machinist at Wheeler's, h 7 Prospect
Gill Geo. F. moulder, h 3 Salem
Gill Geo. W. h 36 Portland
Gill Mark, machinist, h 3 Leicester, N. W.
Gill Thos. boottreer, h 1 Lexington   [h Highland
Gilliard Mrs. H. S. ladies hair work, &c 42 Front,
Gillick James, wiredrawer, h 24 Shrewsbury
Gilman Henry, machinist, bds 1 High st. court
Gilman L. P. carpenter, h Endicott
Gilmore James, laborer, h 4 Tremont
Gimby Edward B. barber, Wash. sq. h 60 Union
Gird Mrs. Elizabeth L. h 71 Summer
Gird Jos. W. bds 71 Summer   [church
Given Wm. moulder, h Exchange, under Zion's
Glasgow Wm. bootfitter, h 24 Chandler
Glathair Wm. amorer, bds 21 Madison
Glazier Henry, clerk at Hood's. h 4 High st court
Gleason Albert H. painter, h 29 Summer
Gleason Mrs. Anna h West Boylston
Gleason Austin, engineer B. R. R. h 8 Salem
Gleason Benj. F. farmer, Ararat
Gieason Bourne, farmer, Lincoln
Gleason David, city messenger, City Hall, h 5 May
Gleason Edwin, bookkeeper at G. & Rice's. h 14
Gleason Geo. W. truckman, h 11 Arch   [Myrtle
Gleason Henry. farmer. West Boylston
Gleason Jonathan R. farmer. Salisbury
Gleason John F. carpenter. h 19 Green
Gleason Miss L. dressmaker, 266 Main
Gleason Robert S. clerk at 21 Wash. sq, h 1 Beach
Gleason Samuel, Prouty lane

Gleason Thos. bootmaker, bds rear Sargent's blk
Gleason Thomas, ice driver, bds Crescent and
Gleason Wm. F. farmer, W. Boylston   [Nashua
Gleasim Miss Martha, h Grafton
Glenon Barney city work, h Cross
Glynn John, bootmaker, bds 2 Hind's court
Goddard Benj. carriage maker, Thomas, h 22 William   [h Ronnd Hill
Goddard Benj. wire manufacturer. S. Worcester,
Goddard Benj. jeweler. 174 Main, h 6 Oxford
Goddard Charles A. (Fiske & G.) bds 14 High
Goddard Charles, stone mason, h Belmont
Goddard Mrs. Clementine, h 3 Clinton
Goddard Delano A. asst. Ed. of Spy, bds Round
Goddard D. B. carpenter, h Newton   [Hill, S. W.
Goddard Daniel, h 14 High
Goddard Ezra, farmer, Chester,
Goddard Frederick, machinist, bds 76 Front
Goddard Geo.W. at G, Rice & Co.'s, bds 24 Orange
Goddard Henry, wiredrawer, h Cambridge, cor. Southbridge
Goddard (Isaac,) Rice (Geo. M.) & Co. (G. S. Barton,) paper mach'y, &c. Union, h 24 Orange
Goddard John, baker, 37 Wash. square
Goddard Leander, shoemaker, h 14 Market
Goddard Lucius P. printer, Palladium office, bds 1 Court hill
Goddard (Luther) & Rand (B. B.) leather, oil and shoe findings, Sargent's block, Main, bds 41
Goddard L. D. bds 14 High   [Pleasant
Goddard N. P. musician, h 79 Summer
Goddard Parley, h 40 Thomas   [Thomas
Goddard S. B. I. counsellor, 141 Main, bds 46
Goddard Silas W. machinist, at G. R. & Co. h 24 Orange
Gogin Richard, at G. Hoppin & Co.'s, h 11 Charles
Goggin Patrick, laborer, h Cambridge
Going Augustus K. tin plate worker, h Highland cor. N. Ashland
Golbert Robert L. last maker, bds 2 Vine
Goldsmith M. watch peddler, bds Bay State house
Gollohr, Michael, boothottomer, h Charles
Gooch Adam. h Oak hill
Goodale D. H. machinist, h 9 Liberty
Goodale Daniel R. machinist, h 23 Hanover
Goodell A. A. teller, City Bank, bds 59 Pleasant
Goodell John M. wood turner, Cypress, h 59 Pleasant
Gooding Edward F. machinist, bds Laurel   [ant
Gooding John Jr. machinist, h 39 Washington
Goodhue J. M. rear 105 Main
Goodman Mrs. Sarah, h 17 Salem
Goodnow Alex. court mill, h 12 Market
Goodnow E. A. wholesale dealer in boots, shoes, &c. 1 Mechanics hall, bds Bay State house
Goodnow Harrison D. pavier, h 7 Hanover
Goodnow Henry H. clerk, bds 7 Hanover
Goodnow John, moulder, h 23 School
Goodnow Lyman II, pattern maker. h 7 Hanover
Goodnow R. E. produce dealer, h 1 Winter
Goodnow Warren, farmer, Lincoln
Goodspeed Charles, carpenter, court mill, h 17 Prescott   [Thomas
Goodspeed Sam'l A. fish market, 14 Thomas, h 3
Goodspeed Wm. C. carpenter, h 18 Wellington
Goodwin Alfred. boot and shoe manuf'r, 301 Main, h 6 Wellington
Goodwin Charles, h rear Advent Chapel, Thomas
Goodwin Francis E. bookkeeper at S. G. & C. G. Reed's, bds 6 Wellington   [Myrtle
Goodwin James H. machinist, bds cor Main &
Goodwin John, shoemaker, 111 Main, h rear of Chapel, Thomas
Goodwin Martin, livery stable, h 15 Austin

GOODWIN Mrs. S. midwife, 15 Austin
Goodwin Wells, hackman, h 17 Austin
GOODWIN WM. S. Life Insurance agt. Clark's Block 257 Main, h 3 John
Gordon Albert A. machinist, bds 3 Belknap
Gordon Joseph, blacksmith, bds rear 54 Exchange
Gordon Wm. H. painter, bds 24 Central
Goff John B. machinist, bds 10 Salem
Goff Wm. hostler at Co. House, h r 72 Mechanic
Gorham Hiram, mason, h 39 Summer
Gormon John, tailor, h 51 Salem
Gorton John, bootmaker, h Mason
Goss Brigham, farmer, h 316 Main
Goss Frank M. Nash. R. R. bds 3 Maple
Goss Peter, laborer, h cor Mechanic & Bridge
Goss Samuel A. carpenter, h 3 Oxford
Goss Wm. farmer, Upland
Goss Wm. jr. farmer, Upland
Gouch Adams, laborer, h Hill
Gouch Franklin J. plane maker, Cypress, cor Exchange, h 16 Mulberry   [Exchange
Gould Aaron M. printer at Times office, h 83
Gould Albert, boot manuf'r, Burnside court, h 2 Portland   [Grafton, h 23 Providence
Gould Chas. M. blacksmith shop, cor Temple and
Gould J. C. clerk, bds 59 1-2 Main
Gould (R. M.) & Andrews (N. H.) grocers, 53 & 55 Main, h 59 1-2 Main
Gould Sylvanus S. clerk, h 82 Chandler
Gould Wm. h Ranks lane   [h 65 Southbridge
Goulding Chas. mechanical engineer, at court mill
Goulding Chas. H. machinist, h 46 Chandler
Goulding Clark, shoemaker, h Abbot
Goulding Henry, h 22 Harvard
Goulding Henry, machinist, h 5 Edward
Goulding John, patent rights, bds Taft's Hotel
Goulding John, gardener, h 6 Brown
Goulding Joseph, laborer at Cyrus Lovell's
Goulding Peter, shuttles, Exchange, h 11 Hanover
Goulding Wm. H. apothecary, 140 Main, bds 22
Grace John, bootmaker, h 24 Temple   [Harvard
Grace Patrick, bootmaker, h 25 Winter
Grady Jeremiah, shoemaker, h 18 Millbury
Grady James, woolsorter, bds 1 Millbury
Grady John, laborer, bds Central
Grady John, laborer, h E. Central
Grady John, moulder, 26 Winter
Grady John C. laborer, h 12 Bridge
Grady Patrick, laborer, h 14 Bridge
Grady Thomas, laborer, h 32 Winter
Graftin James, brakeman, Nor. R. R. h 24 Madison
Gragon Joseph, shoemaker, h Mason
Graham John, Quinsigamond
Granger James, polisher, bds Webster
Grant Francis P. machinist, bds 9 Fulton
Grant Thomas, bootbottomer, bds 2 Hinds court
Graton Henry C. belt maker at T. K. Earle's, h
Graves Mrs. Sarepta, h 13 Market   [28 Grafton
Graves Simon C. painter, h 12 Mason
Graves Walter D. clk at J. H. Clark's, h 58 Austin
Graves Wm. B. painter, h 10 Home   [tin
Gray Christopher, wiredrawer, h 16 Grove
Gray Henry C. printer, h 59 Southbridge
Gray John W. W. clerk at C. Foster's, bds 44 Front
Gray Joshua, wirefinisher, bds 4 Charlton
Gray Patrick, at Grove Mill, bds 19 Blackstone
Gray Wm. L. cigars & fruit, 107 Main, h 20 Thomas
Grayson John, dipper, bds Leicester, N. W.
Green Aaron F. wireworker, bds 26 John
Green Abby R. b 41 Main
Green Alanson, bootbottomer, bds 26 Thomas
Green A. F. barber, bds rear 16 Chandler
Green Charles F. pattern maker, h 25 Bowdoin

Green E. W. saloon, 14 Foster, h Belmont
Green Frank, brass moulder, bds 5 Laurel
Green Henry M. ambrotypist, bds 61 Summer
Green James, druggist, 117 Main, h 12 Harvard
Green J. D. bds Lincoln house
Green Lucius M. clerk, bds 63 Front
Green Mrs. L. H. boarders, h 61 Summer
Green Joel, tinman, bds 23 Exchange
Green Joel W. tinman, bds cor Exchange & Waldo
Green John, physician, bds 102 Main
Green John, machinist, h Harrison
Green John, mechanic, court mill, h 8 Belmont
Green J. W. plumber, bds 26 John
Green M. B. & Co. (J. L. Burbank,) apothecaries,
Green Mrs. Smith, h 26 John   [216 Main, h 3 Oak
Green Wm. E. farmer, Green's lane
Green Wm. N. justice police court, h 75 Summer
Greene Benj. bootfinisher, 40 Newbury
Greene C. C. bootfinisher, h 38 Newbury
Greene Curtis B. bootfinisher, h 84 Southbridge
Greene Harris R. teacher, h Mt. Vernon place
Greene John R. h 2 Madison
Greene Levi, carpenter, h 46 Salem
Greene Wm. A. elocutionist, h 61 Austin
Greene Wm. H. wiredrawer, bds 61 Summer
Greene Wm. S. bds Mt. Vernon place
Greenleaf Mrs. Caroline W. h 26 Mulberry
Greenleaf Levi C. clerk, bds 14 Green
Greenleaf Lewis, rolling mill, h 3 Foyle
Greenleaf Mrs. Mary, h 21 Southbridge cor Myrtle
Greenleaf Wm. counsellor and acct. 82 Main, h 5 Bowdoin   [Mason
Greenman P. S. confectioner, h cor Chandler and
Greenwood Appleton, engineer B.R.R. h 9 Quincy
Greenwood Chas. C. carpenter, h 12 Myrtle
Greenwood Francis, truckman, bds 14 Seaver
Greenwood Henry, printer, bds 7 Maple
Greenwood M. T. machinist, bds 80 Southbridge
Greenwood S. A. truckman, h 6 Cherry
Greer John, shoemaker, h 24 Mechanic
Gregory Peter, laborer, h 12 E. Worcester
Gregson Thomas, machinist, Main N. W.
Griffin Daniel J. carpenter, h N. Ashland
Griffin Dennis, machinist, h 34 Temple
Griffin Henry & Co. grocers, 1 Pleasant, h 24 High
Griffin Henry E. laborer, h cor Brown and Beach
Griffin John, bootbottomer, h 58 Exchange
Griffin Michael, laborer, 2 Canal
Griffin Robert S. carpenter, h 9 Gold
Griggs G. E. shoemaker, bds 52 Mechanic
Griggs John, blacksmith, h 3 Union
Griggs Mrs. Joseph, h 2 Ashland
Griggs Salem, tanner, h 1 Oxford
Grimshaw Henry, tool fixer, h 25 Washington
Griswold Chas. Wm. machinist, bds 1 Bartlet pl.
Grogan Edward, wiredrawer, bds 21 Grafton
Grogan Patrick, wiredrawer, bds 21 Grafton
Gross, (Isaac,) Strauss & Co. French embroideries, &c. 152 Main, h 9 West
Gross Moses, clerk, bds 3 Maple
Grout Francis, farmer, Vernon
Grout Hannah, h Vernon
Grout Jonathan, 239 Main, h 322 Main
Grout Jonathan D. farmer, h Vernon
Grout Wm. h 16 Elliot
Grout Wm. G. farmer, h Greenwood
Grosvenor L. D. carpenter, h Newton
Grover John, bag. mast. W. R. R. h 32 Orange
Grover Lemuel B.R.R. freight house, h 32 Orange
Grover Lowell H. shoemaker, h Dewey
Groves James, moulder, bds 26 Thomas
Groves John, puddler, h 1 Bloomingdale
Guerin Michael, laborer, h Highland

Guider James, bootfinisher, h 20 Shrewsbury
Gulger Geo. butcher, bds 74 Front
Guilfoil Daniel, wiredrawer, h Holden
Guilfoil Dennis, wire temperer, h rear 13 School
Guilfoil John, farmer, Holden
Guilfoil John H. farmer, Chester   [ant
Guilfoil Patrick, laborer at D. W. Lincoln's, Pleas-
Gunderson C. armorer, h 33 Beacon
Gunn John, gas fitter, h Leicester, N. W.
Guuther Julius, clerk at Dewey & Williams, h 20
Gurno Alex'r. moulder, h 12 Market   [Newbury
Gurno Clements, moulder, h 21 School
Gurno John, moulder, h 23 School
Gurry John, at Arcade Foundry, bds 4 Howard
Gustin Andrew J. machinist, at N. Washburn's
Gustin John F. heater, h Mulberry court
Haas Charles, musical inst. maker, h 10 Wash. sq.
Haberthier Bernhart, h Grosvenor
Hacker W. Alfred, h cor. Edward and Glen
Hacker Frederic, weaver, h 5 Millbury
Hacker Rudolph, machinist, bds 5 Millbury
Hacket Edward, painter, h 15 Summer
Hackett James, armorer, h 23 Madison
Hackett Maurice, laborer, h 48 Southbridge
Hacket Michael, roller, at N. Washburn's, h 5
Hacket Thomas, teamster, h 24 Winter   [Temple
Hacket Wm. H. (Howe & H.) bds 76 Main
Hadley Moses C, carriagesmith, h 9 Austin
Hadwin Charles, farmer, Hadwin's lane
Hadwin Obadiah R. garden and nusrery, Lovell
Hagan James, cleaner, h 24 Millbury
Hagan Michael, blacksmith, h 5 Charles
Hagan Owen, blacksmith, h 11 Vine
Hagan Owen, laborer, h 5 Charles
Hagarty Daniel, Nashua R. R. h 5 Charles
Hagarty David, laborer h rear 58 Mechanic
Hagarty Hugh, boottreer, bds 25 Winter
Hagarty Jeremiah, laborer, h 6 Washington sq.
Hagarty John, laborer, bds Mechanic
Hagarty Patrick, nailmaker, bds Tremont
Hagarty Stephen, at Nash. R. R. h 4 Church
Hager Rev. E. W. h 13 High
Haheay Edward, laborer, h cor. Salem & Madison
Hair Charles N. wiredrawer, 14 Lincoln
Hakes Henry B. foreman of forge shop at court
     mills, h 54 Central
Hale Nathan S. truckman, h 28 Hanover
Hale Sumner P. W. R. R. h 60 Summer
Haley Mrs. Ellen, h 11 Hibernia
Haley Thos. laborer, h 63 Mechanic
Hall Charles, h Leicester
Hall Edward, brakeman B. R. R. h 4 Temple
Hall Franklin, counsellor, 157 Main, h Westminster
Hall Rev. H. P, h 7 Newton
Hall John W. file maker, bds 10 Vine
Hall J. T. teller at Quinsig. Bank, bds 80 Main
Hall Judson W. machinist, bds 9 Chandler
Hall Peter, at rolling mill, h Canal
Hall Walter S. laborer, h 25 E. Central
Hall Wm. G. carpenter, h Leicester, N. W.
Hallett Edgar, engineer, h 5 Orchard
Hallock Samuel, h 126 Southbridge
Halloron Edward, bootturner, h E. Temple
Hally Patrick, laborer, h 11 Birt
Haly Daniel, laborer, h 8 Lovell's court
Haly James, hostler, h 15 Blackstone
Haly Thomas, armorer, h 8 Lovell's court
Halpin John, h Franklin   [st. place
Hamant Richard, carriage maker, h 2 Chatham
Hamblin Edwin, cook, 232 Main, h 29 Orange
Hamblin Eleazer, bootmaker, h 3 Chandler
Hamilton Abial, bds 43 Washington
Hamilton C. W. (Jenkins, H. & Hyde,) h 43 Elm

Hamilton Chas. printer c
     change, h 2 Cottage
Hamilton Chas. A. treas.
     Bank block, h 37 Elt
Hamilton Edward, asst.
     Savings, bds 18 Plea
Hamilton Geo. stone cut
Hamilton Geo. S. tinmai
Hamilton M. R. tinman
Hamilton Mrs. Nancy H
Hamlet Reuben B, carri
Hammerbacher J. C. wi
Hammond Andrew H. m
Hammond Elijah, farme
Hammond Fred. farmer,
Hammond Henry, black
Hammond Hugh, labore
Hammond James, at cou
Hammond John, farmer,
Hammond Joseph P. h 3
Hammond Lewis W. cler
Hammond Otis S. clerk
     Highland
Hammond Parley, sec';
Hammond Timo. W. tre
     block, Salisbury
Hampson (Henry F.) &
     cloth manuf'rs, Centr
Hancock Fred. (B. F. N
Hancock Wm. painter, h
Handy Geo. weaver, bds
Hanff Jacob, boarding h
Hanks John W. painter,
Hanlahon Mrs. Michael,
Hanlin Hugh, laborer, h
Hanlin Hugh, laborer, h
Hanlon Jeremiah, groce
Hanlon Joseph. harness
Hanlon Richard, hostler
Hanlon Thomas, eng'r a
Hannagan Barnard, labo
Hannagan David, labore
Hannahan Bridget, h 39
Hannant Richard L. tea
Hanrity James, laborer,
Hansom Edwin A. fire
Hanson C. H. at Bradley
Hapgood Asa, conductor
Hapgood Geo. E. bookke
     & Co.'s, bds 17 Ches
Hapgood Henry R. at 1
Hapgood Nahum R. car
Hapgood Walter J. boo
     cor. William and Ch
Haradon John, machinis
Harbach Palmer, carpen
Harding Edwin B. clerk
Harding Henry A. book!
     & Co. bds 1 Crown
Harding John. peddler.
Harding Lewis, h 20 We
Harding Lorenzo, car bi
Harding (Sam'l D.) & 3
     ton place, h Grafton
Hardy A. D, laborer, h 8
Hardy Chas. A. blacksm
Hardy Geo. H. machinis
HARDY LEVI & Co., 1
     cutters and shear bl
Hargadon Thomas, labo
Harker James & Co. pic
     bds Canal court
Harkness E. A. bookkee

Harkness Mrs. Lucy, h 82 Mechanic
Harkness Nathan, bill poster. h 2 Sycamore
Harlow Elijah S. carpenter, bds 5 Clinton
Harlow Geo. H. Insurance agent, h 18½ Portland
Harlow Geo. P. apothecary, 242 Main cor. Pleasant, bds 15 Portland
Harnet Michael, laborer, h 16 Blackstone
Harney Edward, machinist, bds 74 Pleasant
Harney Michael, hostler, h 16 Blackstone
Harney Michael, laborer, h 2 Charles
Harney Patrick, at court mills, h 2 Charles
Harper Abram, cleaner at Wheeler's, h Hill
Harper Dennis. moulder, h 27½ Union
Harper John, laborer, at W. L. Wood's
Harper Joseph, blacksmith, h 1 Charlton
Harper Joseph. cook, bds 9 Brown
Harper Patrick. peddler, h 9 Brown
Harr James, laborer. h Sargent's ct. Southbridge
Harr Martin, bootsider, h 12 Bridge
Harrington Adam, (Towne & H.) h 22 Mulberry
Harrington Benj. farmer, Harrington court
Harrington Benj. F. farmer. Harrington ct.
Harrington Bartley, lastmaker. bds 24 Exchange
Harrington (Chas. A.) & Co. (J. Marble) wholesale druggists, 50 Main, h 29 Harvard
Harrington Chas. A. milkman, h 1 Fulton
Harrington Chauncy G. at 2 Har. Cor, bds 4 Port-
Harrington Cheney, farmer, Heywood   [land
Harrington C. Albert, machinist,bds 22 Mulberry
Harrington C. N. carpenter, bds 2 Elizabeth
Harrington Daniel, farmer, Harrington ct.
Harrington Edward R. clerk, bds Maple
Harrington Edwin, foreman at A. Rice's, 14 Central, h 53 Chandler
Harrington E. N. h 2 Elizabeth   [Trumbull
Harrington Francis, flour and grain, 39 Front, h 9
Harrington Francis A. clicker, 39 Chandler
Harrington Frank. wire roller, bds 40 Grove
Harrington Frank W. thread store, 180 Main. h 10 Gold   [Salem
Harrington Halloway, jr. (Penniman & H.) h 48
Harrington Henry H. clicker, h 6 Bartlett place
Harrington Henry J. dry goods, 204 Main, h 12 Park
Harrington Henry N. clerk at B. R. R. h 25 Crown
Harrington Isaac S. farmer, Vernon
Harrington Jos. A. milkman, 1 Fulton [325 Main
Harrington Lonmni & Co. grocers, 303 Main. h
Harrington Lucian, freight clerk, W. R. R. bds 4 Edward
Harrington Nathan S. armorer, h 32 Portland
Harrington Mrs. Oliver, h 4 Edward
Harrington Mrs. Samuel, h 82 Salem
Harrington Sam'l P. real estate dealer, h 32 Elm
Harrington Stephen, mason, h 1 Seaver
Harrington Stephen S. h 1 Elizabeth
Harrington Thomas, (Hawkins & H.) h N'thville
Harrington Waldo M. at Angier's refreshment
Harrington Wm. h 4 Portland   [room
Harrington Winslow M. clicker, bds 39 Chandler
Harris Allen, h 14 Elm cor Chestnut
Harris Alfred, carpenter, h 23 Myrtle
Harris Clarendon, Sec. Life Ins Co. 98 Main, h 20
Harris Danforth. armorer, h 12 Charlton   [Elm
Harris Gideon, cotton manuf'r, h 22 Summer
Harris Henry, armorer, bds 23 Myrtle
Harris John J. armorer, bds 23 Myrtle
Harris John, temperer, bds 8 Grafton [Madison
Harris Luther, at D. Tainter's, h cor Orange and
Harris Manton,engineer Prov R. R. h 17 Lafayette
HARRIS O. F. dentist, 158 Main
Harris Wm. brakeman, h 25 Winter[19 Mechanic
Harrison Richard, engineer at N. Washburn's, h

Harrison Richard, laborer, h Lamartine
Harrit Wm. shoemaker, h 23 Myrtle
Harrogan John, at ct. mills, h 6 1 Mechanic
Hart Jacob, confectioner, h 29 Central
Hart John, laborer, h Canal cor Winter
Hart John. roller, h Ward
Hart Mark, h Canal
Hart Michael, laborer, h Ward
Hart Patrick, cook, Lincoln house   [chanic
Hartigan Patrick, brakeman Prov. R. R. h 47 Me-
Harthan S. Emerson, machinist, h cor Newport &
Hartmerm Henry, wiredrawer, h 7 Pink [Edward
Hartshorn Calvin L. farmer, Lovell   [29 Elm
Hartshorn Charles W. counsellor, 206 Main, bds
Hartshorn Geo. F. cashier Cen. bank. h 31 Elm
Hartshorn John W.at Angier's refreshment room
Hartshorn Jonas, farmer, May
Hartwell Alfred, watchmaker, h 81 Chandler
Harty Cornelius, blacksmith h 14 Bridge
Harvey Barney, at Nash. R. R. bds Prescot place
Harvey Charles H. cutter at A. P. Ware's, h 11
Hashell Geo. farmer, bds Howard lane [Thomas
Haskell Calvin, wiredrawer, h 19 Grove
Haskell J. S. wiredrawer, bds 14 Grove
Haskell Joseph, shoemaker, bds 25 Salem
HASKELL S. N. Davis' roofing & paint, Suffolk, h 101 Pleasant
Haskins D. W. law student, bds Tirrell
Haskins Marcena, carpenter, h 226 Prescott
Haskin Harry S. machinist, h 53 Chandler
Hassett James, laborer, h 4 Chandler ct
Hassett Patrick, wheelwright, h 80 Mechanic
Hastings Miss A. C. clerk at hospital
Hastings Geo. machinist, bds 27 Chatham
Hastings Henry W. clicker, h 67 Summer
Hastings Ira, at I. Washburn & Co.'s, bds 12 Thomas   [Central
Hastings Joseph E. at I. Washburn & Co.'s, h 50
Hastings J T. machinist, bds 85 Summer
Hastings Thomas J. machinist, bds 12 Glen
Hastings Washington, Grove mill, h 31 Thomas
Hatch Albert F. machinist, h 21 Hanover
Hatch B. F. h 87 Summer
Hatch William, farmer, h Adams square
Hathaway Dexter B. shoe finisher, bds cor Vine &
Hathaway John E. physician, h 16 Pearl [Front
Hatheway S. W. law student, bds 12 Thomas
Hathorne W. H. clerk, bds 13 Park
Hatton John W. heater, h 5 Fulton [h 16 High
Haven Edwin, constable, 3 Harrington corner,
Haven Henry R. painter, bds 7 Ash
Haven Hollis J. bootmaker, h Grafton
Haven Jubal H. bootmaker, Grafton
Haven Oliver C. (S. Clapp & Co.) h 13 Green
Haven Samuel F. librarian Am. Ant Soc'y, bds Lincoln House   [bds Lincoln House
Haven S. Foster, physician, Foster bl'k, Pearl,
Haverseik Wm. weaver, h Ward   [place
Havey Bernard, Nashua freight house, h Prescott
Hawes Artemas, grocer, 20 Southbridge, h 316
Hawes Mrs. C. J. L. h 23 Austin   [Main
Hawes Frederick, carpenter, h Harrison
Hawes Geo. baggage m'r B R. R. h 14 Oxford
Hawes Russell L. & Co. (G. T. Rice & B. Bottomly) manufacturers, 11 Bank bl'k, h 16 West
Hawes Wm. carpenter, h Harrison
Hawker Mrs. Harriet, washer, h rear 5 Chandler
Hawks Henry, tailor, bds 85 Front
Hawkes Edwin, cabinet maker, h 27 Chatham
Hawkes W. B. clerk 234 Main, bds 27 Chatham
Hawkins (Dan'l A. jr.) & Harrington (T.) wrench manuf'rs, Northville, h N. Ashland cor John
Hawkins John, goldsmith, h 16 Green

11

Hayden Francis W. section master B. R. R. h 34
Hayden Geo. machinist, bds 41 Summer [Mulberry
Hayden Samuel W. carpenter, h 62 Austin
Hayes Mrs. Alice, h 9 Beach
Hayes Mrs. Hannah, h 62 Shrewsbury
Hayes Hugh, shoemaker, bds 25 Blackstone
Hayes John, cabinet maker, bds 8 Union
Hayes Martin, wiredrawer, bds 39 Mechanic
Hayes Patrick, laborer, h 4 Bridge
Hayes Stephen, finisher at Hopeville, h Leicester
Hayes Thomas, laborer, h Madison
Hays Mark, machinist, bds 11 Winter
Hays Wm. farmer, bds 11 Winter
Haynes Charles B. painter, h Eaton place
Hayward Mrs. A. S. h Quincy
Hayward Mrs. Reuben B. h 27 Laurel
Hayward Wm. clerk, bds 27 Laurel
Hazard John, barber, bds 13 Prospect
Hazlebrook John, cigar maker, h Lovell ct.
Hazletine C. B. R. clerk at J. Q. Hill's, bds 13 Ma-
Head Charles, watchman at jail   [ple
Heald Jonas jr. h 8 Wellington
Heald Simpson C. conductor B. R. R. h 60 Pleas't
Heald Solomon O. machinist, h 11 William
Heald Wm. clerk, 24 High
Healy Daniel, laborer, h 14 Hibernia
Healy David, laborer, h Summer at court
Healy James, laborer, h 3 Milk
Healy John, contractor, h cor Salem & Madison
Healy John, armorer, h 1 Temple
Healy John, machinist, h 1 Temple
Healy John, painter, bds 18 Park   [Salem
HEALY JOHN W. pattern maker, Foundry, h 25
Healy Michael, gardener at Dea. Butman's
Healy Patrick, blacksmith, h 36 Mechanic
Healy Thomas, machinist, h 8 S. Irving
Heaney Wm. bds Swan's hotel
Hearn Pierce, laborer, h 43 Green
Heard Nathan, h Belmont
Hearlehy Jerry, wiredrawer. h 30 Winter
Heath Heman A. house-furnishing store,45 Front,
    bds 7 Orange
Heath Jerome A. machinist, bds 12 Glen
Heath Mrs. John W. h 12 Glen   [hotel
Heath Nathaniel, brakeman B. R. R. bds Farmer's
HEATH ORSON N. Poetical Exchange, house fur-
    nishing goods, Bay St bl'k, bds Swan's hotel
Heaton Wm. boottreer, h Apricot
Heavren Michael, laborer, h Cross
Heavren Peter, at rolling mill, h 7 E. Central
Hector Asa, shoemaker, h 60 Union
Hector John, laborer, h rear 16 Chandler
Hector Richard A. barber, 24 Front, h rear 16
    Chandler   [32 Chandler
Hemenway Alexander, F. barber, 8 Mechanic, h
Hemenway Ebenezer, carpet and window cleaner,
    h 32 Chandler
Hemenway Ebenezer, clicker, h 4 Laurel
Hemenway Hannah, wedding cake maker, h May
Hemenway Jos. J. fireman Nor. R. R. bds 32
    Chandler
Hemphill Orson, armorer, bds 7 Orange
Hemphill Wm. A. armorer, bds 80 Southbridge
Henan John, armorer, bds Farmers' hotel
Henchley David, machinist, h 40 Grove
Henchley Eleazer, machinist, h Pink
Henderson James G. machinist, h Adams square
Henriques John, carpenter, h Quinsigamond
Henry Charles, h 42 Summer
Henry Frederick, laborer, h 10 Brown's block
Henry George, teamster, bds 95 Main
Henry Harlan F. wireworker, bds Farmers' hotel
Henry Jacob, armorer, h Lafayette

Henry James teamster, h Cross
Henry James, bootmaker, bds 24 Madison
Henry John, laborer, bds 1 Millbury
Henry John, armorer, bds 10 Sal m
Henry John A. cotton batting, h 151 Pleasant
Henry Lawrence, laborer, h 27 Un on
Henry Peter, laborer, h 47 Shrewsbury
Henry Robert, h Sunny side
Henry Walter, real estate broker, bds 1 Cross
Henry Wm. A. machinist, h Mason
Henshaw Alvin (A. F. H. & Co.) bds 27 Harvard
Henshaw A. F. & Co. (Alvin Henshaw,) manuf'rs
    of machinists tools, Merrifield's building, h
    27 Harvard
Hentz Daniel, machinist, h 58 Exchange
Hergan Timothy laborer, h 23 Temple
Herlihy John, laborer, h Cypress   [Pleasant
Herman Chas. H. gardener at D. W. Lincoln's, h
Hern John, laborer. at Hacker's, h Ward
Hern Patrick, at city coal yard, h S. Irving
Hero Gideon P. car shop, h 28 Shrewsbury
Heron Francis, laborer, h 7 Water
Heron Maurice, stone mason, h 7 Spring
Heron Patrick, bootmaker, h 19 Winter
Heroux Nelson, clicker, h 16 Sh ewsbury
Herrick Wm. A. machinist, bds 42 Summer [mer
Hersey A. W. clerk at 3 Bangs block, bds 30 Sum-
Hersey Charles, real estate broker, 141 Main, h 4
Hersey C. D. mechanic, h 2 Di x   [Stafford
Hersey Henry W. cabinet maker, bds 8 Union
Hersey Wm. foreman at rolling mill, h 9 Wa'er
Hervey A. G. (Pike & Hervey,) bds Waldo house
Hervey Mrs. S. T. h Bowdoin
Hesion Patrick, laborer, h Exchange
Heslin Thomas, machinist, h 99 Summer
Heslor Jacob, (Young, H. & Co.) bds 6 Walnut
Hession John H. machinist, bds 63 Exchange
Hewett Elbridge h 6 Liberty
Hewett George F. h 6 Liberty [stal s, bds 14 Park
Hewitt Ann M. dress making, Clarke's block, up
Heywood Charles H. clerk, bds 3 Everett
Heywood Benj. F. physician, 147 Main
Heywood Henry, h 1 Charlton
Heyw od Reuben, clicker, bbs 27 Laurel
HEYWOOD S. R. boots & shoes, 223 Main, h 14
Heywood Wm. clerk, bds 27 Laurel   [Crown
Heywood Wm. H. farmer, 412 Main
Hibbert Newell, shoemaker, h 21 School
Hickey Daniel D. melter at Washburn's, h 15
Hickey James, laborer, h Cypress,   [Providence
Hickey James. laborer, bds Columbia court
Hickey John, at Nor. R. R. ft. house, h rear Sar-
    gent's block
Hickey Mathew, switchman, h 1 E. Worcester
Hickey Peter, tailor, bds Columbia court
Hickey Thomas, machinist, bds 8 S. Irving
Hickey Thos. laborer, h W. Boylston, Northville
Hicks Elijah W. millwright, h rear Ward
Hick Rev. Joseph, h 17 Wilmot
Hicks Samuel P. millwright, bds rear Ward
Higgins Elon G. paper hanger, h 7 William
Higgins F. W. paper hanger, h 71 Chandler
Higgins Lawrence, laborer, h 3 E. Worcester
Higgins Morris, at W. R. R. b 29 Shrewsbury
Higgins Patrick, switchman, W. R. R. h rear
    Shrewsbury
Higgins Thomas, jobber, h 18 Shrewsbury
Higgins W. F. wireworker. 24 Front, bds 82 Main
Higginson Rev. T. W. h 5 Chatham
Highland School, C. B. Metcalf, Salisbury
Hildreth Mrs Elizabeth E. h Larkin
Hildreth Geo. G. sexton & undertaker, Exchange
    cor. Waldo, h 43 Summer

Hildreth Sam'l E. machinist, Merrifield's building, h 5 Trumbull

H'll Rev. Alonzo, pastor 2d congregational ch. h

Hill Benj. B. wireworker, h 26 Summer

HILL CALVIN A. & THOMPSON, botanic physicians, 82 Main, bds Exchange hotel

Hill Charles P. reed maker, bds 13 Beacon

Hill Cornelius H. case maker, at Taylor & Farley's, h 65 Southbridge

Hill Edwin H. wiredrawer, bds 14 Lincoln

Hill James B. at Childs & Howe, bds 27 John

Hill J. Henry. counsellor, 8 Brinley hall, h Salisbury cor Waldo   [School

Hill John Q. druggist, Mechanics hall, bds 10

Hill Joseph S. ale,38 Mechanic, bds Farmers' hotel

Hill Lyman E. machinist, bds 5 High

Hill Martin, machinist, bds 31 Union

Hill Richard, laborer, h Florence

Hill Wm. A. painter, h 27 John   [Clinton

Hill Wm. B. bookkeeper, at Arcade M. I. Co. h 13

Hills Wm. plowmaker, court mill, h 3 Orchard

Hillyer George, confectioner, h 71½ Main

Hilton John, stoves, 28 Front, h 55 Front

Hilton Levi, boottreer, h 31 Summer

Hilton Wm. weaver, h 33 Green

Hine J. M. artist, h 12 Grove

Hines Edwin W. shoemaker, h 43 Mechanic

Hines John, wiredrawer, h 22 Temple

Hines Mathew, helper, h Oak hill road

Hines Michael, tailor, h Cross

Hinsdale James T. pistol maker, bds 103 Pleasant

Hinsdale Lewis, forger, h Slater's court

Hinkley Frederick, machinist, h 16 Millbury

Hirsch Gustav, clerk, bds Waldo house

Hitchcock David. boots and shoes, Exchange cor. Summer, h 73 Summer

Hitchcock H. S. carpenter, bds 27 Chatham

Hitchcock J. Evarts, armorer, h 10 Salem

Hoar Chas. R. saloon, Harrington cor. h 22 Central

Hoar Geo. F counsellor, 2 Bank block, h Oak av.

Hoar Wm. R. at Harrington cor. saloon

Hobart Anson L physician, h 10 Green

Hobart Emory D. clerk, bds 36 Front

Hobbs George, brick manufacturer, 105 Main, h 12 State cor. Harvard

Hobbs George 2d, machinist, h 55 Chandler

Hobbs Horace, h Lincoln

Hobbs Jairus M. boottreer, h Langdon

Hobbs Miss Louisa, dressmaker, 62 Front

Hobbs Marcus, carpenter, h 10 William

Hobbs S. M. h 7 Chandler

Hobbs Mrs. Wm. h 1 Green

Hobbs Wm. H. bds 12 State

Hodgdon Lemuel M. mechanic, h 37 Mulberry

Hodges Addison S. moulder, h rear 48 Front

Hodges Geo. C. moulder, h 53 Central [Piedmont

Hodgkin Orlando, tends saloon, 232 Main, bds

Hodgkins Daniel, machinist,h Main cor Lagrange

Hodgkins Orrin, machinist, bds 2 Warren

Hogan Jeremiah, wire finisher, h 3 Arch

Hogan John, laborer, h 94 Southbridge

Hogan John, tailor, bds 73 Salem

Hogan John, laborer, h E. Central

Hogan John, mechanic, h Lamartine

Hogg Edward. hostler, h Canal

Holbrook B. E. clerk, bds 36 Front

Holbrook Charles A. attorney, 4 Flagg's block, h 6 George   [2 Am. H. bl'k, h 81 Chandler

Holbrook (Charles W.) & Terry, (Ell) booksellers,

Holbrook DeWitt C. bookkeeper, 59 Chandler

Holbrook Eliphalet, machinist, h 47 Austin

Holbrook Hiram, boot finisher, h 8 Maple

Holbrook John, clerk, bds 44 Front

Holbrook Micah, h 49 Austin

Holbrook Pliny, h 6 Trumbull

Holbrook Sewall, carpenter, h 8 Crown   [Austin

Holbrook Wm. D. (W. H. Dexter & Co.) h 49

Holden Cyrus B. gunsmith, h Blossom cor Russell

Holden Geo. W. clerk W. M. F. Ins. Co. bds 35

Holden Henry H. clerk, h Penn av.   [Lincoln

HOLDEN HOWARD,City mills, Exch. h 44 Front

Holden Nathan, agent for T. Brown, soap & candles, h 20 Providence

Holden Nathan W. (P. & N. W.) bds 20 Providence

Holden Patrick, laborer, at Rural Cemetery, h [21 Pyovidence

Holden Parker, & N. W. flour & grain, 42 Main, h

Holdsworth Henry, machinist, h 66 Summer

Holihan Mrs. Bridget, h Cross

Holihan Michael, hostler, h Cambridge, N. W.

Holland Edward, bootfitter, h 35 Temple

Holland Geo. A. proprietor Sardinian Ointment, h

Holland Henry, machinist, h 5 Shelby   [Newton

Holland Joseph, machinist, bds cor Washington and Plymouth

Hollender J. (Waterman & H.) h 1 Hinds ct.

Holly David, at ct. mills, h 13 Market

Holm Wm. at rolling mill, h rear 70 Mechanic

Holman Cyrus W. farmer, bds May   [place

Holman Horace, at T. K. Earle's, h Russell st.

Holman Moses, at T. K. Earle's, h Providence

Holman Wm. Y. farmer, h Mav

Holmes Albert N. carpenter, rear 22 Thomas, h Edward cor Newport   [port

Holmes Erastus N. carpenter, h Edward cor Newport

Holmes E. S. clerk, bds 89 Pleasant

Holmes Geo. clerk, h 3 Fulton

Holmes Henry, armorer, h 62 Austin

Holmes J. W painter at hospital

Holmes Lewis, Prov. R. R. bds 5 Orange

Holmes Pitt, carpenter, h Cambridge, S. W.

Holmes R. G. improved churns,ct. mills,h 8 School

Holmes Wm. tanner. h Milton

Holohan Patrick, at Crompton's, h rear 10 E. Central

Holt Aaron H. wiredrawer, h N. Ashland   [tral

HOLT MRS EMILY B. medical electrician, 6 Southbridge

Holt George. (Hampson & Holt) h 55 Summer

Holt Hamilton manuf'r of eave troughs, gutters, &c. Union cor Exchange, h 105 Pleasant

Holt H. W. hackman, h 4 Newbury

Holt James, enamelled cloth printer, h 2 Pond

Holt John, enamelled cloth printer, h 12 E. Wor.

Holt Richard, machinist, h 6 Church

Holt Samuel, painter, h 6 Southbridge

Holton Charles S. machinist, h 5 Pond

Holton Josiah C. boottreer, h 50 Front

Holton Lucius N. hackman, h 145 Pleasant

Homer Virgil M. car painter, h 21 Washington

HOMES G. & Co. (C. A. Cushman) China tea store, 230 Main, 12 Congress

Hood Alfred, wheelwright, 11 Central, h 85 Summer   [mer

Hood Frank, brickmaker, h 12 Pond

Hood J. Hamilton, carpenter, bds 13 Salem

HOOD JOHN L. furniture and crockery dealer, 228 Main, h 6 William

Hood Wm. A. machinist, h 16 Carroll

Hooker F. G. saloon, 115 Main

Hooker Mrs. Mary H. h Mason [Main, h Belmont

Hooper Wm. R. editor & publisher Transcript, 206

Hopkins Orrin S. clerk, bds 15 Main

Hopkins Thomas, teamster, 10 Bridge

Hoppin Charles A. machinist. bds 18 Portland

HOPPIN GEO. S. & CO. flour dealers, 7 Mechanic, h 18 Portland

Hopwood Daniel, clicker, 21 Grove

Horan Hugh, farmer, h Grafton
Horan Timothy, laborer, h Ward
Horgan John, blacksmith, ct. mill, 60 Mechanic
Horton John, jeweler, h 16 Green   [5 High
Hoskins Wm. R. painter at O Blood & Son's, bds
Hosmer Mrs. Luther jr. h Leicester, N. W. [av.
Houghton Alba jr. (C. C. H. & Co.) h Harrington
Houghton Alex presser at A.P.Ware's,bds 22 Park
Houghton Augustus,envelopes,h Main opp. Beaver
Houghton Chas. C. & Co. (Alba Houghton, jr.)
    boot manufacturers. h 28 William
Houghton Charles S. farmer. Pleasant
Houghton Daniel F. at Taylor & Farley's. h 65
Houghton Geo. A. machinist,h 37 Salem [Austin
Houghton Hannibal H. (Thayer, H. & Co) h 20
    Plymouth
Houghton Henry, machinist, bds 24 Exchange
Houghton Josiah P.water wheel maker, h 3 Queen
Houghton L. (Dennis & H.) h cor. Main & Austin
Houghton M. H. h 11 Pleasant
Houghton Samuel H. h Penn av.
Houlihan D. M. groceries, 12 Washington square
Hovey Mrs. Wm. h 43 Summer   [4 Reservoir
Howard Alonzo J. F. butcher, 2 Bang's block, h
Howard Ansel B. at ct. mill, h 27 Bowdoin
Howard Chas. A. card maker, bds 3 Fulton
Howard David, bds 12 Thomas
Howard Henry R. clerk, bds Exchange hotel
Howard John R. hair dresser, Piper's block, bds 12
Howard John, machinist,bds 4 Central ct [Thomas
Howard John P. card maker, bds 3 Fulton
Howard Justin, stabler, Exch. hotel, h 16 Lincoln
Howard Mrs. Mary, h E. Central
Howard Michael, laborer. h 65 Exchange
Howard O. 2d. clerk, bds 44 Pleasant
Howard Peter, wiredrawer, h Garden
Howard Mrs. Sarah J. tailoress, h 53 Pine
Howard Thomas, bootturner. h 1 E Central
Howam Thomas, bootmaker, bds 9 Tremont
HOWE A. M. boot & shoe cutters, Armsby's build-
    ing, Central, h 13 Harvard
Howe Daniel, blacksmith, h Bridge cor. Summer
Howe Edward E. cl'k, H. Ayres, bds 20 Pleasant
Howe Geo. A. painter, h Slater's court
Howe Geo. S. & A. J. dealers in manuf'rs articles,
    Bank block, h 19 High   [h 4 George
Howe (Geo. S.) & Hackett (W. H.) groceries, 103
Howe Israel, mechanic. h 14 Grove
Howe John. bootclick, h 31 Portland
Howe John C. armorer, h Benefit court
Howe John W. (Childs & H.) h John St. court
Howe Joseph farmer, Chester
Howe Mrs. Kesiah, h 14 Harvard
Howe Leander, carpenter, h 38 Austin
Howe Levi, blacksmith, h 5 Shrewsbury
Howe Lyman. blacksmith, ct. mill, h 20 Grove
Howe Milton K. wood worker, h 22 Grove
Howe Nathan C. stove dealer, Mason cor. Austin
Howe Samuel G. shoemaker, W. L. Woods
Howe Mrs. Sarah R. millinery & bonnet pressing,
    h 3 Chandler   [h 6 Grove
Howe Thomas R. carpenter, at Ball & Williams,
Howe Wm. bread driver, bds 11 Maple
Howe Wm. B. machinist, bds 42 Central [9 Fruit
Howes Edward S. foreman of gas fitting shop, bds
Howes Geo. W. carpenter, bds 2 Maple pl.
Howes Isaac. bootcrimper, h 9 Fruit
HOWLAND A. H. & CO. (Jos. A. H.) Wheeler &
    Wilson's sewing machines, 239 Main, up str's
Howland Edward P. clerk, bds 16 Summer
Howland Ezra T. lumber yard, Central, h 161
    Southbridge   [Main, h 410 Main
HOWLAND HENRY J. book & job printer, 212

Howland John, moulder, h Slaters ct.
Howland John, carpenter, bds Laurel lane
Howland Jos. A. (A. H. Howland & Co.) h 23
    Bowdoin   [Summer
Howland S. A. ins. agent, Cen. Exchange, h 16
Howland Wm. O. clerk, bds 16 Summer
Howland Wilber, car inspector. h Laurel lane
Hoy James, mason, h 27 Temple
Hoyle Francis, shoemaker, bds 102 Southbridge
Hoyle Wm. machinist, bds 71 Southbridge
Hoyt Geo. L. armorer. bds 378 Main
Hoyt Henry A. wiredrawer, h Quinsigamond
Hoyt Jared, superintendent at N. Washburn's h
    Mendon   [ston
Hubbard Andrew D. wiredrawer, bds W. Boyl-
Hubbard Cyrus K. fruit and confectionery, 248½
    Main, h 10 Chandler   [7 Salem
Hubbard Emmons J. clerk for S. Taft & Son, bds
Hubbard Henry B agt. for H. B. Fay, h 36 Austin
Hubbard Henry M. hackman, h 42 Elm
Hubbard Joel, farmer, h W. Boylston
Hubbard Lorenzo D. carpenter, h 32 Irving
Hubbard Oscar, wiredrawer at Goddard's
Hubbard Oscar A. farmer, bds W. Boylston
Huber Chas. gunsmith, h Lafayette
Hubon Peter E. physician, h 62 Front
Huchins Patrick. laborer, bds 24 Exchange
Hudson Horace, Mill st.   [3 Maple
Hudson James O. at Bowker's bonnet factory, bds
Hudson Leonard R. refreshment room, 115 Main
Hudson Wm. (Cummings & H.) h Westminster
Hughes Patrick. laborer, h 26 E. Worcester
Hughes Richard, roller, bds 7 Burt
Hunt Addison A. school teacher, h 36 Austin
Hunt Daniel E. armorer, h Webster
Hunt Mrs. Fanny C. boarders, h 76 Main
Hunt John A. manuf'r, h Leicester, V. F.
Hunt Marcus B. bread driver, bds 59 Pleasant
Hunt Phillips, boot manufacturer, 309 Main, h 53
Hunt Stephen W. h 41 Green   [Chatham
Hunt Thomas A. machinist, h 8 Liberty
Hurgin Timothy, currier, h 28 Temple
Hurlburt Chas. on Nash. R. R. h 21 Southbridge
Hurlburt John, cook at Exchange saloon, h 12
Hurlburt Mrs. Thomas N. h 7 William   [Grove
Hurly Daniel. laborer, h 7 E. Central
Hurly John, laborer, h 80 Salem
Hurly John, laborer, h 73 Salem
Hurly John. wiredrawer, h Greve
Hurly Lawrence, laborer. h 4 Chandler ct.
Hurly Patrick, tailor, h 85 Front
Hurly Thomas, machinist, h 56 Exchange
Huse Geo. W. millwright, h 32 Newbury
Huse Wm. E. jobber, h North Newton
Hushins Patrick, laborer, bds 24 Exchange
Hutchins Asa, map agent, bds Waldo house
Hutchins C. L. carpenter, h 101 Pleasant
Hutchins Eli H. moulder, bds cor Beacon and
    Charlton
Hutchins Freeman M. shoemaker, bds 3 Maple
Hutchins F. P. at Wm. H. Dexter & Co. h cor
    Chandler and Irving
Hutchins H. H. bookkeeper, h 36 Newbury
Hutchins James D. machinist, h 37 Mulberry
Hutchinson Andrew, boot & shoe store, 49 Front
Hutchinson Benj. E. harnesses,172 Main h 34 Elm
Hutchinson Gerry, painter. Mechanic, h 4 West
Hutchinson Mrs. Nelson, h 1 Market
Hutchinson Wm. truckman, h 14 Grafton
Hyde B. W. clerk, 213 Main, h 20 High
Hyde Charles, blacksmith, h rear 195 Pleasant
Hyde Daniel H. carpenter, h Downing   [ton
Hyde E. F. (Jenkins, Hamilton & H.) h 5 Charl-

Hyde John, engineer Nor. R. R. h 30 Mechanic
Hyde James R. h 19 Myrtle
Ide Henry M. machinist, h 24 Green
Ingall Seth, carpenter, h 31 Austin
Ingalls Geo. machinist, bds 41 Summer
Inman Edwin S. bootmaker, h Mason
Inman Francis H. (Pratt & I.) h Westminster, near
Inman Otis M. machinist h 16 Elliot   [Vernon
Ingraham L. P. machinist, bds Farmer's hotel
Jackson Andrew, plowmaker, h 35 Green
Jackson Charles. clicker, h 38 Newbury
Jackson Dwight S. brush peddler, h 1 Gold
Jackson John, stone mason. h 14 Winter
Jackson Jonathan C. machinist, bds 5 High
Jackson Joseph P. printer, bds 7 Prescott
Jackson Levi. h 7 Prescott
Jacobi Ferdinand. confectioner, 38 Front, h Me-
Jacobs Darius S. farmer, l.ds 65 Front   [chanic
Jacobs Martin, bootfitter, h 65 Front
Jacobs Matthew, laborer. h 22 Temple
JACOBS J. NELSON. manuf'r patent paper file,
     15 Central Exchange. h 15 Congress
Jacobs Mrs. Simon T. h 15 Congress
Jacobs Wm. H. h 61 Southbridge
James Benj. (R. K. & B. James,) h 3 Jamesville
James Rev. Horace, bds 294 Main
James John. roller, h Ward
James John K. machinist, h 2 Jamesville
James R. K. & B. manufacturers of knit goods,
     Jamesville   [ty
Janes Jos. L. at Bay St. planing mill, h 19 Liber-
Jankins Wm. H. barber, under Am. House block
     h 13 Prospect   [House block
Jankins Mrs. Wm. H. hair work, 1 American
Jaques Geo. h 21 Wellington
Jaques John C. h 21 Wellington
Jay Joshua, carpet cleaner, h 60 Union
Jefferson Thomas, bootheer, h Cypress
Jefts Albert M. moulder, bds 41 Main
Jefts Frederick, carpenter, Mechanic h 1 Blossom
Jefts Wheelock, carpenter. Mechanic. h 3 Blossom
JENCKS C. H. dentist, 239 Main, h 6 West
Jenkins (J. H.) Hamilton (C. W.) & Hyde (E.F.)
     dry goods, 146 Main, h 11 Elm
Jenks Horace L. machinist, h Mill, N. W.
Jenks H. B. boot manuf'r, 1 Park, h 11 Sycamore
Jennings H.J. electro-plater, 239 Main, h 5 Clinton
Jennison Geo. tinman at Russell's, bds 53 Central
Jennison Mrs. Samuel. h 15 Pearl
Jennison Wm. h 13 Chestnut
Jerome Moses, polisher, bds Northville
Jessup Rev. Lewis. h 42 Summer
Jewett Eben., (Davis & J.) bds Holden
Jewett Ebenezer. farmer Holden
Jewett Joseph. farmer, Holden
Jillson Clark, clerk police court, h 17 Chatham
Jilson Simeon, fireman Nash. R. R. bds Farmer's
Johnson A. H. laborer, h 16 Union   [hotel
Johnson Charles A. lather, h Bluff
Johnson Clark, farmer, Pleasant, Tatnick
Johnson David, wiredrawer, bds Quinsigamond
Johnson D. W. mastic roofing, Suffolk, office cor.
Johnson Mrs. Emily. h Mill | Front & Bridge
Johnson Eli, bootmaker, h Mill, Tatnuck   [Main
Johnson E. P. peoples' dining rooms, 91 & 91½
Johnson Gardner, shoemaker, h Adams square
Johnson Geo. A. painter, h 35 Summer
Johnson Geo. H. lather, h Bluff
Johnson Geo. P. shuttlemaker. bds 79 Exchange
Johnson Geo. P. harnessmaker, bds Taft's hotel
Johnson Geo. R. whitewasher, &c. h 66 Union
Johnson Geo. S. axe-helve maker. b 9 Foundry
Johnson Jas. J. hairdresser, 109 Main, h 30 Laurel

Johnson John F. clerk. bds Maple ct.
Johnson Joseph, machinist, h 13 Myrtle
Johnson Levi. watchmaker, 144 Main. h John
Johnson Levi L. loombuilder, h 40 Chandler
Johnson Lincoln L. boottreer, 122 Chandler
Johnson Micah. farmer, Mill
Johnson Nathaniel K. farmer, Mower
Johnson Peter, blacksmith, h Cambridge. N. W.
Johnson Richard. marble cutter, bds 22 Winter
Johnson Richard, h Beaver
Johnson Robert H. jobber, h 62 Union
Johnson (Rodney A.M.) & Co. (D.Tainter) manuf'rs
     spinning machinery. Union, h 5 Hanover
Johnson Samuel. shoemaker, bds 1 Millbury
Johnson Timothy, farmer, h Shrewsbury
Johnson (T. W.) & Bulah, (Chas.) painters, 77
     Main, h 28 Wilmot
Johnson Wm. painter, bds Bluff
Johnson Wm. M. machinists, h 43 Thomas
Jones Albert, laborer, h 37 Washington square
Jones Alfred P. cutter at Parker's, l.ds 300 Main
Jones David, carpenter, h 85 Summer
Jones Dexter W, (Warden & J.) bds 57 Front
Jones Henry P. mason, h Bloomingdale   [Front
Jones Horace, insole & stiffenings, 37 Front, h 57
Jones Rev. J. D, E. sup't of schools, City hall. h
Jones John, h 300 Main   [45 Providence
Jones John, moulder, bds 11 Temple
Jones John P. machinist, bds 3 Maple
Jones Mrs. Samuel, h 4 Central court
Jones Samuel A. bds 85 Summer
Jones Sylvester, foreman Junction Foundry, h
     cor. Charlton and Beacon
Jones Rev. Thomas H. h 13 Austin
Jones Timothy, h 79 Front
Jones Willard (Earle & J.) h 16 Oxford
Jordan A. H. tinman, h 26 Southbridge
JORDAN EDWIN D. pump maker, 1 White's bl'k,
     h 18 Myrtle   [1 Southbridge
JORDAN JOHN W. stoves, &c. 16 Southbridge, h
Joslin Benj. F. improved fire arms, S. Junction,
     h Beaver   [Co 's. 296 Main
Joslin C. H. bookkeeper, at Barnard, Sumner &
Joslin Geo. C. clerk, bds 59½ Main
Joslin James, machinist, bds 1 Green
Joslin Jos. N. janitor Ladies' College Institute
Joslyn Isaac R. machinist, h 1 Fulton
Joslyn J. E. machinist, bds 6 School
Joslyn Miss T. millinery rooms, 121 Main [chard
Jourdan Chas. E. clerk Nashua ft. house, h 22 Or-
Jourdan Wm. H. supt. trans. P. R. R. h 17 Green
Joyce James, farmer at Darius Rice's, Grafton
Joyce Martin, laborer, h Cross
Joyce Martin, carpenter, h 51 Shrewsbury
Joyce Thomas, teamster, h E. Worcester
Joyce Timothy, at N. Washburn's, h 7 Beach
Jube Joseph, walter at Lincoln house
Judge Andrew, machinist, h 92 Southbridge
Judge Mrs. Bridget, h cor. Winter and Canal
Judge Daniel. moulder, bds 31 Mechanic
Judge Dominick, moulder, bds 31 Mechanic
Judge James, wiredrawer, h Canal
Judge Lackey, machinist, bds Mill
Judge Patrick. bootmaker, bds 8 E. Central
Kabley Arnold, moulder, bds 90 Southbridge
Kalaher Cornelius, bootcrimper. bds 2 Chandler
Kane Jeremiah, constable, h 12 Temple   [court
Kane Jerry, machinist, bds 3 Green
Kane John, laborer, h 9 Beach
Kane John, at rolling mill, h rear 53 Salem
Kane John, laborer, h 5 Blackstone
Kane Martin, moulder, h 35 Mechanic
Kane Morris, laborer, h 16 Brown

Kane Owen, at rolling mill, rear 10 E. Central
Kane Patrick, laborer, at Hacker's coal yard
Kast Mrs. Elizabeth, h rear 12 Plymouth
Kathern A. J. rolling mill, h Grafton
Katlng John, tailor, h rear 68 Front
Katlng Patrick, laborer, h Gold
Kavanagh Mrs. Catharine. h 1 Brown
Kay Thomas, at rolling mill, h 37 Temple
Keuch Nelson, laborer at Chas. Bowen's
Kean Michael, carpenter, h Mason
KEAN (Wm. B.) & CO. (J. Toulmin,) manuf'rs
    patent binders' shears, N. W. h Webster
Kearney Thomas, bootbottomer, h 8 S. Irving
Kearning Thomas, puddler, h 1 Hibernia
Keefe Daniel, laborer, h 26 Winter
Keefe Dennis, moulder, h 4 Howard
Keefe John, laborer, h Gold
Keeven Edward, rolng mill, bds 1 Burt
Keeven William, laborer, h 23½ Winter
Kehoe Mrs. Wm. h Hill
Keily Martin, laborer. h Grove
Keith Alonzo, acct. at T. S. Stone's, bds 1 King
Keith Henry, (J. Keith & Co.) bds 20 Pleasant
Keith Henry B. clerk, bds 44 Pleasant
Keith Henry R. Ins. and real est. broker, Flagg's
Keith James R. h 21 Orchard   [block
KEITH JOHN & CO stationers and blank book
    manuf'rs, 208 Main, bds Lincoln house
Keith Mrs. L. A. h 44 Pleasant   [Howard
Kelaher Timothy, at Arcade iron foundry, h 4
Kelley Abner, farmer, Millbury avenue
Kelley Charles, mason, h rear 21 Winter
Kelley Edward, laborer, h Cross
Kelley Francis, wirecleaner, 8 Cross
Kelley F. H. physician, h and office 36 Front
Kelley James. moulder, bds 18 Central
Kelley J. Clawson, analytical physician, 142 Main
Kelley John, laborer, h 99 Summer
Kelley John M. tailor, h Cypress   [tine
Kelley John P. tailor, 12 Mechanic, h 20 Lamar-
Kelley Michael, engineer at N.Washburn's, h Burt
Kelley Orrin A. grocer, 15 Arch
Kelley Patrick, hostler, h 6 Bridge
Kelley Patrick, laborer, h 3 Chandler court
Kelley Patrick, bootfitter, h E. Worcester court
Kelley Patrick, laborer, h Ward
Kelley Patrick, junk dealer, h rear 10 E. Central
Kelloy Patrick, currier, bds 83 Front
Kelley Phillip, laborer, h cor. Canal and Cherry
Kelley Thomas, blacksmith, h 33 Lafayette
Kelley Thomas, laborer, h Quinsigamond
Kelley Thomas, laborer, h 40 Shrewsbury
Kelley Thomas. teamster, h 21 Summer
Kelley Wm. spinner, h Leicester. V. F.
Kelley Wm. laborer, h 18 E. Worcester
Kelley Mrs. Winnifred. h 20 E. Worcester
Kelliher Michael, blacksmith, h 16 Shrewsbury
Kelloy Charles C. carpenter, bds 7 Orange
Kelsey Orlando, roller. bds 2 Warren
Kelton Ira J. gunsmith, bds 83 Exchange
Kemmerer P. L. polisher, bds 2 Mechanic
Kempston Joseph, gasfitter, bds 3 Carlton
Kendall Albert G. stationery, &c. at Boston depot,
    h 9 Washington
Kendall Asa G. bds 8½ Trumbull
Kendall Caleb, weigher at City coal yd, h 21 Park
Kendall Dana C. engineer B. R. R. bds Farmers
    hotel
Kendall Edward, furniture painter, h 16 Trumbull
Kendall Francis, bonnet bleacher, rear Flagg's
    block, h 5 Irving
Kendall Geo. H. with M. Stowe, h 85 Pleasant
Kendall Mrs. H. H. h 8½ Trumbull

Kendall H. J. painter,
Kendall H. J. clerk, b
Kendall John, clerk, J
Kendall John G. agen
Kendall Maro, hat stor
Kendall Sanford M.(J.
Kendall Smith, chair p
Kendall Wm. F. at Bo
    Plymouth
Kendrick (Geo. P.) &
Kendrick John A. farn
Kenir Connor, wire cle
Keniston Wm. H. ston
Kennedy Daniel, boot
Kennedy Edmund, h 1
Kennedy John, at B.
Kennedy Michael, at r
Kennedy Michael, boo
Kennedy Patrick, labo
Kennedy Patrick, boot
Kenny Emmons S. car
Kenney John, painter,
Kenney Michael, tailor
Kennily Edward, black
Kennington John, carp
Kennington Moses, sh
Kent Ezra, job wagon,
Kent S. W. light mach
    dard & Rice's, h 14
Kenyon John, tinman,
Kerber Frank, saloon,
Kerin James, laborer,
Kern Frank, machinis
Kern John, wire clean
Kern Mrs. Mary, h 13
Kerns Murt, laborer, h
Kerr Mrs. John, h 22 T
Kervick Patrick, porte
    Main, h rear 20 Th
Kervin Dennis, laborer
Kerwin Mark, spinner,
Kett Henry F. clerk, b
Kettell Daniel, bds cor.
Kettell James F. clerk,
Kettell James S. hatte
Kettell John P. hats
    Thomas
Kettell Thos. J. whitew
Keven Patrick, bootma
Keves Solomon, bootm
Keyes Chas. A. painte
Keyes David D. grocer
Keyes Edward, at A. M
Keyes Israel N. (J. L.
Keyes John L. & I. N.
    Exchange, h 17 Sc
Keyes Justin L. Weste
Keyes Shurbern. fish 1
Keyes Thomas, heater,
Kickam Wm. moulder,
Kidder Geo. M. painter
Kies Erastus, armorer.
Kilburn Charles, headv
Kildae Martin, laborer,
Kiley Michael P. moul
Kiley Wm. laborer, roll
Kilgour James, blacker
Kilgour Wm. boot crin
Killeps John, engineer
Kimball G. B. clerk at
Kimball Juliette W. dr
Kimball Leonard, farm
King Charles A. carpe

King Charles W. wirefinisher, h 1 Salem
King Daniel, currier, h 21 Prescott
King Edward W. machinist, h 15 Gold
King E. J. machinist, b 3 Maple   [Quincy
King Francis L. counsellor, 4 Cen. Exchange, h 2
King Geo. T. baker at hospital, h 91 Summer
King Henry J. machinist, American house block
King James M. moulder, bds 41 Summer
King James M. wiredrawer, h Cambridge
King Wm. hostler, Exchange
Kingale August, gigger, bds 1 Millbury
Kingsbury George, miller for W. W. Patch, h Mill
Kingsley Geo. pistol maker, bds 7 Mechanic
Kinney B. H. sculptor and cameo cutter, 188 Main
   h 6 Laurel
Kinney Geo. W. bootmaker, bds 103 Summer
Kinney Wm. P. machinist, h 25 Salem
Kinnicutt (F. H.) & Co. (S. Woodward,) hardware,
   162 Main, h 1 Chestnut   [Lincoln house
Kinnicutt Thomas, counsellor, 6 Brinley hall, bds
Kinsley Daniel, messenger of courts, h rear Ct. H.
Kirby Charles, armorer, h Piedmont
Kirby Geo. E. whipmaker, bds 9 Thomas
Kirby Mrs. James, h Adams square
Kirby Tyler C. (Richardson & K.) h 9 Thomas
Kittredge A. W. paper hanger, h 5 Gold
Kittredge L. W. mason, bds 5 Gold   [22 Thomas
Kittredge M. H. at Prouty's provision market,bds
Kivnay Dominick, laborer, 31 Mechanic
Klein John, barber, h Lafayette
Knapp Alfred, B. bonnet presser, bds 1 Eden
Knapp Henry E. fancy goods, Waldo block, h 5
Knapp John, wiredrawer, bds 30 Grove   [Elliot
Knapp Judson, laborer, h E. Worcester
Knapp Mrs. L. E. h 48 Elm
Kneeland Andrew, gardener, h 13 Brown
Kniffen L. G. bds Exchange hotel
Knight Albert A. farmer, h Burncoat
Knight Alden B. milk dealer, h Burncoat
Knight Edwin A. painter, h Burncoat
Knight Elijah W. freight, W. R. R. h 32 Orange
Knight Elijah, woodsawer, h Mason
Knight Franklin H. acct. & collector, h 13 Salem
Knight Mrs. Harriet, teacher Orphan's home, 64
   Shrewsbury
Knight James, truckman, h 67 Summer
Knight Mrs. Jerusha, h 27 Oxford
Knight Joseph A. belt maker, h 20 Central
Knight Prentiss, farmer, Burncoat
Knight Willard P. carpenter, h Brattle
Knight Wm. foreman at Nash. R.R. shop, h 3 Lib-
Knights Frank, teamster, bds 13 Grafton   [erty
Knights Henry W. h 17 Crown   [h 28 Pleasant
KNIGHTS JONA. H. hat & cap store, 163 Main,
Knights Otis H. carpenter, h 80 Southbridge
Knowles Wm. machinist, bds 63 Austin
Knowlton Mrs. Asa, h Prescot
Knowlton Charles H. carpenter, bds 3 Fulton
Knowlton (Chas. L.) & Dutch (J. C.) Bay State
   shoe store, h 40 Summer
Knowlton Daniel W. (Freeland & Co.) h 7 Seaver
Knowlton Geo. carpenter, bds Bloomingdale
Knowlton Nathan M. attendant at Hospital
Knowlton J. S. C. sheriff, & publisher of Palladi-
   um, 9 Central Exchange, h Salisbury
Knowlton Mrs.Lucy,bds cor Webster & Cambridge
Knowlton Luke, machinist, h 1 Chandler
Knowlton Pomeroy, box maker, h 14 Chestnut
Knowlton Samuel, wood worker, h 7 Arch
Knowlton Thomas W.ship carpenter, h Hammond
Knowlton Wm. F. carpenter, h 95 Summer
Knowlton Wm. M. wood dealer, h 93 Pleasant
Knox Henry F shoemaker, h 44 Newbury

Knox Jerome, tinner, bds 2 Bartlett place
Knox (Joseph B.) & Lang (C.) die sinkers and
   engravers. Harrington cor. h 1 Sycamore
Knox Robert R. shoemaker, h 3 Ash   [Lincoln
Knox Samuel A. plow pattern maker, C. mill, h 4
Kobler Conrad, spinner, h 22 Millbury
Koch Ernest, carriage maker, h 9 Washington
Kochan Jephrey, laborer, h Lovell's court
Kolman Jacob, laborer, h Lamartine
Kough Michael, laborer, h 15 Summer
Kuhl Frederick, hatter at Knights', h 32 Exchange
Kyle Mrs. Chas. A. 8 E. Central
LaBanister Wm. machinist, bds 81 Exchange
Lackey Albert, h 343 Main
Lackey A. W. shoe manuf'r, h 8 Wellington
Lackey Rufus A. couchman at hospital
Lacross Cyprian, moulder at court mill
Lacy Michael, soap driver, h 15 Millbury
Ladd Vernon A. grocer, 6 Green, h 14 Green
Lahry James, planer, 23 Temple
Lodoux Ezra, engineer at H. S. Washburn's, h
   Bloomingdale
Lakeman Ebenezer, mason, bds Farmer's hotel
Lally James, city laborer, h E. Central
Lamar John, helper, h 23 Winter   [Summit
Lamb Chas. wire manuf'r, Washington st, h 3
Lamb Chas. H. card wiredrawer, bds 3 Summit
Lamb Edward, carpenter, Cypress, h 8 Hanover
Lamb Isaac, farmer, Brooks
Lamb Jairus B. tinman, h 12 Church
Lamb Jeremiah B. wiredrawer, h 5 Orchard
Lamb John G. wiretemperer, h 8 Grove
Lamb Thomas M. watchmaker, 275 Main, h 36
   Pleasant
Lambert James, weaver, h rear 24 Millbury
Lamberton Henry, blacksmith, bds 1 Carroll
Lamphere Charles H. steam & gas fixer, bds 30
Lamson A. J. overseer, Valley Falls   [Thomas
LAMSON ELI B. & Co. (Joseph Curtis,) auct'rs,
   66 and 68 Main, h 79 Pleasant
Lamson Henry H. clerk, bds 79 Pleasant
Lainson James W. finisher, h Parsons
Lamson Wm. C. car builder, h 5 Austin
Lancton Timothy, hostler, h Cypress
Lancton Mrs. Jane F. h 44 Washington
Landers Michael, grinder, Blossom
Lane Arthur W. cook at Hoar's, Harrington cor
Lane Fred. farmer, bds 3 Salisbury
Lane John, horseshoer, bds 24 Exchange
Lange William Henry, wiredrawer, bds 1 Millbury
Lang Chas. (J. B. Knox & Lang,) h 13 Congress
Langlois Paul, blacksmith, h 22 Carroll
Langway Louis, shoemaker, 33 Shrewsbury
Lanpher Horace V. blacksmith, h 65 Summer
Lao David, armorer, h 26 Madison
Larasey James, shoemaker, h 3 Orchard
Larken Michael, laborer, h 7 Howard
Larken Richard, shoemaker, h 14 Madison
Larkin Elias, merchant tailor. 245 Main, h 20 Bow-
Larned Abel, laborer. h 3 Summit   [doin
Larned Mrs. E. h 1 Walnut
Larock Antoine, farmer, Burncoat
Larvin Daniel, laborer, h Canal
Latham John,shoemaker,Central Exchange,Main,
   h 26 Chandler
Latham Wm. picker, h 22 Millbury
Lathe Martin. (Shepard, L. & Co.) h 14 Walnut
Lathrop A. H. carpenter, bds 5 High
Lathrop Edward, armorer, h Benefit place
Lathrop W. P. at C. C. Coleman's, bds 2 Oxford
Laughlin Jeremiah, laborer, h Quinsigamond
Laughlin Patrick, machinist, bds 1 Millbury
Laughlin Patrick, laborer, bds Quinsigamond

Laverty James F. fireman, h 11 Temple
Laverty John, shoemaker, h 1 Temple
Laverty Joseph, wrenchmaker, bds 65 Chandler
Laverty Joseph, wrenchmaker, bds 4 Pond
Laverty Oliver P. bootbottomer, h Forest
Laverty Philip engineer at Washburn's, h 4 Pond
Laverty Robert, carpenter, h 8 Pond
Laverty Wm. H. machinist, bds 8 Pond
Lawler Lawrence, teamster, h 15 Pond
Lawler Michael, farmer, Chester
Lawler Thomas, currier, Grafton, h 28 Grafton
Lawrence Edward R. bookbinder, bds 1 Court hill
Lawrence Edwin P. carpenter, bds 46 Newbury
Lawrence Edwin S. card maker, h 24 Grafton
Lawrence Frederic J. ornamental painter, Foster, h 11 Salem
Lawrence Geo. F. machinist, bds N. Ashland
Lawrence J. C. soap manufacturer, h 46 Newbury
Lawrence James K. wiredrawer, bds 12 Grove
Lawrence Jos. B furniture, American house bl'k, h 33 Summer   [land, cor Bowdoin
Lawrence S. E. machinist at court mill, h N. Ash-
Lawrence Wm. bowling saloon, 14 Front, h 4 Salem
Lawson Geo. machinist, h 2 Langdon
Lawton Job G. carpenter, h 2 Assonet
Lawry David F. student, bds 1 Congress
Laying George, machinist, h N. Ashland
LAZELL NATHAN, leather dealer, 199 Main, h
Lazell Nathan E. bds 6 Sudbury   [6 Sudbury
Lazell Nathan W. h Hudson
Leach Mrs. Eliza, bds 8 Edward
Leach Henry, mule spinner, h Northville
Leach Wm. machinist, h 2 Canal
Leahy Daniel bootsider, bds 5 Spring
Leahy Edward, at freight, West R. R. h 9 Charles
Learned Isaac G. clicker, bds 7 Park
Learned Mrs. Jeremiah, h 3 Queen
Learned P. A. iron fences, h 20 Beacon
Leary Bartholomew J. blacksmith, h 2 S. Irving
Leary Daniel, marble polisher, h Larkin
Leary Francis, laborer, h 58 Shrewsbury
Leary Humphrey, laborer, h Locust
Leary Patrick, laborer, h 9 Spring
Leary Patrick, laborer, h 2 S. Irving
Leary Patrick, at court mill, h North
Leary Patrick, knife scourer, Bay State house, h 15 Blackstone
Leary Patrick, currier, h 12 Winter
Leary Timothy, wire roller, bds Pink
Leathers Elliot G. machinist, bds 16 Congress
Leavens Daniel, h Canal
Leavens James L. teamster for J. S. Hill, h 2 Vine
LeBaron Mrs. Mary D. h 23 Harvard
Lebo Alexander, spinner, Leicester
Lebo Peter, spinner, Leicester
Lee B. F. bookkeeper at Witt & Pratt's, bds Waldo
Lee Dennis, blacksmith, h 17 E. Central   [house
Lee Harry O. bonnets, &c. 154 Main, bds Bay St. H.
Lee Henry A. (Dennis & L.) Union st. h 2 Crown
Lee James, watchman Nash. R. R. shop, h 6 Church
Lee John M. laborer, W. R. R. h 13 Foundry
Lee Pardon, carpenter, bds 6 Park
Lee Mrs. Samuel P. h 7 Fruit
Lee Wm. bootfitter, h 34 Shrewsbury
Lee Zebina, carpenter, h 181 Pleasant
LeHur Theodore, stone cutter, h 3 Goddard
Leigh Stephen, hostler, h 25 Laurel
Leighton Ariel H. tin peddler, h Abbot
Leighton Walter H. bds 2 Sudbury
Lejare Eugene, millinery & fancy goods, Waldo block, h 153 Main
Leland Aaron, bds Exchange hotel
Leland Edson, wheelmaker, bds 25 Mechanic

Leland James, machinist, h 5 Fulton
Leland John, machinist, h 5 Fulton
Leland L. B. boarders, h 25 Mechanic
Leland R. F. machinist, bds rear 44 Thomas
Leland Samuel R. music teacher, pianos, 48 Front h 46 Front
Leland Thomas E. wheelmaker, bds 25 Mechanic
Leonard Fred. S. Boston Express, 1 Lincoln house block, h 31 Harvard
Leonard Feran, shoemaker, bds 8 S. Irving
Leonard James, laborer, h 30 Shrewsbury
Leonard John, at city coal yard, h Locust
Leonard John, hostler, h 16 Blackstone
Leonard Martin, bootmaker, 22 Winter
Leonard Patrick, bootmaker, bds rear Sargent's
Leonard Samuel S. h Harvard place   [block
Leonard Thomas, laborer, h 38 Shrewsbury
Leseur Mrs. Mary M. h 36 Pleasant
Lester John, laborer, 24 Lafayette
Lesure Mrs. L. millinery, 156 Main
Lewis Mrs. Asa, h 18 Chatham
Lewis (Benj.) & Thayer (Benj.) eating house, 232 Main, h 4 Sycamore   [Mechanic
Lewis Benj. R. livery stable, 15 Mechanic, h 26
Lewis Geo. C. marble worker, bds rear Unit. ch.
Lewis John, moulder, bds 13 Mechanic
Lewis Joseph, moulder, h E. Worcester court
Lewis Joseph, marble yard, Market, h 10 Market
Lewis Joshua O. manuf'r, Cambridge cor. South-bridge
Lewis R. L. boottree manuf'r, h 1 Hanover
Lewis Thomas, moulder, h E. Worcester place
Lewis Thomas, marble worker, 20 Mechanic, h rear Unit. Ch. Main
Lewis W. Dean, clerk, bds 18 Chatham   [ard
Lewis Westley, clock repairer, Wash. sq. h 1 How-
Lewisson Louis, clothing bazaar, 259 Main, h State cor. Harvard
Libby Lavine, teamster, h 16 School
Lichtenfels Geo. confectioner, h 100 Southbridge
Light Edward F. machinist, Lagrange   [Hanover
Light Gardner, chief engineer, Merrifield's, h 4
Light Jos. F. (Wood, L. & Co.) h Lagrange
Lilley A. J. (Taft & L.) h 9 Harvard
Linaham John, hostler, h 16 Blackstone
Lincoln Ambrose, machinist, h 31 Washington
Lincoln Chas A. agt. at June. denot, h 15 Oxford
Lincoln Daniel W. nursery, &c. 125 Pleasant
Lincoln Edward W. h 1 Oak
Lincoln Levi, office 105 Main, h 25 Elm
Lincoln Levi, 2d. carpenter, Salisbury
Lincoln Sanford W. carpenter, h 24 Grove
Lincoln Wm. S. farmer, h May   [Mechanic
Lindsay Frank J. fireman Wor. & N. R. R. bds 15
Lindsay Ira, machinist, 27 Central
Linnell Dr. J. E homœopathist, 9 Elm   [Chatham
Liscomb Nathaniel S. clerk at Eldred's, bds 17
Little Wm. bootmaker, h Russel st. place
Littleton Mathew, moulder at Arcade Iron Co. h 26 Winter   [chanic
Littleton Michael, harness maker, bds 39 Me-
Littleton Stephen, blacksmith, h 94 Southbridge
Livermore Chas F. clerk, h 5 Prescott   [bridge
Livingston Albert T. cabinet maker, bds 71 South-
Livingston Geo. st. repairer, bds 71 Southbridge
Livingston John, street repairs, h 71 Southbridge
Lloyd John C. roofing, h Bridge cor. Mechanic
Lochner John, tailor, h 12 Temple
Locklin Frederic, machinist, bds 1 Millbury
Lock Oliver P. carpenter, bds 26 Thomas
Lock Thomas M. blacksmith, h Edward cor. Elliot
Loftus Michael, oyster saloon, under Zion's ch. h 19 E. Central

ı Parsons lane
r, h 23 Winter
bds 24 Exchango
rear 72 Mechanic
lst, 228 Main, bds 31

t, bds 15 Hanover
ı Elizabeth
r High School
l & Co.) h 15 Hanover
r, bds 5 High
ı Nor. R. R. h S. Irving
Jypress, h 22 William
ıgate
r, bds 29 Portland
ard
repairs, h Margin
h 19 Spring [Charlton
. at Freeland's, bds 15
reeland, bds 15 Charl-
st, 12 Chandler [ton
Jharlton
Bridge
h 87 Southbridge
Jypress
bds 56 Exchange
st, bds 266 Main
', h 18 William
h 8 Vine
ier, 2 7 Main [Ashland
ı, h Highland cor. N.
h 38 Pleasant
ıwer
ıker, h 1 Harris [coln
ıes, 73 Main, h 32 Lin-
ıear 28 Newbury
', rear Quinsigamond

ıer, h 20 Plymouth
ı Hermon
mill, bds 7 Burt
Central
ıut's, h E. Wor. court
ı 24 Central
O. bds Sunny Side
ıain
ıtain
untain
ıain
bds Mountain
ıwland's, bds 378 Main
May
warehouse, 248 Main,
　　　[h 18 High
y Side
25 School
ı 7 Ash
h 26 William
y State house
an, h 12 Brown's bl'k
ə　　　[ton
man B. R. R. h 6 Ful-
', h 36 Thomas
', Mountain
ıge Holy Cross
' 70 Mechanic
l Exchange
', bank, bds 390 Main
ır, bds 39 ı Main
ı Canal [Southbridge
Goddard & Rice, h
ıentral　　　[Central
vare &c. 2 Pearl, h 13

Ludington James, oysters, 10 Foster, h 19 Oxford
Lumbard Wm. miller, Chelsea　　[Reservoir
Lund Ebenezer, watchman at I. Washburn's, h 5
Luther Benj. S. wholesale clothier, Allen's bl'k,
　　bds Lincoln House
Luther Jonathan, h 10 Irving
Luther Robert, plowmaker, h Kendall hill
Lynam James, blacksmith, h 30 Liberty
Lynch Cornelius, wire cleaner, h rear 16 Shrews-
Lynch Dennis, tailor, h 11 Blackstone　　[bury
Lynch Edward, spinner, bds 1 Millbury
Lynch Jeremiah, laborer, rear 3 Spring
Lynch Peter, express driver, bds 175 Pleasant
Lynch Thomas, farmer, Brattle
Lynes John, bootbottomer, bds 8 Mechanic
Lynes Patrick, at Grove mill, h 6 E. Central
Lyon Mrs. Amos, h 13 Portland
Lyon Edward, carpenter.shop 15 Central,h 9 John
Lyon John, mason, bds Linwood place
Lyon Mrs. John, h 12 Vine
Lyon Jonathan, bds Lovell
Lyon Jonathan jr. farmer, h Lovell
Lyon Joshua B. farmer, Prouty lane
Lyon Michael, tailor, bds 41 Mechanic
Lyon Wm. baker, bds 115 Main
Mack Mrs. M. h 6 Home
Macullar Edmund P. bootmaker, h Dewey
Maddan James, wiredrawer, h Ward
Maddan John, soap boiler, 1 E. Central
Maddan Martin, farmer, h Providence court
Madden John, laborer, h 10 E. Central
Madden Thomas, wiredrawer, h 5 E. Central
Madigan John, boarding house, 5 Spring
Magennis Michael, laborer, h Canterbury
Magennis Thomas, sexton, h 17½ Temple
Magone Peter, marble cutter, bds 5 Charles
Magone Phillip, old iron dealer, h 14 Pond
Magoun Isaac W. mason, h 32 Exchange
Magoun Mrs. Margaret, b 32 Exchange
Mahan Francis, moulder, h 21 Summer
Mahan Patrick, laborer, h 28 Temple
Mahan Thomas, tailor, bds 70 Mechanic
Maher Dennis, laborer, h rear Temple, cor Canal
Maher Edward P. at T.K. Earle & Co h 19 Grafton
Maher Michael, moulder, bds 12 Thomas
Maher Patrick, laborer, h 12 Brown
Mahon John, spinner, h 8 Millbury
Mahoney Cain, tanner, h 7 Tremont
Mahoney Cornelius, laborer, bds 83 Front
Mahoney Dennis, laborer, Canterbury
Mahoney Edmond, armorer, h 9 Charlton
Mahoney Frank, laborer, h rear 3 E. Central
Mahoney James, laborer, h Grove　　[bridge
Mahoney Kane, repairer West. R. R. h 94 South-
Mahoney Morris, armorer, h 94 Southbridge
Makepeace Geo. L. carpenter, h 93 Pleasant
Malay Mrs. Lawrence, h 64 Mechanic
Malay Martin. tailor, h 45 Mechanic
Malay Wm. laborer, h 12 Winter
Mallican Michael, court mill, h 66 Mechanic
Malley Henry, laborer, bds 69 Mechanic
Malloy James, laborer, h W. Boylston, Northville
Malloy James, boottreer, h 49 Mechanic
Malloy Wm. tailor, h 69 Mechanic
Malone Dennis, at rolling mill, h 1 Burt
Malone John, laborer, h 11 Franklin
Malone M. wiredrawer at Goddard's
Malony David, blacksmith, 20 Pink
Malony James, helper, h 9 Spring
Malony Michael, blacksmith, h 76 Mechanic
Malony Robert, at Wellington's, h S. Irving
Malvina Patrick, laborer, h Apricot
Manahan Wm. H. machinist, bds 27 Chatham

Mann Mrs. Abigail, h 76 Front   [bridge
Mann Albert G. stone cutter at Junc. h 85 South-
Mann B. F. engineer, h 4 Winter
Mann Charles A. machinist, bds 76 Front
Mann Geo. E. bds 20 Salem
Mann John, clerk, bds cor May and Mason
Mann John, farmer, Brooks
Mann John jr. farmer, bds Brooks
Mann Mrs. Narcissa E. h 20 Salem
Mann Owen, h Cypress
Mann Wm. W. farmer, Pleasant, Tatnick
Manning A. C. supt. for C. Washburn & Son, h Quinsigamond
Manning D. boot manufacturer, h 7 Newton
Manning Frank, at R. H. Blair's, Pleasant
Manning John, boot crimper, bds 3 Columbia ct.
Manning Lowell, ice driver, bds cor Crescent and
Manning Michael, fuller, Cambridge   [Nashua
Manning Michael, laborer, b rear 58 Mechanic
Manning Wm. carpenter, h Highland   [land
Manning Wm. C. sign & fancy painter, bds High-
Manning Wm. J. machinist, bds 27 Chatham
Mannix Cornelius H. grocer, 37 Temple
Mannix John, laborer, h 12 Vine
Manson Otis L. h 22 Green
Maple Mrs. Angeline, h 41 Main
Maple Zebedee, moulder, bds Pink
Mar M. P. moulder, bds 12 Thomas
Marble Edwin T. machinist, h 3 Trumbull
Marble Francis, spinner, bds Valley Falls
Marble Francis R. machinist, bds Vernon
Marble H. G. freight master W. R. R. bds 22 High
Marble Holland, millwright, h 22 High   [cott
Marble Jerome, (C. A. Harrington & Co.) h 1 Pres-
Marble John P. h 1 Prescott   [Chatham
Marchant J. W. cutter at A. P. Ware & Co.'s, h 14
Marchessault Jos. carriagesmith, bds 32 Mechanic
Marcy Albert, at ct. mills, h 16 Walnut
Marcy Charles, bds 22 High
Marcy Chas. D. carpenter, h 14 Bowdoin
Marcy Chauncy L. pattern maker, h 7 Vine
Marcy Geo. farmer, Gates lane
Marcy Hosea J. farmer at hospital
Marcy Jeremiah S. machinist, h 8 Union
Marcy Merrick D. machinist, h 14 Trumbull
Marky James, moulder, h Benefit
Marlar Mrs. Mary, h rear Bangs block
Marley Michael, presser, bds 1 Millbury
Marion Owen, bootsider at Rice & Meacham's
Maroney Patrick, h E. Central
Marra John, melter, h 4 Washington square
Marra Michael, tailor, h Cypress   [5 Cherry
Marrs Augustus, confectioner, &c. 151 Main, bds
Marsden Anthony, fileforger, rear 12 Cherry
Marsh Alexander D. h Southbridge, S. W.
Marsh Alex. barometer manuf'r, 7 Central Ex-
change, h 33 Elm
Marsh Mrs. A. R. h 42 Pleasant
Marsh B. C. coffin maker, h 42 Elm
Marsh Mrs. Clara B. h 27 Oxford
Marsh C. W. clicker, h 2 King
Marsh Edward A. machinist, bds 42 Central
Marsh Mrs. Eunice A. tailoress, h 27 Oxford
Marsh Geo. shoemaker, bds Mason
Marsh Henry A. teller Central Bank, bds 33 Elm
Marsh Mrs. M. W. h 28 Grove
Marsh S. B. shoestitcher, 8 Jackson
Marsh Samuel N. machinist. h rear 20 Thomas
Marshall E.H.bookbinder.239 Main,bds 20Pleasant
Marshall Geo. F. machinist, bds 5 Orange
Marshall Geo. S. clerk at J. L. Hood's,h 312 Main
Marshall James E. carpenter, h 5 Queen
Marshall Joshua J. hostler, h rear 7 Pearl

Martin Andrew, spinn
Martin Chas. wiredra
Martin Emery E. pedd
Martin Frederick, eng
Martin Jas. R.clothes c
Martin J. Harlow, gro
Martin Geo. F. wiredr
Martin Levi P. machi
Martin Michael, bootb
Martin Oramel, physic
Martin Owen, wiredra
Martin Patrick, garde
Martin Peter, gigger,
Martin Wm. B. machi
Marvel Mitchell, black
Marvin Chas. planer a
Mason Alonzo, 6 New
Mason Chas. F. carpe
Mason H. agent, bds
Mason Isaac, window
Mason James, moulde
Mason John, at clerk
Mason John C. Prest.
Mason Jos. cl'k of cou
Mason Jos. dealer in b
Mason Jos. W. h 4 Hi
Mason Lemuel G. mac
MASON LYMAN L. w
Mason Theo. L. clerk
Mason Thomas B. cler
Masterson Christophe
Mather Jerome S. boo
Mathews Benj. farmer
MATHEWS HENRY.
Hemans
Mathews Isaac D. for
Mathews John, labore
Mathews Wm. J. plum
Mathewson John, mas
Matthews Edmund, la
Matthews Eli, wheelu
Matthews Hugh, at A
Matton James H. fore
Maud John, at Curtis'
Maudsley Wm. bootr
Mawhinney John, last
Mawhinney Samuel, (
Maxwell Wm. B. coun
May Chas. F. pattern
May Edward F. butch
May Elijah, laborer, h
May Elijah T. laborer
May Mrs. Harriet, dre
May Mrs. Samuel, h c
May John B. painter,
May Oliver W. carpen
Mayberger Cosmer, b
Madison
Mayberger John, arm
Mayer Martin, brushn
Maynard Ezra, h 30 V
Maynard John A. carp
Maynard John Q, cler
Congress
Maynard Jos. A. (Sto
Maynard Leonard, bd
Maynard Lyman A. b
Maynard Malcom W.
Maynard Mander A. t
Maynard Mrs. Mary, h
Maynard Mrs. Mary
Maynard Reuben S. ca
Maynard M. Williams

Maynard Samuel A. farmer, Burncoat
Maynard Wm. G. at Taft & Lilley's, h 38 Summer
Maynard Wm. L. repairs pumps at Tucker's, h 18 Newbury
Mayo Wm. supt. Fox's mills, bds Vernon
McAlister John carpenter, bds 27 Mechanic
McAllecr Reynolds, harnessmaker, bds 82 Central
McArdle John, bootmaker, bds 18 Central
McArdle Owen, tender, bds 9 Millbury
McArdle Patrick, moulder, h 27 Union
McAtee Rev. F. prof. belles lettres, &c. College Holy Cross
McAvoy James, tailor, bds 23 Winter
McAvoy James, laborer, h Quinsigamond
McAvoy Michael, gigger, bds 9 Millbury
McAvoy Patrick, laborer, h 45 Mechanic
McAvoy Thomas J. hostler at W. B. Fox's, h cor Ward and Vernon
McCabe Henry, laborer, h Canal
McCaffaray Dennis, laborer, h Winter court [lem
McCafferty M. J. counsel'r, 3 Flagg's bl'k.h 52 Sa-
McCambridge Mrs. Alexander, h 19 Washington
McCambridge Francis, trader, 19 Washington
McCan Charles, wiredrawer, h 7 Bridge
McCan Edward, gasfitter, h 13 School
McCan Mrs. Eliza, h 13 Blackstone
McCan Felix, stone mason, h 47 Mechanic
McCan Hugh, stone mason, h 23 Blackstone
McCan James. bootmaker, h rear 70 Mechanic
McCan John, U. S. stable, h 24 Mechanic
McCan Owen, gas works, h School
McCan Patrick, gas works, h 19 Pink
McCan Patrick 2d, gas works, h Linwood place
McCan Thomas, gas fitter, h rear 34 Green
McCan Thomas 2d, gas works, h Pink
McCann Ross, helper, h 25 Blackstone
McCann Thomas, bootfitter, h rear 70 Mechanic
McCannen Charles, loomfixer, bds 1 Millbury
McCannen Charles, wiredrawer, bds 1 Millbury
McCannen James, machinist, bds 1 Millbury
McCarty John, heater at N. Washburn's
McCarty Mrs. John, h 62 Shrewsbury
McCarty John, laborer, h 87 Front
McCarty Mrs. John, h 13 Blackstone
McCarty Michael, wirecleaner, h O'Rourke place
McCarty Michael, coachman, h 30 Oxford
McCarty Michael J. wiredrawer at Goddards
McCarty Patrick, bootmaker, h 10 Pond
McCarty Patrick, heater, h 8 Mulberry
McCarty Peter, laborer, h 37 Temple
McCarty Thomas, laborer, h Lincoln
McCauliff Michael, grocer, h 25 Shrewsbury
McCausland James F. machinist, bds 15 Chandler
McClennan Wm. H. clerk at Knight's, h 5 Home
McClosky John, harness maker, bds 34 Elm
McClosky Patrick, at Pratt & Inman's, h Millbury cor Foyle
McCombe John, bootmaker, 4 Foster, h 1 Winter
McConvill Henry, cardmaker,cor Park&Trumbull
McConvill M. S. druggist, 24 Trumbull, cor Park
McConvill Peter J. machinist, bds cor. Park &
McCormick James, laborer, h 34 Green[Trumbull
McCormick James, laborer, h rear 72 Mechanic
McCormick James, laborer, h 39 Mechanic
McCormick John, laborer, h Lynde
McCormick John J. armorer, bds 34 Green
McCormick Patrick, Quinsigamond
McCourt Owen, laborer, h 99 Summer
McCoy Joseph, wiredrawer, h Wall
McCoy Michael, laborer, 34 Shrewsbury
McCuddy Cornelius, laborer, h 33 Temple
McCue Martin, laborer, h 2 Howard
McCue Thomas, clicker, h 23 Summer

McCullagh, grinder, rear of 25 Winter
McCullugh James, gas works, h 47 Mechanic
McCune Owen, laborer, h 63 Exchange
McCune Thomas, laborer, h 28 Millbury
McDermot Bernard, laborer, h Lynde
McDermot Francis, striker. h 5 Howard
McDermot Henry, waiter, Bay State house
McDermot James, laborer, h rear Bangs bl'k
McDermot James, hackman, bds 32 Southbridge
McDermot John, walter, Bay State house
McDermot Mathew, laborer, h 35 Shrewsbury
McDermot Patrick, laborer, h 23 Winter
McDermot Mrs. Sarah, h 32 Southbridge
McDermott John, tailor, h 12 Bridge
McDermott John, laborer, 4 Bridge
McDivitt ——, ropemaker, h 56 Shrewsbury
McDolan Archibald, baker, bds College
McDolan John, farmer, h College
McDolan John jr. engineer, Southgate
McDolan Moses, farmer, bds College
McDonald Peter. truckman, h 36 Shrewsbury
McDonnald Alex'r, at T. K. Earle's, h 2 Lagrange
McDonnald Alex'r, wiredrawer, Quinsigamond
McDonnald James, moulder, h 7 Charles
McDonnald James, farmer, h Webster
McDonnald James, laborer, h 20 E. Worcester
McDonnald John, teamster, h 3 Foyle
McDonnald John, boottreer, h 33 Temple
McDonald John A. moulder, bds 32 Thomas
McDonnald Michael, laborer, h 7 Bridge
McDonnald Patrick, laborer, h 2 Howard
McDonnel Peter, laborer, h 2 Charles
McDonnel Patrick, laborer, h 3 E. Worcester
McDonough Peter, at Fox & Rice, bds 10 Millbury
McFadden James, moulder, h 11 Orchard
McFadden Samuel, moulder, h 5 Howard
McFarland David, jr. manuf'r of card setting machines, Junction, h 34 Portland
McFarland E. D. at Arcade Iron Co. h 10 Cherry
McFarland Hosea, bootmaker, h Salisbury
McFarland Ira, farmer, Pleasant   [Providence
McFarland Jas. overseer at county house, h 17
McFarland John L. painter, 48 Central, h 50 Central   [15 Park
McFarland Warren, agt. Arcade Mal. Iron Co. h
McFarland Wm. bootfinisher, bds 50 Front
McFarran John. laborer, bds Lodi
McGaddy Jeremiah, moulder, h N. Ashland
McGaddy Michael, laborer, h 15 Summer
McGaffy B. B. laborer, h Canterbury
McGarr Barnard, wiredrawer, h 21 Pink
McGarr Edward, Wellington's coal yard, h 17
McGarr John. machinist, h 12 Grafton[Blackstone
McGarr Patrick, laborer. h 24 Pink
McGarvis James, gardener, h Pink
McGee John, bootfitter, h 7 Bridge
McGenness Michael, helper, h Canterbury
McGillycuddy Cornelius, grocer, 4 Wash. Square
McGillycuddy P. polisher, h 39 Shrewsbury
McGirl James, h 16 Bridge
McGirl John, laborer, h 22 Winter
McGirl Peter, hod carrier, h Hill
McGoun Patrick, laborer, h E. Central
McGourty Michael, h Ward
McGourty Owen, laborer, h Oak avenue
McGowen Felix, fish peddler, bds Cross
McGowen Michael, laborer, h 5 E. Worcester
McGowen Neal, at Hacker's, h E. Central
McGrath Edward, laborer, h 5 Bridge
McGrath James, laborer, h King
McGrath Mrs. Jane, h 16 Bridge
McGrath John, at Wellington's, h 56 Mechanic
McGrath Lawrence, laborer, h Grove

McGrath Michael. currier, h Temple
McGrath Michael, laborer, h 62 Salem
McGrath Michael, laborer, h S. Irving [chanic
McGrath Michael, mason tender, h rear 70 Me-
McGrath Michael, well digger, h King
McGrath Peres, laborer, h 72 Salem
McGrath Thomas, laborer, bds Linwood place
McGrath Wm. stone mason, h King
McGregor Mrs. Alexander, h 7 Myrtle
McGregor Alex. painter, h 7 Myrtle
McGregor Wm. armorer, h 4 Lafayette
McGuigan Lawrence, wheelwright, h 99 Summer
McGuilhicuddy Thomas, farmer. h Cypress
McGuire Francis, blacksmith, bds 5 Spring
McGuire Richard. bootcrimper, h 54 Mechanic
McGunigal Barnard, at roll'g mill, h 70 Mechanic
McGunigal James, hostler, h 70 Mechanic
McGurty Michael, wiredrawer, bds 5 Belmont
McHugo Michael, bootsider, bds 31 Union
McIntire David, machinist, bds 2 Lafayette
McIntire Elijah, street repairs, bds 309 Main
McIntire John, wiredrawer, h Cambridge
McIntire Joseph, machinist, h 13 Temple
McIver David H. machinist, bds 2 Warren
McIver Wm. B. machinist, bds 1 Warren
McKenna Geo. mason, h 6 Temple
McKenna James, mason. h cor. Beach & Brown
McKenna James, h 22 Winter [Cross
McKenna M J. professor languages, College Holy
McKenna Patrick, mason, h 6 Temple
McKenna Thomas, carpenter, bds 18 Central
McKennon James, machinist, bds 1 Millbury
McKenzie Robert C carriage painter,bds 4 Central
McKeon Bartholomew, laborer, h 24 Liberty
McKeon John, moulder, bds 8 Bridge
McKeon Michael, bootmaker, h 10 Bridge
McKeon Patrick, stone mason, h 10 Brown
McKeon Thomas, clerk, bds Liberty
McKeon Thomas, clicker, h 11 Orchard
McKeone Owen, blacksmith, h 7 Charles
McKerns Chas. wiredrawer, h Bridge
McKinley Charles, wirecleaner. h Gold
McKinley John. at gas works, h Carbon
McKnight Gilbert, boarders, h 3 Maple
McKnight Gilbert L. machinist, bds 3 Maple
McKnight Mrs Harriet,dress maker,Bloomingdale
McKoy Mrs. Clarissa H. h Grafton
McLaflin, James, gas fixer, bds 3 Carlton
McLane Miss Cynthia D. bds 5 High
McLane James, carpenter, bds 1 Goddard
McLane John, painter, bds 1 Goddard
McLaughlin Andrew, bootfinisher, h 26 Winter
McLaughlin Andrew, laborer, h Heard
McLaughlin Dan'l.marble polisher,bds 9Mechanic
McLaughlin James, bootmaker, bds 15 Temple
McLaughlin Michael, bootfinisher at J. Walker &
McLaughlin Michael, clicker, h 27 Austin [Co's.
McLeer Mrs. Mary, h rear 31 Union
McLeer Reynolds, harness maker, bds 31 Union
McLellan Edwin B. rollingmill.h cor Sum'r&How-
McLellan Geo watchman, bds 87 Summer [ard
McMahan Michael, laborer, h 21 Franklin
McMahan Phillip, moulder, bds Columbia
McMahan Phillip, engineer at Arcade,h Columbia
McMahon Edw'd, at Arcade I.works,h 3 Columbia
McMahon Ed. machinist & roll turner, h Millbury
McMahon James, at Arcade I.foundry, 6 Columbia
McMahon James. laborer, h Franklin
McManus Bernard, roller. h Quinsigamond
McManus Dominic, wiredrawer, h 4 Pond
McManus Joseph, bootmaker, h rear Bangs bl'k
McManus Patrick, moulder, h 16 Winter
McMurray Anthony, laborer, h 19 Blackstone

McMurry Farrell, laborer, h 24 Liberty
McNamara Jeremiah, laborer, h 22 Pink
McNamara John, brakeman, h 7 E. Central
McNamara Michael, ct. mill, bds 39 Mechanic
McNamover John, Quinsigamond
McNanay Cornelius. moulder, bds Bridge
McNauy Edward, moulder, bds 31 Mechanic
McNaughton Daniel, boottreer, h N. Ashland
McNulty Francis, teamster, h 49 Mechanic
McNulty Patrick, laborer, h 12 Brown
McNulty Patrick, laborer, h 35 Mechanic
McPartlan James, clicker, h 15 Vine
McQueeny Patrick, wiredrawer, h Ward
McSweeny Brian, laborer, 19 Blackstone
McSweeny John, laborer, h 3 Milk [33 Temple
McSweeny Patrick, liquor store, 27 Wash sq. h
McSweeny Patrick, porter at I. Cary's, bds 2 Milk
McTeirnan Mrs. Catherine. h 74 Mechanic
McTyge John, laborer, h 36½ Shrewsbury
McTyre Josephine, doctoress, 1 Prescott
Meacham Benj. (Rice & M.) h 22 Salem
Meade Mrs. Harriet W. h 12 Portland
Meadowcraft James, boottreer, h 66 Exchange
Meadowcraft John, cordwainer, h 55 Summer
Meadowcraft Robert, boottreer, bds 66 Exchange
Meagher James, wiredrawer, bds 10 Grove
Meany Thomas, coachman at A. H. Bullock's, h
 30 Southbridge [block, h 2 Crown
Mecorney Wm. merchant tailor. 7 Lincoln H.
Mecrea Daniel, machinist, bds 27 Mechanic
Meinhard Rodolph. wiredrawer, bds 2 Mechanic
Melanefy James, coll. & cl'k of Wor. gas Co. h 34
Melaven Morris.blacksmith,h 54 Mechanic[Green
Melican Michael, at ct. mill, h 66 Holden
Mellen (Edward) & Davis (W. S.) counsellors,
 188 Main, bds Bay State House
MELLEN EDWARD jr. bookstore, 239 Main, bds
Mellon Henry, mason, bds 11 Myrtle (Bay St. H.
Mellen Mrs. James 11 Temple
Meller Conrad, beer saloon, 11 Mechanic
Mellish G. Herbert, printer, bds Lincoln house
Mel'on Thomas, h 199 Pleasant
Mellor James, boottreer, h 1 Beach
Melsop Joseph, baker, bds 115 Main
Melsop Thomas, gardener, h 14 Shrewsbury
Mende Robert, musical instrument maker, bds 7
Merriam Chas. carpenter, h 1 Vernon [Mechanic
Merriam Charles J. turner, h Dewey
Merriam F. H. B. & W. R. R. h 52 Mechanic
Merriam Geo. D. wirefinisher. h 14 Portland
Merriam Rufus N. foreman J. A. Fay & Co.'s, h
 300½ Main
Merriam Thomas, machinist, bds 27 Mechanic
Merrick Francis T. h 6 Ashland
MERRICK JOHN M. & CO. (A. L. Rounds &
 T. R. Timby)barometer manuf'rs, 7 Cen. Exc.
Merrick Lewis, clerk, h 16 Lincoln
Merrifield Mrs. Alpheus, h 53 Summer
Merrifield Francis N. farmer, h Holden
Merrifield Henry K. student, bds Highland
Merrifield Lucius. music teacher, h 18 Austin
Merrifield Wm. F. bds Highland
Merrifield Wm. T. office Exchange, h Highland
Merrill Daniel, h 11 Bowdoin
Merrill D. M. G. printer, bds 11 Bowdoin [West
MERRILL ENOCH. variety store, 221 Main. h 10
Merrill Geo. E. bookkeeper Mech. bank, bds 11
Merrill Geo.F. machinist,bds 5 Orange [Bowdoin
Merrill J. M. bookkeeper at Quinsig. bank,bds 80
Merrilles Wm. gardener. h 7 Elizabeth [Main
Meritt Edson, grocer, 21 Wash. sq. h 23 Washing-
Merritt F. T. machin'st, h 18 Liberty [ton
Merritt Jesse S. moulder, h Palmer

Merritt John A. machinist. bds 4 Central
Merritt Oscar J. wiredrawer. h Highland cor N.
Meservey Geo S. machinist, h 54 Elm [Ashland
Messenger Dan'l F. tailor at Parker's, h 13 Myrtle
Messinger A. embroideries, &c., 112 Main
Messinzer David S. h 10 Chestnut
Metcalf Alfred E. machinist, h 14 Congress
Metcalf Caleb D. Highland School for Boys, Salls-
Metcalf Rev. David, h 61 Front   [bury
Metcalf Mrs. L. A. milliner and dressmaker, 61
Metcalf Mary R. boarding house, 5 High [Front
Methven John, machinist, h 3 Lamartine
Methven John F. machinist, bds 29 Southbridge
Meyer Francis, printer, h 43 Green
Midgely Mrs. Elizabeth, h 21 Grafton
Midgely James, cleaner at Crompton's. h 2 Water
Midgely John, boot packer, bds 66 Exchange
Midgely Joseph, boottreer, h 33 Mulberry
Miett Oliver, spinner, bds Northville
Mignault Peter B. physician, 23 Green
Milan John, wire cleaner. 58 Mechanic
Miles Chas. M. Sec. W. M. F. Ins. Co. court h. h
      35 Lincoln
Miles Wm. T. clerk, h Newbury cor Chatham
Millea Andrew, tailor, h 4 Bridge
Millen Thomas, coachman at Hacker's,bds Central
Miller Benjamin, painter at court mill
Miller Clifford, roller, h Ward
Miller Eli, roller, h Ward   [Pearl
MILLER HENRY W. hardware &c. 46 Main,h 22
Miller John, at Whiting & Woodbury.h 37 Wash.
Miller Miss Lucy, boarding house, 11 Main   [sq.
Miller Riley A. attendant at hospital
Miller (Seth P.)& Chamberlin dentists, 142 Main,
Millet John, wirecleaner, h Belmont [h 1 Harvard
Millet Michael, wire cleaner, h rear Bangs block
Mills Frank, fireman P. R. R. bds 39 Salem
Mills George, carpenter, h 6 Lincoln
Mills Isaac, farmer, Forest
Mills Isaac M. farmer, Forest
Mills James, car inspector, P. R. R. h 39 Salem
Mills Marshall, mason, h May
Mills Richard, mason, h 42 Pleasant
Minahan John. at Grove mills, bds Larkin
Miner Edward M. agent, h 11 Chandler
Minot Jonathan E. blacksmith, h 42 Summer
Minot Joseph N. eave troughs, h 38 Summer
Minter Henry, machinist, h 15 Salem
Minter James, blacksmith, h 23 Myrtle
Mirick Horace, bootcrimper, h 7 Congress
Mirick John A. clerk at Wyman's, h cor Wm. &
      N. Ashland   [Orange
Mirick John T. clerk at Ellis & Flagg's, bds 46
Mirick J. D. at Ellis & Flagg's, bds 46 Orange
Mirick M. D. machinist, bds 63 Front
Mirick Wm. H. music teacher, h N. Ashland
Mitchel Henry, rolling mill, h 20 Grafton [Irving
Mitchell John, gardener at N. Washburn's, h S.
Mitchel Patrick, laborer, bds Lynde
Mix Isaac C. iron worker, bds Bloomingdale
Mixer Charles P. mechanic, h 43 Exchange
Mixter G. C. shoemaker. bds 1 Carrol
Mixter Rufus, bds 2 Sudbury
Moen H. A. R. clerk, bds 11 Main
Moen Phillip L. (I Washburn & Co.) h 4 Ashland
Moffit Ambrose. farmer, Mountain
Moffit Oliva, h Grafton
Mooney Robert, laborer, h Lovell's ct.
Monaghan John. butcher, May
Monaghan Mrs. Mary, h 16 Hibernia
Monaghan Thos. hostler, h 14 Bridge
Monahan Alexander, moulder, bds 5 Brown's bl'k
Monahan Maurice, moulder, bds 5 Salem

Monahan Thomas, butcher, h 4 Vine
Monarch Matthew, Central st. dye house & soap
      manufactory
Monger John M. clerk, bds 20 Pleasant
Mongoven James, laborer, h 19 Franklin
Monihan Timothy, blacksmith, h Larkin
Monroe Addison, pat'e of water wheel, 73 Front,
Monroe Addison R. moulder,bds 3 Vine [h 3 Vine
Monroe Charles H. at A. Davis, bds 2 Sudbury
Monroe Henry, laborer, bds 1 High
Moody Alvin Jr. carpenter, bds 5 Orange
Moody Edwin, h 20 Trumbull
Moony Andy. Prov. R. R. h Benefit
Moony John, laborer, h 5 S. Irving
Moony Mrs. Richard, h S. Irving
Moony Richard, bootmaker, bds 24 Madison
Moony Richard, laborer. h 47 Mechanic
Moore Mrs. Abigail, nurse, h 8 Prospect
Moore Amory, carpenter, h Edward cor Earle
Moore Ashley, farmer, Pleasant
Moore Charles, carpenter, bds 11 William
Moore Calvin, carpenter, h 9 Shelby
Moore Charles, carpenter, h 6 Lincoln
Moore Charles A. farmer, bds Ashley Moore's
Moore Charles A. machinist, h 6 Lincoln
Moore David, bootmaker, h Stafford
Moore Geo. barber, 6 Foster
Moore Geo. W. machinist, bds 27 Mechanic
Moore Harrison, farmer, Mower
Moore H. S. wireworker, 44 Front
Moore J. wiredrawer at Goddard's
Moore Rev. J. C. vice pres't College Holy Cross
Moore John, laborer, h Columbia
Moore John E. carpenter, h Lamartine
Moore J. H. dancing teacher, h 29 Crown
Moore John R. clerk at B. R. R. bds 51 Chandler
Moore Levi, jr. farmer, 5 Piedmont
Moore Lewis, h 5 Highland
Moore L. D. clerk, 21 Hanover
Moore Luther, carpenter, bds 43 Summer
Moore Luther G. farmer, cor.W. Doylston & Moun-
Moore Marcus, carpenter, h 21 Carroll   [tain
Moore Michael, laborer, h 1 Howard
Moore Nathaniel C. farmer, Salisbury
Moore Nicholas P. h 1 Lynn
Moore Oliver J. stable, rear Taft's hotel, h 3 Thos.
Moore Patrick, Quinsigamond
Moore S. B. farmer, Malden
Moore Samuel H. h 51 Chandler
Moore Miss Sybil, h 8 Prospect
Moore Thomas, boottreer, h 43 Mechanic
Moore Wm. farmer, bds W. G. Moore's
Moore Wm. B. moulder, bds 9 Summer
Moore Wm. G. farmer, Pleasant   [court
Moore Wm R. grocer, 15 Exchange. bds Slater's
Moran Bartholomew, bootfitter, h 9 Howard
Moran Charles, watchman, Southgate
Moran John, laborer, h 87 Front
Moran Patrick, bootfitter, h 31 Mechanic
Moran Thomas, laborer, h 3 Belmont
Morey Charles, city watchman, bds 1 Orange
Morey John, bowling, Norwich, h 32 William
Morey John jr. h Bowdoin
Morgan John, laborer. h Cross
Morgan John, laborer, h near Jamesville
Morgan Patrick, at Wheeler's, h 97 Summer
Morgan Wm. H. gardener, at J. C. Mason's
Moriarty Mrs. Hannah, h 14 Hibernia
Moriarty Morris, laborer, h 4 K. Central   [place
Morril David L. counsellor. Bank bl'k, h Chatham
Morrison Frank, at ct. mills, h rear 58 Mechanic
Morrison Frank C. clerk, bds 5 Orange
Morrison Mrs. V. W. boarding house, 5 Orange

Morrissey John, laborer, h 9 Charles
Morrissey John, laborer, h 48 Southbridge
Morrissey Patrick, laborer, h Gold
Morrissey Stephen, laborer, h Foyle   [ison
Morrissey Thomas, laborer, h cor.Salem and Mad-
Morris Joseph, at rolling mill, h 37 Temple
Morse Chas. H. clerk at M. B. Greene & Co.'s, bds
    4 Madison
Morse Chas. T. acct. at M. Stowe's, bds 7 Park
Morse Edward, machinist, h 107 Pleasant
Morse Edwin, carpenter, h Salisbury
Morse Edwin, (Shepard, Lathe & Co.) h 23 Chatham
Morse Elisha H. patent gutters, h 5 Central ct.
Morse Geo. L. painter, h 36 Pleasant
Morse Hezekiah D. bds 2 Sudbury
Morse Horace A. Bloomingdale
Morse Isaac, farmer, h Bloomingdale
Morse Jas. C. lumber yard, Grove, h 7 Park
Morse Jas. S. melodeon maker, h 41 Salem
Morse John G. wiredrawer, bds Bloomingdale
Morse John N. cabinet maker, bds 12 Thomas
Morse Mrs. Maria, h 25 Orange
Morse Mason H. carpenter, h 11 Elm   [40 Austin
Morse Milton M, melodeon manuf'r, 263 Main, h
Morse Norris, bootmaker, h 22 Elliot
Morse Rufus E. painter, bds 3 Harrington av.
Morse S. A. at Lawrence's furniture store, h 11
Morse Samuel jr. carpenter, h 3 Mason   [John
Morse Simeon B. mason, h 35 Salem
Morse Wm. M. carder, bds Webster
Morton David, h 55 Chandler
Morton Ephraim S. machinist, bds 39 Washington
Morton John, moulder, court mill, h 3 Howard
Morton Mrs. Relief, h 23 Exchange
Morway Felix, clerk, h 8 Burt
Moses Samuel A. armorer, bds 81 Exchange
Moss Rev. Lemuel, (1st Baptist,) h 23 Oxford
Mosher Frank, shoemaker, bds 32 Mechanic
Moules Chas. R. dentist, h & office, 19 Pleasant
Moulton Austin N. melter, h 22 Thomas
Moulton B. C. envelopes, h 22 Park
Moulton Charles A. bootsider, bds 1 Market
Moulton Charles O. clicker, h 126 Southbridge
Moulton Orson, moulder, h 10 Jackson   [Elliot
Mowbray J. G. paper hanger, &c. 26 Union, h 26
Mower Ebenezer, bds 8 Washington square
Mower Ephraim, farmer, 321 Main
Mower Mrs. M. E. milliner, 104 Main,bds 102 Main
Mowry Charles D. plowmaker, h 1 Orange
Mowry David, h 41 Salem
Mowry Geo. J. bookkeeper, bds 41 Salem
Moynahan Daniel, laborer, h 56 Front
Mulany Charles A. bootbottomer, bds 76 Front
Mulcahay James, farmer, Burncoat
Mulcahay John, wiredrawer, bds Liberty
Mulcahay Michael, laborer, h Franklin
Mulcahy John F. printer, bds 12 Thomas
Mullen John, laborer, h 9 Bridge   [Winter
Mulligan Francis, at Arcade Iron Foundry, h 32
Mulligan Patrick, moulder, h 35 Madison
Munger Mrs. Cyrus C. h 4 Bartlett place
Munger J. M. clerk, bds 20 Pleasant   [lett place
Munger Watson F. clerk at W.Allen's,bds 4 Bart-
Munster John, amorer, bds 90 Southbridge
Munyan Patrick, laborer, bds 19 Blackstone
Murdock E. H. clerk at Pinkham's, bds 43 Salem
Murdock John, baker, 72 Southbridge
Murley Cornelius, laborer, h 3 Spring
Murley Michael, laborer, h Southbridge
Murphy Arthur, horse nail maker, h 89 Front
Murphy Daniel, ginder, h 23 Pink
Murphy David, painter, bds 15 Summer
Murphy Dennis, laborer, h Larkin

Murphy Edward, laborer, h Cross
Murphy Edward, moulder, bds 24 Exchange
Murphy Mrs. Ellen, h 2 Milk
Murphy Mrs. Ellen, h 10 Charles   [Bridge
Murphy Florence, Arcade Iron foundry, bds 4
Murphy James, carpenter, h 13 Hibernia
Murphy Jeremiah, carpenter. h 22 Madison
Murphy John, laborer, h 21 Franklin
Murphy John, laborer, h 3 Foundry
Murphy John, laborer, h rear 11 Market
Murphy John, laborer, h Linwood place
Murphy John, laborer, h 3 Brown
Murphy John, nail maker, h 89 Front   [Brown
Murphy Jonn L. bookkeeper at H. Doherty's, h 4
Murphy Maurice, horse nail maker, h 13 Foundry
Murphy Michael, laborer, h 18 Blackstone
Murphy Patrick, engineer Bay St. planing mills,
Murphy Patrick, laborer, Winter ct.   [bds 2 Milk
Murphy Patrick, laborer, h 9 Hibernia
Murphy Patrick, laborer, 18 Shrewsbury
Murphy Patrick, bootmaker, bds 11 Brown's bl'k
Murphy Patrick, farmer, Millbury avenue
Murphy Patrick, tailor, h Columbia ct.
Murphy Richard, at rolling mill, h 15 Franklin
Murphy Thomas, wiredrawer, bds 1 Water
Murphy Thomas, at rolling mill, h Cross
Murphy Thomas, laborer, h 23½ Winter
Murphy Timothy, Arcade iron foundry, h 9 Burt
Murphy Timothy, A. I. F. h 13 Hibernia
Murphy Timothy, shoemaker,bds 11 Brown's bl'k
Murray Charles M. bootmaker. h Russel place
Murray Edward, law student, bds 26 Temple
Murray Edward, tin plate worker, bds Wash. sq.
Murray F. E. currier, bds 103 Summer
Murray Frank S. farmer, bds Jefferson
Murray Henry, carpenter, h 26 Temple
Murray Henry J. carpenter, bds 26 Temple
Murray Jabez, brass moulder, bds 5 Laurel
Murray John, laborer, bds 26 Madison
Murray John F. wire plater, h 41 Green
Murray Kerrion, rolling mill, bds 1 Burt
Murray Mrs. Mary, h 24 Liberty
Muzzy Chas. A. blacksmith, h Cambridge
Muzzy Chas. bootmaker, h Newton
Muzzy Edwin A. (L. Stow & Co.) h 2 Elliot
Muzzy F. A. shoe dresser, h 9 Carroll
Muzzy James M. carpenter, h 15 Gold
Muzzy Lewis C. accountant at J. Gates', bds 9
Muzzy Mrs. Nathan, h 9 Market   [Market
Muzzy Nathan M. machinist, h 17 Thomas
Myer Joseph, laborer, Burncoat
Mynihan Mrs. Ellen, h 5 Brown's block
Mynihan Timothy, blacksmith, h Larkin
Nash Chas. farmer, Pratt
Nash James H. machinist, h 7 Webster
Nason Chas. hackman, h 47 Pleasant
Nason Edward S. music teacher, Clark's block, h
    Jackson cor Beacon
Nason Samuel, bds 47 Pleasant
Naylor P. spinner, bds 1 Millbury
Neagle David, washer, h 22 Millbury
Nealan John, at rolling mill, h Burt
Nealan Mary, h E. Central
Nealan Mrs. Mary, h Cross
Nealan Michael, laborer, h E. Worcester place
Needham Chandler, moulder, h 30 Providence
Nell James, wiredrawer, h 155 Southbridge
Nell Joseph, wiredrawer, h Goddard's lane
Neligan Morris, boottreer h 24 Shrewsbury
Nelson David, painter, h 92 Summer
Nelson Jonathan, h 16 Park
Nelson Marcus, pattern maker, h 33 Summer
Nelson S. W. machinist, bds 92 Summer

Nelson T. L. (Rice & N.) h Kendall
Nettleton E. B. dentist, cor Main and Park
Nevins P. gardener, h Endicott cor Ward
Nevins Patrick, laborer, h 12 Brown
New England Tea Co. 210 Main
Newbury Albert, acct. bds Quinsigamond village
Newcomb Austin, shoemaker, 8 1-2 Myrtle, h 25
Newcomb Henry K. h 8 Elm   [Chandler
Newcomb Mis. M. L. h 262 Main
Newell Rev. C. h 1 Forest road
Newhall Geo. N. silver plater, h 29 Orange
Newhall Mrs. H. h 31 Myrtle
Newland Wm. A. clerk, bds 44 Front
Newton Albert, painter, h 8 Liberty
Newton Albert H.cutter atD.H.Eames',h45 Pleas't
Newton A. H. at Firth's, h 17 Maple
Newton Misses Almira & Alvira, h 13 Shelby
Newton Chas. blacksmith, 42 Union, h 16 Arch
NEWTON CHAS. manuf'r cave troughs,gutters,
    &c. Merrifield's building, h 29 Newbury
Newton Courtland, boot manuf'r, White's bl'k. h
Newton Dennis, farmer, Millbury av. [11 Shelby
Newton Ezekiel, farmer. Brattle
Newton Ezra, farmer. Brattle
Newton Geo. A. shuttlemaker, bds Webster
Newton G. F. dentist, 1 Harr. cor. bds Bay S. H.
Newton Geo. F. clicker, h 11 Salem
Newton James. teacher, bds 13 Main
Newton John C. mason, h 1 Orange •
Newton Leonard, carpenter. h Granite
Newton L. D. clicker, h 20 Beacon
Newton Myron J. wiredrawer, bds 12 Grove
Newton Rejoice, counsellor, h 2 State
Newton Rufus W. machinist, bds Harrington av.
Newton S. B. butcher, Ripley's market, bds 23
Newton Wm. B butcher, 32 Main   [Exchange
Neylon Michael, roller, h Quinsigamond
Nichols Abijah, pattern maker, h 329 Main
Nichols Amos, bootmaker. h Leicester, N. W.
Nichols Chas. P. (Chase & Nichols) h 288 Main
Nichols Eben W. (T. Smith & Co.) machinist, h
Nichols Geo. h 3 Madison   [28 Chandler
Nichols Henry B. machinist, h 14 Portland
Nichols Henry P. agent West. R. R. h 55 Thomas
Nichols Horace, wiredrawer at Goddard's
Nichols J. bookkeeper at People's Ins. office, bds
Nichols John, spinner, h Millbury   [329 Main
Nichols John, shoemaker, bds 8 Quincy
Nichols John B. bds 286 Main
Nichols John M. agent, h cor Union & Penn av.
Nichols John M. peddler, h 3 Franklin
Nichols Joseph, h 1 Plymouth
Nichols L. B. homœopathic physician, 112 Main
Nichols P.E. fruit dealer, 303 Main, h 32 Newbury
Nichols S. B. cigar maker, h 286 Main
Nichols W. L. h 181 Pleasant
Nicholson John, spinner, h 6 Millbury
Nickerson Francis, h 19 Austin
Nickerson Spencer P. jobber, h 26 Portland
Niles Geo. A. machinist, h 2 Water
Nitcher Wm. W. machinist,bds 2 Central [George
Nixon Hamilton, watchmaker at Fenno's, bds 4
Nixon Mrs. Harriet, h Bridge,rear Mission chapel
Nixon John A. wheelmaker. 23 Summer
Nixon Solomon, grocer.h Webster corCambridge
Nolan David, gardener, h rear 68 Front
Nolan Dennis H. machinist, bds 27 Mechanic
Nolan James, tailor, h 10 Spring
Nolan John, blacksmith, bds 16 Summer
Nolan Patrick, gardener, h 24 Madison
Noon Patrick, blacksmith, h Border
Norcross Otis C. att. at hospital
Norton F. B. & Co. (F. Hancock) stone ware

manufacturers, Wash. sq. h 14 Mulberry
Nourse Adonis H. farmer, h Heard   [Church
Nourse B. F. provisions &c. Southbridge, h 5
NOURSE (Joel), MASON & CO. (Samuel Davis &
    Peter Harvey,) manufacturers of agricultur-
    al implements, court mill
Nourse Silas, wiredrawer, h 1 Salem
Nourse Stephen, farmer, Heard
Noyes Chas. F. machinist, bds cor Main & Beaver
Noyes Daniel, farmer, h Millbury
Noyes Francis H. sash & blind maker, h 2 Cen-
Noyes L. D. bds Millbury   [tral court
Noyes Richard P. painter, h 78 Front
Noyes Thomas, carpenter, Main, N. W.
Nugent Charles, h 1 Shrewsbury
Nugent Patrick, marble cutter, 9 Mechanic
Nugent Thomas, laborer, h 16 Bridge
Nure Mrs. Achsah, 1 Leicester
Nye Edwin W. baker at Stearns', h 51 Austin
Nye Marshall P. butcher, h 46 Orange
Nye Sam'l D. acct. N, Washburn's, h 7 Oxford
Nye Sewall, butcher, h 14 Seaver
Oakley Wm. F. truckman, h Gold court
Oaks Barney, hostler, h Cypress
Oaks Wm. temperer, h Ludlow
Oatley Rowland S. brakeman B. R. R. h 16 Gold
Oberer Fidel, blacksmith, h Lamartine
Oberer Freien, blacksmith, bds Lamartine
Obey Michael, laborer, bds 35 Temple
O'Brien Charles, bootsider, bds 31 Mechanic
O'Brien Conner, laborer, h 6 Bridge
O'Brien Daniel, soap boiler, h 16 Shrewsbury
O'Brien Francis, moulder, h 12 Bridge
O'Brien Mrs. Hannah, h 19 E. Central
O'Brien James, laborer, h 33 Madison
O'Brien John, currier, h rear 19 Winter
O'Brien Michael H. farmer, bds West Boylston
O'Brien Morris, laborer, h 12 Charles
O'Brien Thomas, laborer, h S. Irving
O'Brien O. hostler, bds 6 Bridge
O'Brien Wm. farmer, West Boylston
O'Brien Wm. laborer, h Salem cor Madison
O'Byern, Francis, boottreer, h Canal
O'Connell Daniel, bootmaker, 3 Tremont
O'Connell Daniel, law student, bds 3 Burt
O'Connell Mrs. Ellen, h 3 Burt
O'Connell Michael, tailor, h Cypress
O'Connell Patrick, bootmaker, h 47 Mechanic
O'Connell Peter, laborer, h Webster
O'Connell Phillip, coachman at L. Lincoln's
O'Conner Dan'l, repairer N. R. R. h 14 Shrewsbury
O'Conner Dennis, grocer, h 2 Washington Sq'r.
O'Conner Mrs. Mary, h 12 E. Worcester
O'Conner Thomas, shoemaker, h 4 Bridge
O'Connor Dennis, grocer, cor Larkin & E. Wor.
O'Connor James, shoemaker, h 17 Temple
O'Connor Michael. bootmaker, bds Mechanic
Octavius Joseph, waiter, Bay State house
O'Day Dennis, wiredrawer, h 58 Mechanic
O'Day Patrick, laborer, h 58 Mechanic
O'Day Patrick, laborer, h 15 Franklin
Odd Leonard, wirewinder, h Margin
Odlin Chas. H. carriage maker, h Houchin av.
Odlin Willis H wheelmaker, h Houchin av.
O'Donnel John, laborer, h 26 Southbridge
O'Donnel Maurice, bootmaker, bds 26 Madison
O'Donnell Thomas, moulder, h Madison
O'Driscoll John, at Firth's
O'Gorman John J. tailor, h 51 Salem
O'Hagan Owen, blacksmith, h 11 Vine
O'Hagan Patrick, blacksmith, h Cross
O'Harra Barney, moulder, h rear Winter
O'Harm Patrick, city coal yard, h Lovell's court

O'Keefe Cornelius, dyer, bds 1 Millbury
O'Keefe Mrs. Eliza, h 24 Madison
O'Keefe John, gardener at Mrs. A. D. Foster's
O'Keefe Michael, bootmaker, bds 24 Madison
O'Keefe Patrick, R. R. contractor, h 12 Green
O'Keefe Patrick, bootmaker, bds 24 Madison
O'Keefe Phillip, student, bds 1 Millbury
Olds Nathan jr. engraver for Knox & Lang, bds 1 Walnut
O'Leary Jeremiah, blacksmith, 33 Temple
O'Leary John B. blacksmith, 3 Burt
O'Leary Timothy, boottreer, h 5 Brown
Olin Frank M. blacksmith, bds Bloomingdale
Oliver C. P. Henry, harness maker, bds 69 Front
OLIVER FRANCIS P. stoves &c. 108 Main, bds
Oliver James L. tinman, h 1 6 Main   [102 Main
Oliver J. T. clerk, bds 106 Main
Olney George. painter, bds 25 Mechanic
O'Locklin Brien, laborer, bds 9 Bridge
O'Neal Arthur, painter, h Canal near Cherry
O'Neal John, blacksmith,W.R.R. h 35 Shrewsbury
O'Neal John, heater, h Bloomingdale
O'Neal Thomas, laborer, h 41 Mechanic
O'Neil Mrs. Bridget. h Ward
O'Neil Charles, machinist, bds Ward
O'Neil Daniel, laborer, h 4 E. Central
O'Neil Daniel H. watchmaker, bds 44 Front
O'Neil James, machinist, bds 8 Winter
O'Neil Michael, h Prescott place
O'Neill Joseph, wiredrawer, S. Worcester
O'Neill Wm. machinist, h Ward
Onion Mrs. Clara, h Wellington
O'Regan John. painter, h 3 Burt
O'Reilly James A. house & sign painter,h 49 Salem
O'Reiley Patrick H. tinman, bds 49 Salem
O'Reilley Antony, watchman, h 49 Salem
O'Reilley Rev. Patrick T. bds 20 Temple
Orfall Joseph, boarding house, 7 Mechanic
O'Rourke Charles B. carpenter, h Ward cor Foyle
O'Rourke H. wiredrawer at Goddard's
O'Rourke John, gardener, h 33 Shrewsbury
O'Rourke Patrick, carpenter, h Ward cor Foyle
Orvis John M. clerk, h 21 Bowdoin
Osgood Jas. H. express agent, 1 Lincoln H. bl'k, h Academy hill
Osgood Samuel W. carpenter, h 20 Liberty
Osmer Alba C. eave troughs, h Abbott
O'Sullivan John, currier, bds 18 Temple
O'Sullivan Timothy, moulder, h 21 Salem
Otis Benj. B. boot manuf'r and leather dealer, 5 Bangs block, h 15 Orchard
Otis Benj. F. h 15 Beacon
Otis Harrison G. clicker, h Plantation
Otis John C.boot manuf r,Bangs bl'k,h 11 Bowdoin
Ott Leonard, wiredrawer, h Margin
Otto Frederick, weaver, h 6 Millbury
O'Tool Michael, machinist, bds 2 Hinds court
Ouimette Camille L. armorer. bds 42 Summer
Overend Henry, wiredrawer, h Chelsea
Overend John, wiredrawer, h Goddard's lane
Overend Matthew, wiredrawer, h Benefit
Overend Robert, wiredrawer, h Goddard's lane
Overend Samuel, wiredrawer, bds Goddard's lane
Overend Wm. wiredrawer, h Quinsigamond
Owen Peter, blacksmith, bds 1 Millbury
Owens Richard, laborer, h 13 Millbury
Packard Lucius B. machinist, h 15 Elliot
Packard Wm. A. machinist. h 19 Mechanic
Paddock John D. clerk at Barnard, Sumner & Co. bds 8 Maple
Padleford John, coal dealer, h Belmont
Page Christopher, laborer, h Sutton's lane
Page Dexter, machinist, h 20 Chatham

Page Jesse, laborer at Levi Moore's, Pleasant
Page Nelson, court mill, h 23 Bowdoin
Page Samuel, physician, bds Lincoln house
Paille Paul, watchmaker, 2 Bay St. bl'k, bds Bay State House
Paine Charles, h 28 Elm
Paine David H. machinist, bds 27 Portland
Paine Francis N. tinsmith, h 42 Washington
Paine Frederick Wm. treas. Wor. Ins. Co. h 34
Paine Mrs. Gardner, h 14 West   [Lincoln
Paine Geo. P. machinist, h 17 Central
Paine Mrs. Gideon, h 199 Pleasant
Paine Henry M. inventor, h 5 Stafford
Paine James P. farmer, 34 Lincoln
Paine Nath'l, cashier City Bank, bds 14 West
Paine Thomas J. shoemaker, h cor Main & Lagrange
Paine Jefferson, shoemaker, h Main cor Lagrange
Painter Thomas, box maker, h 12 Church
Palmer A. B, bootmaker, bds 31 Mechanic
Palmer Addison, (H. & A. P.) h 11 William
Palmer Anthony, bootmaker, bds 31 Mechanic
Palmer C. H. wiretemperer, bds 14 Liberty
Palm r Fred. B. carpenter, bds 11 William
Palmer Henry & A. P. carpenters, h 88 So'bridge
Palmer James, h Leicester, V. F.
Palmer James W. machinist. 29 Green
Palmer Jonas G. boottreer, h 14 Liberty
Palmer Joseph S. clicker, h 76 Front
Palmer Michael, bootmaker, bds Bridge
Palmer Paul T. truckman, 1 Seaver
Palmer Rosalinda H. teacher Col. Institute
Palmer Sam'l, collector. h 1 Dewey
Palmer Stephen J jeweller.226 Main,h 1 Piedmont
Palmer Terrence, bootmaker, bds Bridge
Park Daniel H. carpenter, Plantation
Park Geo. machinist, h 50 Chatham
Park Russell, farmer, h Abbott
Park Sidney M. conchman at Mrs. Burnside's
Park Wallace M. Sawyer's music store, bds rear 7 William   [33 Thomas
Parks Ada M. operator on sewing machine, bds
Parks Cyrus,overseer at County House,h 72 Pleas't
Parks Mrs. Lucinda C. h 5 Orchard
Parke Robert, moulder, bds Benefit
Parker Aaron, carpenter, Sunny Side
Parker Abner G. news agent, W. & Nashua R. R. bds Waldo house
Parker Alfred, livery stable, School, h 18 School
Parker Chas. G. depot baggage master, B. & W. R. R. h 3 Cottage
Parker Chas W. & Co. (E. H. Parker) provisions, 2 Bangs bl'k, h 8 Belmont
Parker Dexter F. clicker, Exchange hotel
Parker Edward B. breaddriver, bds Belmont
Parker Edward H.(C. W. Parker & Co.)h 6 Grove
Parker Eli, acct. bds Taft's hotel
Parker Geo. A. shoemaker, bds 63 Southbridge
Parker Geo.C.at Fitch's, Sargent bl'k,h 98 Chan-
Parker J. B. car painter, bds 45 Summer   [dler
Parker Joel K. planer at Baker's, bds 12 Thomas
Parker Porter A. carpenter, bds 5 High
Parker Robert, carpenter's pin maker, 4 Milk
Parker Robert D. farmer, Granite
Parker Samuel, tailor, 139 Main, h 9 Hanover
Parker Thomas D. joiner, h 41 Summer
Parker Mrs. Wyman, h Belmont
Parkhurst Nathaniel R. manuf'r, V. F. h 376 Main
Parsons Anthony, laborer, h 11 E. Worcester
Parsons Orrin, fireman B. R. R. h 21 Mechanic
Parsons Samuel B. surveyor, Apricot
Parsons Solomon, farmer, h Apricot
Parsons Solomon jr. h Apricot

Partridge Mrs. Amoret. h 23 Salem
Partridge B. F. jr. bds 72 Pleasant
Partridge Elbridge G. h 28 Chatham
Partridge Ezra, carpenter, h 4 John
Partridge Geo. carpenter, h John
Partridge Horace. stair builder, h Highland
Partridge John M. clicker, bds Waldo House
Partridge Micajah, carpenter, h 7 Clinton
Patch L. A. wire manuf'r, h 14 Green
Patch Leander C. painter, h 19 Summer
Patch Mrs. Maria, tailoress, h 15 Market
Patch Wm. W. farmer and miller, May
Patch Wm. W. jr. miller, Mill
Patterson Albert, cutter at Walker's, h 40 Pleas't
Pattison Everett W. teacher at Oread Institute
Pattison Miss Frances, teacher at Oread Institute
Pattison Rev. R. E. principal Oread Institute
Paul Geo. W. (Freeland & Co.) h 21 Arch
Paulk Mrs. Ephraim, h 3 Cottage   [mont
Payne Richard, gardener at J. Grout's, h 1 Clare-
Peabody Bradford I. wheelmaker, bds 5 High
Peacock John, stitcher, h 6 Carroll
Peacock Richard, boottreer, h 10 Glen
Pearo Joseph, striker, bds 32 Mechanic
Pease A. G. tinman, h cor Chatham & Clinton
Pease Vashni, brass moulder, bds 5 Laurel
Peaslee (Abram) & Co. (Thos. W. Davis) provis-
   ions, 3 Pleasant, h 21 Pleasant
Peck Augustus E. auc'r, 145 Main, h 1 Maple pl.
Peck Chas. H. (Tourtelott & Peck) h 24 Austin
Peck Earl, saloon, 59 Main
Peck Tyler, shoemaker, bds 81 Exch.   [Wilmot
Peckham Geo. R. cylinder manuf'r, 2 Laurel, h 26
Peirce Daniel, bootbottomer, h 7 Brown's block
Peirce Harding, machinist, h 38 Grove
Peirce J. T. M. clicker, bds 36 Front
Peirce Levi, blacksmith at Bickford's, h 4 Grove
Peirce Thos. boot manuf'r, 339 Main, h 6 Salem
Pelton Charles H. clerk at Jenkins, Hamilton &
   Hyde's, bds 59 1-2 Main
Pendleton Daniel, gardener, h Garden
Penniman Geo. D. bootmaker, h Dewey   [Main
Penniman Geo. F. clerk, Leonard's Ex. bds 158
Penniman Henry H. express F. R.R. h 20 Central
Penniman Marcus L. Osgood's Ex. messenger, h
   158 Main   [Main, h 8 George
Penniman (Silas) & Harrington (H.) grocers, 7
PENNIMAN T. S. boot and shoe dealer, 7 Pleas't,
   h 5 Newbury
Penny James H. carpenter, bds Farmer's Hotel
Perkins B. W. shipmaster, h Edward cor Newport
Perkins Joseph, h 86 Southbridge
Perkins Wm. dresser tender, h Northville
Perkins Wm. P. barber, h 107 Summer
Perris Reuben, fish dealer, h 10 Mulberry
Perry Dexter H. farmer, Quinsigamond
Perry Mrs. Elizabeth, h 17 Winter
Perry James, farmer, h Hudson
Perry James jr. at C. Paine's, 28 Elm
Perry Jehu, clicker, h 2 Lodi
Perry John A. clerk at Taber & Chollar's, bds 57
Perry J. G. farmer, Quinsigamond   [Chandler
Perry John S. carpenter, h 21 Washington
Perry Nathan F, farmer, 9 Vernon
Perry Rowland, pattern maker, h 23 Washington
Perry Samuel, farmer, Vernon
Perry Samuel D. last turner, h 3 Lexington
Pettegrew David L. clerk, bds 44 Front
Powiress Samuel L. potter, h 65 Summer
Peyton Wm. H. painter, bds 39 Austin
Pfeifer Matty, shank beer, 82 Front   [chanic
Phalan John, trader, 66 Mechanic, h rear 72 Me-
Phelan Patrick, laborer, h 12 Lovell's court

Phalan Richard, engineer at C. Baker's, 14 Bridge
Pheir Wm. tailor, h 3 Hinds' court
Phelps Catherine, h Fenn av.   [Bartlett place
PHELPS FRANKLIN F. stoves, &c. 67 Front, h 2
Phelps Geo. bookkeeper at T. W. Wellington's, h
   24 Irving   [Mt. Vernon
Phelps Henry, picture frames &c. 145 Main, h
Phelps Horatio, h 8 Lexington   [wood place
Phelps John E. wire finisher, Grove mill, h Lin-
Phelps Joseph E. at court mill, h Linwood place
Phelps Miss Lucy A. millinery &c. Clark's block,
   up stairs, bds 1 Portland
Phetteplace Simon W. wheelwright, h 105 Pleas't
Phillips Ivers. President Fitch. R R. h 17 Portland
Phillips Luther, blacksmith at F. Willard & Co 's,
Phillips Silas, shoemaker, h Plantation [h 3 Laurel
Phillips Sydney W. clerk, bds 3 Laurel
Phillips Thomas, laborer, bds 19 Washington
Phillips Wm. P. clerk at Swan's Hotel
Pickering Geo. grinder, h 59 Salem
Pickett Josiah, painter, h Chatham cor Clinton
Pickford Chas. J. cl'k at Pinkham's, bds 20 Pleas't
Pickford John F. satinet manuf'r, Pleasant place
Pickford John K. L. satinet manuf'r, Pleasant pl.
Pickup James, tin plate worker, h 10 Market
Pierce Arba, decorator & designer, bds L House
Pierce Calvin W. stone mason, h 18 Plymouth
Pierce Charles, carpenter, bds 41 Summer [liam
Pierce Chas. L. at arcade iron foundry, h 21 Wil-
Pierce Edw'd L. moulder at Wheeler's foundry,
   bds 17 Liberty
Pierce Edwin, clerk, bds 18 Plymouth
Pierce E. W. wireroller, bds 16 Central
Pierce Geo. M. at arcade iron foundry, h John
Pierce Gilbert, carpenter, h 22 William
Pierce James A. pattern maker at Northville, h
   2 Millbrook   [Providence
Pierce James B. carpenter at Western station, h 31
Pierce James D. mail carrier, h 13 Exchange
Pierce James R. landlord's agent, h cor Main &
Pierce Joseph F. moulder, bds 17 Liberty [Austin
Pierce Royal S. porter at C. A. Harrington's, h
Pierce Sylvester S. teamster, h 1 Vine [17 Liberty
Pierce Wm. H. boottreer, h Locust
Pike Amos. stone cutter, h 13 Elliott
Pike (D. E) & Hervey (A. G.) soap makers, New
   Worcester, bds Waldo House
Pike Edwin S. carpenter, bds Auburn place
Pike James S. moulder, h 25 Oxford
Pike Nathaniel, carpenter, h Pleasant, Tatnuck
Pike S. E. carpenter, 30 Exchange, h Auburn pl.
Pike Wm. P. finisher, h Leicester.
Pinkham Albert H. clerk, bds 17 High
Pinkham James S. dry goods, 233 & 235 Main, h
Pinkham Joseph E. clerk, h 21 Portland [17 High
Piper James, wiredrawer, h 23 Grove
Piper John, farmer, Mill, Tatnuck
Piper John J. Register of Probate, brick ct.house
Piper P. Simeon, armorer, h 29 Austin
Piper Wm. h 9 Irving
Piper W. H. bds 9 Irving
Plant Charles jr. carriage maker, bds rear 32
Plant John. moulder, bds 1 Millbury [Thomas
Platt Frederic C. painter, h 2 Assonet
Platt Juliette. supervisor at hospital
Ploch G. Charles, blacksmith, h 9 Brown's block
Plunket Michael, bootsider, bds 9 Tremont
Plummer Frank, machinist, bds 51 Summer
Plimpton Frederick W. clerk, bds 11 Laurel
Plympton Alden B. carpenter, h Quinsigamond
Plympton N. A. clerk, bds 6 Oxford
Podver James, blacksmith, bds 27 Mechanic
Pohler Herman, wiredrawer at Goddard's

Poland L. F. salesman, bds 296 Main
Pollard Leonard L. pattern maker, h 40 Portland
Pollock James, painter, h 6 Chandler
Pomroy Alonzo, farmer at J. Brittan's
Pond Ezra P. waiter at Spurr & Priest's
Pond John F. farmer, Winthrop   [h 13 Laurel
Pond Luclus W. manuf'r machinists' tools,Union,
Pond Thos M. walter at Spurr & Priest's
Pond Willard F. farmer, h Providence court
Poole Francis N. machinist, h 91 Pleasant
Poole Horace W. machinist, bds 36 Front
Poole Leonard, blacksmith, 22 Mechanic, h 29
     Mechanic   [ison
Pope Lemuel S. clicker at H. B. Fay's, h 1 Mad-
Porter Alfred, spinner, h 41 Green
Porter C. H. moulder, Cambridge
Porter Samuel A. machinist, h 36 Main
Potter Augustus, shoemaker, bds 17 Summer
Potter Otis, h 4 Plymouth
Potver Gilbert, machinist, h 18 Union
Power James J. machinist, bds 8 Winter   [bury
Power Rev.J.J.pastor St.Anne's ch. h 23 Shrews-
Power Lawrence, machinist, bds 8 Winter
Power Maurice A. clerk at gasworks, h 1 Belmont
Power Nicholas, machinist, bds 8 Winter
Powers Mrs. Catherine, h 8 Winter
Powers Charles, machinist, h 23 Grove
Powers David, at N. Washburn's, bds 55 Front
Powers David, bootsider, bds 1 Wash. sq.
Powers James, wiredrawer, h 15 Summer
Powers James, helper, h 66 Mechanic
Powers James, court mills, h Lovell's court
Powers John, laborer, h King
Powers John, laborer, bds Quinsigamond
Powers John laborer, corner Park and Trumbull
Powers Lawrence, machinist, bds 8 Winter
Powers Mrs. Margaret, h 3 Chandler court
Powers Martin, laborer, h Gold
Powers Martin, laborer, h Vine cor Foundry
Powers Michael, walter at Lin. h. h 23 Temple
Powers Michael, laborer, 30 Oxford
Powers Michael, laborer, Main, N. W.
Powers Morris, laborer, h 80 Salem
Powers Mrs. Nancy, laundress, h 105 Summer
Powers Nicholas, laborer, h W. Boylston, North-
Powers Nicholas, machinist, bds 8 Winter   [ville
Powers Nicholas, painter, h 10 Vine
Powers Patrick, laborer, h 9 Beach
Powers Patrick, at court mills, h Gold
Powers Peter, laborer, h cor Pond and Winter
Powers Pierce, laborer, bds Benefit
Powers Richard, wire puller, h Grove
Powers Terrence, boottreer, bds 73 Salem
Powers Thomas, laborer, bds 35 Madison
Powers Thomas, laborer, h cor Salem & Madison
Powers Wm. laborer, h King
Powers Mrs. Winifred, h 15 Vine
Pratt Chas. J. marble manuf'r, 3 Market
Pratt Chas.B.submarine navigator,h12Providence
Pratt Daniel R. h 12 Wellington
Pratt Elnathan, farmer, Salisbury
Pratt Geo. Dexter, clerk div. 42, bds 44 Front
Pratt Mrs. Harriet, h 7 Walnut
Pratt Harrison W. machinist, h 27 Mechanic
Pratt Henry S. clerk, bds 18 Pleasant
Pratt James C. printer, 12 Thomas
Pratt James H. saloon, Front, bds 151 Pleasant
Pratt John, jeweller, bds 4 Oxford
Pratt John A. marbleworker, 3 Market
Pratt John B. gardener, fruit, &c. h Salisbury
Pratt (Jos.) & Inman, (F. H.) iron & steel, Wash.
Pratt Joseph, tailor, h 20 Chatham [sq. h Grafton
Pratt Sylvanus, h 12 Park

Pratt Samuel A. jr. agent N. E. P. Union, div. 42,
     20 Front, h 59 Austin   [12 West
PRATT SUMNER, manuf'rs supplies,22 Front, h
Pratt Wm. stencil cutter, h Benefit
Pratt Wm. teamster, bds 13 Grafton
PRATT WM. W. real estate broker and auction-
     eer, Flagg's block, h 7 Walnut
Pray Ebenezer, blacksmith, h 6 Union
Prendergast Mrs. Catherine, h 2 Spring
Prentice Benj. farmer, h Southbridge, S. W.
Prentice Benj. W. machinist, bds So'bridge, S. W.
Prentice Geo. H. butcher, bds Belmont
Prentice Harrison S. butcher, 35 Front,h 72 Front
Prentice Henry, highway commissioner, h Bel-
Prentice Levi, bds Belmont   [mont
Prentice Robert, h 4 Queen
Prentice Vernon F. machinist, Southbridge, S.W.
PRENTISS ADDISON, engraver,over City Bank,
     Main, h Crescent   [Front
Prentiss Chas. G. counsellor, 157 Main, bds 58
Prentiss Geo. M. h Mt. Vernon place
Prentiss Henry C. apothecary at hospital
Prescott E. A. armorer, h 83 Southbridge
Prescott John, jobber, bds 90 Southbridge
Pressey Cyrus, boss repairer, Nor. R. R.
Preston Charles L. truckman, bds 19 Orchard
Preston Mrs. Eliza B. boarders, Webster
Preston Geo. W. teamster, bds 11 Arch
Preston Samuel H. watchman, h 11 Arch
Preston Wm. laborer, h Quinsigamond
Price Allen B. carpenter, h 6 Home
Price John, cleaner, h Canterbury
Price Joseph, peddler, h 32 Temple
Priest Lucien J. (Spurr & P.) bds 9 Maple
Prince Alpheus, carpenter, h Millbury, Quinsig.
Prince David, shoemaker, h 29 Irving
Prince James M. shoemaker, h Quinsigamond
Prince Lucian, carpenter, 26 Union, h 14 Wilmot
Prince Mrs. Mary W. boarding house, 7 Orange
Proctor C. F. wheelmaker, h Abbot
Prouty Calvin L. h 30 Chatham
Prouty Cutler, butcher, bds 22 Thomas
Prouty Daniel W. wiredrawer, h 15 Prescott
Prouty G. W. wiredrawer, bds 76 Main
Prouty (Joseph H.) & Allen, (Asa M.) brads and
     nails, Union, h 91 Pleasant   [Thomas
Prouty Lauriston M. butcher, 16 Thomas, h 22
Prouty Wm. wiredrawer, h 31 Thomas
Prouty Wm. D. varnisher and polisher, 1 Central,
     h Eden   [Thomas
Prouty Winthrop, wiredrawer, grove mill, h 29
Provan Thomas, blacksmith, h 6 Goddard
Pryor Joseph H. finisher, h 10 Brown
Puffer J. M. h 5 Home
Pushee Sidney A. blacksmith, h 57 Summer
Putnam Mrs. Adeline M. h 5 Cottage
Putnam Alex. auctioneer, h 13 Main   [Lincoln
Putnam Alonzo S. mechanic at court mill, h 8
Putnam Chas. L. Sec. Ins. Co. 98 Main, h Linden
Putnam (Chas. V.) & Clark (Sewell) auct'rs, 143
     Main, h 4 Laurel
Putnam Clark, millwright, h Ward
Putnam Darius, clerk at W. L. Clark's, h 41 Sum-
Putnam Mrs. F. H h 1 Congress   [mer
Putnam Geo. h Highland
Putnam Henry, farmer, Belmont   [Goddard
Putnam Horace, foreman Prov. freight depot, h 10
Putnam Jason, manufacturer of harness frames,
     Cypress, h 46 Salem   [302 Main
Putnam J. R. leather and oil dealer, Wash. sq. h
Putnam Leander, Prov. freight depot, h 11 Ply-
     mouth
Putnam M. M. clerk, bds cor Chandler & Queen

Putnam Otis E. (Barnard, Summer & Co.) bds Lincoln House
Putnam Philander, carpenter, h 1 Queen
Putnam Salmon, carpenter, h 77 Chandler cor.
Putnam Samuel, farmer, Belmont [Queen
Putnam Samuel jr. farmer, h Adams
Putnam Samuel H. bds 77 Chandler
Putnam Sibley, grocer, 26 Green
Putnam William, farmer, Shrewsbury
Putnam Wheelock, clerk, bds 1 Queen
Quackenboss Abram E. at Prov. freight house, h
Queen John, laborer, h Millbury [17 Washington
Quimby Andrew J. h 249 Pleasant
Quimby Henry, moulder,h 12 Cherry[Providence
Quimby Smith, foreman mall. iron foundry, h 10
Quinlin Edward, blacksmith, h 21 Summer
Quinlin Frank, at Wellington's, bds Howard
Quinlin Peter, laborer, h 23 Madison
Quinlin Patrick, blacksmith, h 3 Belmont
Quinn Dennis, laborer, bds Quinsigamond
Quinn John, laborer, h 13 Spring
Quinn John, teamster, rear 58 Mechanic
Quinn Michael H. blacksmith,h Cambridge,N.W.
Quilty John, bootfitter, h 2 Chandler court
Quint John, bds 80 Front
Quint Theodore, at Washburn's, h 80 Front
Quirk James, at Dr. Heywood's
Qu'rk Jeremiah, bootfitter, h Hibernia
Quirk Michael. tailor, h 2 Wash. square
Quirk Michael, tailor, h 66 Front
Quirk Morris, laborer, h Margin
Quirk Patrick, bootmaker, h 7 S. Irving
Quirk Timothy, laborer, h 24 Shrewsbury
Rabb Richard, court mills, h 13 Summer
Rafferty Geo. stone mason, h 49 Mechanic
Rafferty James, laborer, h rear 13 School
Rafferty Michael, laborer, Grove mill, h 65 Ex-
Ragan Thomas, laborer, bds 31 Mechanic [change
Raitt John B. machinist, bds 21 Arch
Rall Rosa, h 5 Bridge
Rand B. B. (Goddard & R.) Sargent's block, h 318
Rand James S. at Browning's, h Eden [Main
Rand Wm. A. clerk, bds 24 Portland
Rand Wm. D. mason, h 24 Portland
Randall A. G. counsellor, Main
Randolph Mrs. M. F. h 23 Austin
Ranger S. W. truckman, h 14 Seaver
Ratigan Patrick, wiredrawer, h E. Central
Ratigan Patrick E. moulder, h 1 E. Central
Rawson Charles B. carpenter, bds 16 Central
Rawson David N. confectionary, bds Benefit ct.
Rawson Deering J. fruit & confectionary, 2 South-
bridge, h Benefit court
Rawson Elisha J. R. R. repairer, h 11 Plymouth
Rawson E. O. at Smith's woodyard, h Highland
Rawson Gilbert N. planer, h 24 Summer
Rawson Henry A. hostler, h 20 John
Rawson Henry C. confectioner, bds Benefit ct.
Rawson J. D. saw manufacturer and repairer, 236
Main. h 8 Glen
Rawson K. P. carpenter, bds 16 Central
Rawson Lewis A. painter, 12 School, h 11 John
Rawson Oscar F. cigar maker, bds cor Central &
Ray James, carpenter, h East [Summer
Ray John, carpenter, h rear 20 Wilmot
Raymond James, carpenter, h 15 School
Raymond Jos. D. telegraph repairer, h 89 Pleasant
Raymond Michael, laborer, h Canterbury
Raymond Tilley, carpenter. h 6 George
Raymore James F. h 23½ Thomas
Raymore James H. h 95 Main
Read Robert, printer, h 55 Shrewsbury
Reardon Partick, moulder, at court mills

Redding Chas. L. penny post, h 15 Charlton
Redican James, umbrella maker, h 5 E. Central
Reeby Richard M. cabinet maker, Heywood's
building, Central, h Woodland
Reed Anson, machinist, bds 26 Thomas
Reed Arba, laborer, h 12 Linco
Reed A. P. (J. W. Bartlett & Co.) bds 3 High st.
Reed Mrs. A. S. dressmaker, h 26 Salem [court
Reed Benj. h 13 Maple
Reed C. D. h 30 Mechanic
Reed Chas. G. (S. G. & C. G.) h 22 Portland
Reed Dwight, h 13 Hanover [88½ Southbridge
Reed Elbridge H. at Prov. R. R. engine house, h
Reed Eugene T. headwaiter, Bay State house
Reed E. J. clerk, bds 3 Everett
Reed Geo. N. clerk, bds 84 Pleasant
Reed Henry C. porter Bay State house [b 5 High
Reed Henry J. daguerrean,16 Harrington Corner,
Reed John, farmer, Southbridge, So. Worcester
Reed John B. clerk, h 3 High st. court
Reed L. R. S. clerk, h 50 Austin
Reed S. G. & C. G. wheel makers, Merrifield's
building, h 22 Portland
Reed Mrs. Sophia, h 86 Chandler
Reekie James. h N. Ashland
Reeves Geo. W. finisher, h 20 Grafton
Regan John, painter, h cor Milk & Burt
Regan John 2d, painter, 9 Central, h N. Ashland
Regan Thomas, laborer, bds 31 Mechanic
Reid Jacob, stonemason, h 14 Newbury
Reid Robert, painter, bds 57 Larkin
Reid Wm. bootcrimper, h 6 Pink [11 Providence
Remington John H. laborer at West. R. R.station,
Reynolds Mrs. Elizabeth W. boarders, Webster
Reynolds Franklin, shoemaker, h 29 Irving
Reynolds Geo. tinman at Miller's, h 18 Austin
Reynolds John, shoemaker, h 2 Lagrange
Reynolds Owen, bootmaker, h 9 Vine
Reynolds Werden, president Female College
Reynolds Rev. Werden P. h Jefferson
Rice Albert L. machinist, bds 10 Hannover
Rice Allen, boarding house, 18 Pleasant
Rice Augustus, manuf'r Taft's patent shears, 14
Central. h cor Main and May
Rice Benj. baker, Fairmount
Rice Benj. P. baker, h and shop, Fairmount
Rice Calvin L. engraver, 195 Main. h 6 Sycamore
Rice Calvin N. car builder, bds 7 Maple
Rice Denzil S. carpenter, bds 27 Chatham
Rice Charles, farmer, rear Lakefarm [dler
Rice Chas. H. cook at Taft & Lilley's, h 30 Chan-
Rice Chas. W. watchmaker at Fiske & Goddard's,
Rice Curtis, farmer, Lincoln [h Linden
Rice Darius, farmer, Grafton
Rice Dexter,sign and ornamental painter, Piper's
block, h 13 Bowdoin
Rice Edwin N. clerk at C. Foster & Co.'s, bds 36
Rice Edward A. acct. bds 7 West [Front
Rice E. Beaman, farmer, West Boylston
Rice E. F. at Bradley's car shop, bds 7 Maple
Rice Emerson K. carpenter, h 2 Summit
Rice Francis B. h Elm cor West
Rice Frank H. asst. physician at hospital
Rice Geo. O. farmer, Rice court [45 Summer
Rice Geo. F. manuf'r hay cutters &c. Cypress, bds
Rice Geo. M. (Goddard. Rice & Co.) h 30 Elm
Rice Geo. T. president Nash. R. R. h 260 Main
Rice Geo. T. jr. (Fox & R.) bds Lincoln house
Rice Henry C. att'y, 4 Brinley hall, bds 18 Pleas't
Rice Henry H. baker; bds Fairmount
Rice Henry S. printer, bds 11 Maple
Rice Hiram, blacksmith at C. mill, h Reservoir,
Rice Jabez, farmer, Rice court [cor East

Rice James D. clerk, bds 10 Fruit
Rice J. Marcus, physician, 12 Pearl
Rice John, acct at ct. mill, h 1 William
Rice (John 2d,) & Mencham (Benj.) calf boot manuf'rs, cor Main & Pleasant, h 13 Beacon
Rice John, mason, h 4 Tremont
Rice John A. clerk ct. mill, h Linwood place
Rice Joseph O. machinist, bds 6 Wellington
RICE JOSIAH, saw repairer & dealer, over 242
Rice Mrs. Julia, h 37 Salem   [Main, h 7 Union
Rice Lawrence, farmer, h 22 Chandler
Rice Lorenzo D. bootmaker, h 5 Mason
Rice Lucius W. boxmaker, bds 63 Main
Rice Mrs. Mary, bds 47 Austin
Rice Milton J. clerk, bds 5 High
Rice Minot, trader, h 39 Chandler
Rice Nathan P. carpenter, h 37 Salem
Rice Norman, telegraph repairer, bds 13 Bowdoin
Rice Peter, spinner, h Sutton lane
Rice Peter, agent, h 2 Newbury
Rice R. B. blacksmith, bds 8 Laurel
Rice Rodney M. farmer, Rice court
Rice Mrs. Rufus, h 7 West
Rice Mrs. Samuel, h 17 Prospect
Rice Sewall, wirefinisher, h 3 Arch
Rice Thomas H. horseshoeing, 47 Exchange, b
Rice Wm. h 10 Fruit   [Harrington av.
Rice Wm. H. machinist, bds 1 Market
Rice (Wm. W.) & Nelson (T. L.) counsellors, 7 Bank block, h 33 Lincoln
Rich Marcus L. shoe finisher, h 26 Myrtle
Rich Miss Eliza, h 167 Summer
Rich Peter, musician, h E. Worcester place
Rich Peter, teamster, h 9 Arch
Rich P. S. b'acksmith, C. mill, h 15 Lincoln
Richards Chas. J. boot pattern maker, h 5 Newton
Richards Geo. boot crimper, h 11 Portland
Richards Raymond, machinist, h 17 Temple
Richards Samuel C. clicker, h Central court
Richards Seth, boot crimper, h 1 Harris
Richardson Albert, moulder, bds 26 Thomas
Richardson Albert F. carpenter, bds 4 Glen
Richardson (A. P.) & Mawhinney (Samuel,) last manuf'rs, Union, h 308 Main
Richardson Charles, h 7 Everett
Richardson G. Byron, bootfinisher, h 43 Exchange
Richardson G. N. machinist, h 1 Bowdoin   [Elm
Richardson Geo. W. president City Bank, h 9
Richardson H. A. (J. A Fay & Co) h 6 Wellington
Richardson (Jonathan) & Kirby (T. C.) fish dealers, 10 Mechanic, h 3 Carlton
Richardson Lysander, painter, bds 12 Eliott
Richardson Rev. M. pastor Salem st. Church, h 28 Orange
Richardson O. P. manuf'r shuttle mountings, Cypress, h 1 Queen cor Austin   [ct.
Richardson Orlando W.stone cutter,bds 1 High st
Richardson Wm. machinist, h 37 Green
Richardson W. A. cutter at Freeland's, bds Exch.
Richardson W. H. machinist, bds 53 Central
Richmond A. K. painter, Mechanic, h 7 Ash
RICHMOND CHAS. fancy box shop, Clark'sbl'k, h 12 Chatham   [Pleasant
Richmond Willard, merchant tailor, 265 Main, h
Ricker A. P. wiredrawer, bds 3 Belknap
Ricker Freeland, wire straightener, bds 3 Belknap
Ricker Chas. P. printer, h cor Elm & Russell
Rideout Joseph, pattern maker, h 6 Bartlett place
Rider A. S. laborer, h Grove
Rider Benjamin, machinist, h 6 Cottage
Rider Mrs. Mary, h Border
Ridler Wm. plow maker, bds Mason
Riedle John, boarders, 2 Mechanic

Riggs Albert, hostler, bds 26 Mechanic
Riggs Calvin, blacksmith, bds 10 Cherry
Riggs Ira J. carpenter, h 1 Fountain
Riley Mrs. Ann, h 103 Summer
Riley Bernard E. bootmaker, bds 9 Tremont
Riley James, wiredrawer, h Quinsigamond
Riley John, moulder, h 14 Plymouth
Riley Joseph O. machinist, bds 6 Wellington
Riley Margaret, washer and ironer, h 12 Pond
Riley Michael, brakeman Nash. R. R. h 3 Tremont
Riley Owen, laborer, h North
Riley Patrick, laborer, h Foyle
Riley Robert, bds 64 Front
Ring John, gardener, h 2 Pink
Ring Sanford B. machinist, h 9 Thomas
Riordan James, currier, h 24 Shrewsbury
Ripley John C. cashier Citizen's Bank, h 399 Main
Ripley S. B. provisions, 7 Exchange, h 38 Pleasant
Ripley S. F. painter, h Slater's ct.
Roach James, laborer, h 41 Mechanic
Roach Michael, boottreer, h 25 Winter
Roach Samuel J. machinist, h 41 Exchange
Roach Thomas, boottreer, h 25 Winter
Roath Albert, conductor Nor. R. R. h 8 Portland
Roath Louis P. engineer Nor. R. R. h 26 So'bridge
Robb James, baker, bds 115 Main
Robbins Benj. W. shoemaker, 130 Southbridge
Robbins C. B., M. D. h 10 Hanover
Robbins Ezra L. Nor. R. R. engine house, h 27 Southbridge
Robbins Geo. B. farmer at Walter Bigelow's
Robbins John, clerk, bds 266 Main
Robbins John M. h Stafford
Robbins Samuel L. farmer, h Salisbury
Robbins Silas B. grocer, 307 Main, h 21 Park
Roberts Chas. machinist, h Pond st court
Roberts David, barber, h rear 25 Central
Roberts Edward A. heater, bds Quinsigamond
Roberts Leo, machinist, h 15 Salem
Roberts Milton, mechanic, h 33 Mulberry
Roberts Samuel, heater, bds Quinsigamond
Roberts Thomas, heater, bds Quinsigamond
Roberts Wentworth, mechanic, h 6 Lincoln
Roberts Wm. file cutter, h rear 12 Cherry
Robinson Alexander, moulder, h 29 Washington
Robinson Augustus A. daguerrean, 16 Harrington corner, bds 5 High
Robinson Geo. F. machinist, bds 5 Carroll
Robinson Henry P. h 11 Maple
Robinson J. H. author, h 19 Chestnut
Robinson Miss M. Imogene, academy of fine arts, Clark's bl'k, 257 Main
Robinson Richard, barber,197 Main,bds 109 Sum'r
Robinson Thaddeus, machinist, h 5 Carroll
Robinson Thomas B. machinist, h 35 Grove
Robinson Thomas B. farmer at Newton's, Pleas't
Robinson Wm. L. at Nor. ft. house, bds 81 Exch.
Roby Edwin A. coppersmith, bds Farmer's hotel
Rockwood Calvin R. milkman, h 96 Chandler
Rockwood Edward P. bds 8 Salem
Rockwood Elias J. plowmaker at ct mill,h 21 East
Rockwood Miss Fannie E. h 6 Park
Rockwood L. R. blacking agent, h 3 King
Rockwood Miss M. E. h 6 Park
Rockwood Mrs. Rebecca, h 8 Salem
Roe D. E. wireworker, h 3 Irving
Rogers A. machinist, h 27 Summer
Rogers Albert. laborer, h 151 Pleasant
Rogers Austin L. h Wyoming site
Rogers Caleb, carpenter, h 1 Queen, cor Austin
ROGERS E. F. coal dealer, Southbridge, office Central Exchange, h 6 Arch
Rogers Geo. P. farmer, Holden   [46 Central
Rogers Geo. W. grocer, cor Main & Exchange, bds

Rogers Mrs. Henry, h 296 Main
Rogers Israel M. farmer, Adams sq.
Rogers Jeremiah, farmer, Hollen
Rogers Seth, physician, cor Arch and Fountain
Rogers Thos. M. (Southgate & R.) h 21 Chatham
Rollins Jesse, h Oak avenue
Rolston David, tinman, h E. Worcester
Rome Geo. R. engineer, b 7 S. Irving
Romerskirck D. wiredrawer, h Belmont
Rooney James, at city coal yard, h 9 Tremont
Rooney Mrs John, h Lynde
Rooney Michael W. machinist, bds 1 Millbury
Rooney Patrick, bootbottomer, bds 18½ Park
Rooney Peter, weaver, h 24 Millbury
Root J. B. teamster, h Quinsigamond
Rosenthall S. clerk at Lewisson's, bds Waldo H.
Ross Rev. Albion, cor Pleasant and Newton
Ross Mrs. Eliza, h 81 Summer
Ross John G. pattern maker, bds 23 Salem
Ross Luther, pattern maker, ct. mill, h Forest
Hill Cottage, cor Forest and Channing
Ross Nathaniel, at court mill, h Kendall hill
Ross Wm. painter, Central, h 25 Bowdoin
Ross Wm. mason, h 7 Austin [Oxford
ROSENBUSH JOS. optician, 172½ Main, h 17
Rounding Wm. shoemaker, bds 14 Market
Rounds A. L. (J. M. Merrick & Co.) bds B. St. H.
Rourke Daniel, bootbottomer, h 15 Hibernia
Rourke John, moulder, bds 76 Mechanic
Rourke John, at ct. mill, h 65 Exchange
Rourke Michael, farmer, Oak avenue
Rourke Michael, moulder, h 64 Front
Rourke Wm. moulder, h 3 Orange
Rouse A. B. at Kinnicutt & Co.'s, bds 3 Pearl
Rowe David, wireworker, h 30 Irving
Rowe David, laborer, h 12 Lovell's court
Rowe Geo. machinist, h 10 Hanover
Rowe Ichabod. blacksmith, h 11 Market
Rowe James M. harness maker, h 30 Irving
Rowland Daniel, Union Art Gallery, 197 Main, h
Rowland John, millwright,h 21 Bowdoin [10Fruit
Ruby Sanford, machinist, h 52 Central
Rudy Henry, laborer, 28 Liberty [Queen
Rugg Albert J. painter at Chase & Nichols, h 1
Rugg Chas. F. clerk, bds 12 Prospect [pect
Rugg Geo. W. soap and candles, h & shop 12 Pros-
Rugg Gilbert J. machinist, bds 46 Central
Rugg Mrs. Mary, h 1 Market
Ruggles Chas. M. counsellor, 3 Brinley Hall, bds
Ruggles Draper, h 1 Catherine [16 Green
Ruggles John H. carpenter, h Westminster, cor
Ruggles W. G. h 210 Pleasant [Mt. Vernon
Ruhmpohl A. broadcloth finisher, 59 Front, h 13
Rumery John B. carpenter, h 50 Mechanic [Vine
Russ James J. carpenter at Dennis & Lee's, h 20
Russell Addison,tinman,bds4 Trumbull [Chatham
Russell Charles, machinist, h 14 Market [Pearl
Russell E. Harlow, elocutionist, 6 Warren block,
Russell Geo. W. (A. Tolman & Co.) h 11 Harvard
Russell Hiram H. S. machinist, h 25 Washington
Russell Isaiah D. stoves & tin ware, 88 Front,
h 4 Trumbull
Russell James, boiler maker, h 32 Irving [stitute
Russell Jennie H. teacher at ladies' Collegiate In-
Russell Joseph C. boarder, h 32 Mechanic
Russell Julius, h Plantation
Russell Lewis, at court mills, h 20 Grove
Russell Martin, carpenter, h 1 Concord
Russell Mrs. Mary E. h Columbia
Russell Thomas, gunmaker, h 55 Summer
Rutter Alfred A. wool sorter, h Mason
Ryan Andrew, wire worker, h Prescott place
Ryan B. D. musician, bds 79 Southbridge

Ryan Edward E. woolsorter, bds Claremont
Ryan James, laborer, h Prescott place
Ryan John, laborer, h Winter st. ct.
Ryan Michael, grocer, Larkin
Ryan Patrick, mechanic, h 25 Blackstone
Ryan Patrick, boottreer, h 23 Madison
Ryan Patrick, hostler, h 5 Bridge
Ryan Thomas, wiredrawer, h Orchard
Ryan Timothy, farmer, h Leicester
Ryan Wm. farmer at Paine's, h Lincoln [Church
Ryan Wm. baggage master, Nashua R. R. h 5
Salisbury Wm. S. h 5 Exchange
Salisbury Stephen, prest. Wor. Bank, h Highland
Sampson Aaron,carriagemaker, Union, h 5 Wash-
ington
Sampson Joseph N. bootbottomer, bds 41 Main
Sampson P. H. painter & paper hanger,h 20 Pleas't
Sampson Reuben, carpenter, h 7 Vine
Sampson Wm. machinist, bds 17 Orange
Sampson Wm. M. machinist, h 2 Plymouth
Samson J. H. cornpopper, h 8 Bartlett place
Sanders Charles, clerk at court mill, h 13 Wil'm
Sanders Erl, carpenter at court mill, h 8 Lincoln
Sanders Henry, musical instrument maker, h 8
Brown's block [William
Sanders Samuel, woodworker, court mill, h rear 9
Sanford E. H. & Co.(C. B.Eaton,) hosiery & glove
store, 4 Flagg's block, h 15 Chestnut
Sanford G. L. clerk, bds 46 Pleasant
Sanford Wm.H. bookseller, 184 Main, h 46 Pleas't
Santon Joseph, moulder, h rear 32 Thomas
Santon Wm. moulder, h 32 Thomas
Sargent Joseph, physician, 256 Main
Sargent Simon D. S. at H. B. Fay's, h 214 Pleas't
Satchwell Benjamin, blacksmith, h 11 Foundry
Savage Jeremiah, weaver, h 26 Shrewsbury
Savage Seth, head waiter Bay State House
Savage Wm. boottreer, h 27 Crown
Sawin Chas. H. machinist, Grove mill, h 33 Grove
Sawin Chas. M. watchman at B. R. R. h 9 Seaver
Sawtell Charles, clerk at Albert S. Brown's, bds
Sawtell Homer, planer, h 9 Carroll [42 Summer
Sawtell Wm. W. clerk, bds 46 Orange
Sawyer Andrew W. music store, 2u7 Main, h 15
Sawyer Augustus, forger, bds 15 Charlton[Beacon
Sawyer Chas. H. machinist, h 20 Wilmot
Sawyer Ezra, woodworker, h 5 Crown
Sawyer Isaac G. wiredrawer, h Benefit court
Sawyer John, boottreer, bds 12 Thomas
Sawyer Stephen, clerk at Jenkins, Hamilton &
Hyde's, h 9 Park
Sawyer W. A. (Bassett & S.) h 34 Portland
Sawyer Wm. L. shoemaker, bds 25 Mechanic
Sayer Adolf, at Crompton's, bds 3 Water
Scanlan James, at Crompton's, bds 1 Towpath
Scanlan James, brakeman, E. Worcester
Scanlan James, laborer, W. R. R. h 10 E, Worc.
Scanlan John, weaver, h 5 Millbury
Scanlan Richard, hostler at W. A. Wheeler's
Scanlan Terrence, weaver, bds 1 Towpath
Scanlan Thomas, weaver, bds 1 Towpath
Scannall Dennis, laborer, h Larkin
Schneider Henry, machinist, h 47 Front
Schofield W. John, at Fox's mill, h 12 Gold
Scholan James, moulder, bds 4 Cherry
Scholan John, carpenter, h 4 Cherry
Scholin Andrew, wiredcleaner, bds Liberty
Schollay Michael, laborer, h 2 S. Irving
Schmidt G. Albert, court mill, h 25 Grove
Schreyer John, heater, h rear 12 Cherry
Schubert Anton, wiredrawer, h Langdon
Schwartz David, bootmaker, h & shop cor Waldo
& Exchange

Schwartz Geo. shoemaker, 8 Mulberry
Scott A. B. gas fitter, h 37 Mulberry
Scott David, druggist, 251 Main, h Goddard place
Scott Edson, Quinsigamond   [h 34 Temple
Scott (Gilman) & Ellis, (N. B.) grocers, 99 Front,
Scott John R. laborer, h 6 Lafayette
Scott Nelson R. at Scott's drug store, h 10 Salem
Scott Mrs. R. W. h 12 Salem
Scott Mrs. Samuel B. h 47 Thomas   [Tremont
Scrymgeour Thomas, horseshoer, bds Front cor
Seagrave Daniel, job printer, Spy Office, h 6 Crown
Seagrave J. D. & Co. (Geo. Fisher,) shoddy mill, So.
    Worcester, h 50 Elm
Searles Orville, shoemaker, h 149 Pleasant
Searles Edwin, machinist, h 2 Harris
Sears Alden H. h W. Boylston
Sears Philander, farmer at Chase's, W. Boylston
Sears Sylvanus, farmer, Salisbury
Seaver A. Milton, wire annealer, bds 40 Grove
Seaver A. H. silversmith, bds 40 Grove
Seaver Augustus W. bread driver, h 4 Winter
Seaver James M. clicker, h 21 Carroll
Seaver Wm. clerk at I. D. Russell's, h 2 Burt
Seavey Chas. L. carpenter, h 12 John
Segur Chas. bootmaker, h Bartlett place
Seibert Jacob, h 14 Millbury
Serell Henry M. hackman, bds Lincoln house
Sessions Francis E. pat'rn maker, ct mill, h 27 Main
SESSIONS GEO. city sexton & undertaker, 53
    Front, h 63 Front
Sessions Nath'l, farmer at hospital
Sexton Jerre, teamster, h cor Exch. & Blackstone
Seymore Edward, tailor, h 8 Chandler
Shaff John, spinner, V. Falls
Shallay Cornelius, helper, bds 7 Winter
Shangood Joseph, clerk, bds 266 Main
Shannon Patrick, laborer, h 4 Water
Sharp Hugh, tailor, bds 18 Central   [house
Shattuck Oliver P. at M. E. Shattuck's, bds Waldo
Shattuck R. W. h Lincoln
Shattuck Samuel F. boarding, h 56 Main   [house
Shattuck M. E. cigar store, Piper's bl'k, bds Bay St.
Shaw Geo. W. engineer at Goddard, Rice & Co's,
    bds 3 Winter
Shaw Henry, machinist, h 20 Summer
Shaw John, boot crimper, h 2 Pink
Shaw John B. manufacturer, 5 Salem
Shaw Joseph W. coppersmith, h 3 Winter
Shaw Samuel, farmer, h Leicester, V. Falls
Shaw Thomas W. blacksmith, h 17 Orange
Shay Patrick, bootmaker, h rear 16 Shrewsbury
Shea Florence, boot & shoemaker, bds rear 89
Shea James. laborer, h 60 Salem   [Summer
Shea John. blacksmith, h 14 Brown
Shea Michael, bootcrimper, h 78 Mechanic
Shea Thomas, laborer, h 35 Temple
Shea William, currier, h 23 Winter
Shearer Henry, watchman at Fox's, h 7 Millbury
Sheedy John, crimper, h 4 Spring
Sheedy Thomas, clicker, h rear Bangs block
Sheehan Dennis, shoemaker, bds 9 Fulton
Sheehan James, laborer, h 24 Shrewsbury
Sheehan Michael, laborer, h 3 E. Central
Sheehan Patrick, laborer, h rear 12 Grafton
Sheehan Patrick, laborer, h 5 S. Irving
Sheehan Thos. laborer, W. R. R. h 24 Shrewsbury
Sheehan Thos. fireman at Hospital, h 29 Shrews-
Sheffield Chas. P. teamster, h 19 Grafton   [bury
Sheilds Daniel, bootmaker, h 62 Salem
Shelby Charles H. Nor. engine house. h 13 Myrtle
Sheldon Gilbert W. wheelmaker, h 48 Chatham
Sheldon Hiram Z. machinist, h 9 Reservoir
Sheldon Horace, clerk at Pinkham's, h 4 West

Sheldon Nelson L, woodworker, h cor. Quincy &
    Chatham
Shepard Constant, agt. & collector, h 4 Charlton
Shepard Mrs. C, O. boarders, h Leicester, V. F.
Shepard Felton, wool sorter, h 130 Southbridge
Shepard Geo. W. at Lee Sprague & Co., bds 17
Shepard James, h 314 Main   [Prospect
Shepard James, spinner, bds 1 Millbury
Shepard John, halfway house, Millbury
Shepard Moses, laborer, bds Leicester, V. F.
Shepard Paul, laborer, Fowler
Shepard (Russell R.) Lathe (Martin) & Co. (Edwin
    Morse) machinists' tools, Junction, bds 1 Con-
Shepard Sam'l, machinist, h 71 So'bridge   [gress
Sherman Aaron, machinist at Willard & Co's, h 20
    Union
Sherman Nath'l H. armorer, bds 15 Austin   [mot
Sherman Wm. H. engineer at hospital, h 12 Wil-
Sherwin Waldo, carpenter, h 2 King
Sherry J. T. tailor, bds 7 Maple
Sherwood Hiram, machinist, h 24 Washington
Shields Robert, plumber, h 23 Pleasant
Shippee H. J. wiredrawer, h 14 Arch   [Bowdoin
Shippen Rev. Rush R. past. ch. of the Unity, h 6
Shonyard Joseph, salesman, bds 266 Main
Short Charles S. machinist, bds 7 Charlton
Short Timothy W. machinist, bds 7 Charlton
Short Mrs. Timothy W. h 7 Charlton
Shortell John, laborer, h 44 Shrewsbury
Shortell Patrick, shoemaker, bds 44 Shrewsbury
Shove Baxter, farmer, h 6 Newport
Shuckrow James, laborer, h 15 Hibernia
Shuckrow Patrick. laborer, h 13 Hibernia
SHUMWAY EMORY L. boottree manuf'r, Wash-
    ington, h 22 Orange
Shumway Stephen, watchman, h 2 Woodland
Shurtlieff Sam'l H. pump maker, 69 Front, h 10
Shute Chas. carpenter, h High st. ct.   [Grafton
Sibley Chas. bds 18 Pleasant
Sibley Chas. M. mason, h rear 12 Gold
Sibley Cyrus, (Woodward & S.) bds 19 Washing-
Sibley David, farmer, Harrington   [ton
Sibley J. B. deputy sheriff, 3 Central Exchange
Sibley Wm. carpenter, h 13 Central
Sibley Wm. E. machinist, bds 12 Salem
Sibley Wilson, shoemaker, Lamartine
Siegars Gilbert G. bonnet presser, bds 2 Sudbury
Sikes Mary, bds Exchange Hotel
Sikes Sarah, bds Exchange Hotel
Silcox John, machinist, h 4 Lexington
Simmons Charles E. carpenter. bds 16 Plymouth
Simmons John, carpenter, h 16 Plymouth
Simmons John A. carpenter, h 16 Plymouth
Simonds Elijah, bootcrimper, h 5 Edward
Simonds James M. farmer, h Salisbury
Simonds Miss Miranda, dressmaker, 93 Main
Simonds Nathan J. boot counters, Sargent's bl'k,
    h 65 Southbridge
Simonds Sullivan, bds 63 Southbridge
Simonds Sullivan jr. shoemaker, h 63 Southbridge
Sinclair James, blacksmith, h 14 Blackstone
Sinclair Robert, baker, h 17 Beach
Sisco Savory, laundress, h rear Bangs bl'k
Sisson Wm. S. machinist, bds 44 Central
Skahan Dennis, laborer, h 24 Winter
Skallay Thomas, bootbottomer, bds 64 Front
Skerrett Mrs. Catharine, h 5 Foyle
Skiff Geo. W. farmer, Pleasant, Tatnuck
Skinner Mrs. Catharine, h 17 Myrtle
Slater Mrs. Nancy, h 14 Grove
Slatery Thomas, laborer, h 5 Cross
Sloan Robert, moulder, h 31 Union
Sly Timothy, carpenter, h Mason

Smith Aaron, wire plater, bds 43 Summer
Smith Adelbert S. plow maker, h Sunnyside
Smith Albert C. attendant at hospital
Smith Albert D. (E. & A. D. Smith) h 7 Cottage
Smith A. H. wiredrawer at Goddard's
Smith Alfred, carpenter, h 98 Chandler
Smith Andrew, laborer, h Quinsigamond
Smith Bernard, wirecoater, h Temple
Smith Charles, mechanic, h 28 Laurel
Smith Charles B. att. at hospital
Smith Charles L. carpenter, h rear 1 Queen
Smith Coradon, shoemaker, h Cambridge
Smith Daniel B. machinist, 17 Winter
Smith Edward, moulder. h 72 Salem
Smith E. D. saloon, 97 Main, bds Taft's Hotel
Smith E. H. cabinet maker, bds 4 Newbury
Smith Elliot T. grocer, Shrewsbury cor Mulberry, bds rear 18 Mulberry
Smith Elisha, gentleman, Forest
Smith Ephraim, waiter at Lion Saloon
SMITH ESTES & ALBERT D. hats, caps and trunks, 239 Main, h 7 Cottage [bury
Smith Ezekiel, plane maker, Exchange, h 4 Newbury
Smith Ezra C. wiredrawer, bds 16 Grove
Smith Francis, machinist at ct. mill, h Lynde
Smith Fred. E. walter, Bay State House
Smith Geo. shoemaker, bds 91½ Main
Smith Geo. A. machinist, bds 44 Front
Smith Geo. E. (Smith & Brother) 144 Main, h 32
Smith G. H. machinist, h 9 Shelby [William
Smith Geo. H. shoe manufacturer, 3 Southbridge, h 21 Portland [Co.'s
Smith Geo. R. bootmaker at Geo. S. Farnum &
Smith Geo. W. sole leather clicker, bds 27 Mechanic [h 1 Home
Smith Henry D. agent Swan, Brewer & Tileston,
Smith Henry M. machinist at G. & Rice's, h 47
Smith H. P. moulder, h rear 10 Prospect [Central
Smith Hiram, machinist, h 1 Otis
Smith James G. grinder, bds 33 Beacon
Smith Jarius W. saloon 47 Main, h 45 Main
Smith Jesse, clerk, bds rear 18 Mulberry
Smith J. Baxter, attendant at hospital
Smith John, h Foyle
Smith John, bootireer, h Grove
Smith Mrs. John A. h 11 Irving
Smith John D. watchman Merrifield's building, bds Farmer's Hotel
Smith John F. (Smith & Brother,) h 3 Prescott
Smith John M. blacksmith, bds Farmer's hotel
Smith John M. wiredrawer, bds Bloomingdale
Smith John P. armorer, h 10 Chandler
Smith John W. bds rear 18 Mulberry [Providence
Smith Rev. Jos. treas. & steward Fem. Coll. h 43
Smith Joshua, at ct. mill, h Concord
Smith Mrs. Julia A. h Mason [Penn. av.
Smith Larkin, real estate broker, 236 Main, h
Smith Lewis, lime dealer, Shrewsbury, h rear 18
Smith Mrs. Lydia, h 23 Orchard [Mulberry
Smith Monroe F. moulder, h cor Charlton & Beacon
Smith Moore, carpenter, h 18 Lincoln [con
Smith Morton, machinist, h 37 Summer
Smith Moses B. farmer, h Ward
Smith M. Myron, farmer, bds Ward
Smith Paris, machinist, h 9 Shelby
Smith Patrick, teamster, h 21 Grafton
Smith Patrick, laborer, h Stafford
Smith Rodney A. mechanic, h 1 Lafayette
Smith Roswell A. painter, h 1 Lafayette
Smith Samuel, city clerk, City hall, h 57 So'bridge
Smith Samuel, laborer at B. Converse's
Smith Samuel C. currier, Burnside ct. h 1 School
Smith Sanford J. shoe dresser, L 126 Southbridge

Smith Simeon A. at court mill, h Sunnyside
Smith Sidney, h 30 Chandler
Smith Thos. & Co. (Wm. Conkey & E. W. Nichols,) machinists, Cypress, h 2 Otis
Smith Thos. F. merchant tailor, 229 Main, h 2
Smith Wm. horse shoer, h 20 Exchange [Everott
Smith Wm. A. asst. clerk of courts, h 5 Harvard
Smith Wm. L. moulder. h 5 Cherry [cott
Smith Wm. P. wire roller, Grove mill, h 19 Prescott
Smith Woodbury C. machinist, bds 57 So'bridge
Smyth Robert L. 12 Foster, h 3 Glen
Smyth (Wm. A. S.) & Brother, (R. L.) shoe manufacturers, 12 Foster, h 13 Orchard
Snow Alonzo, armorer, h Southgate
Snow Mrs. Betsey, b 16 Shrewsbury
Snow Joseph, blacksmith, h 17 Summer
Snow W. N. dentist, office 153 Main, h Salisbury
Snow James R. armorer, bds Southgate
Son Joseph, moulder, h 104 Southbridge
Son Levi, blacksmith, h Green
Souther Rev. Samuel, h 7 1-2 Shelby
Southgate John P. h 10 Church
Southgate R. H. (Rogers & Southgate,) shoefindings, cor Main & Pleasant, bds 20 Pleasant
Southwick J. E. agt. for barometers, bds 32 Mosspalding Edward L. clerk, bds 76 Pleas't [chanic
Spalding Mrs. Susan H. T. h 76 Pleasant
Spaulding Edmund, clerk at Draper & Clark's, h
Spaulding Edwin, h 3 Fruit [1 Lafayette
Spaulding Elisha K. jobber, h 9 Gold
Spaulding Geo. overseer court mill foundry, h Lincoln cor Kendall
Spaulding Geo. H. bds Lincoln cor Kendall
Spaulding John E. carpenter, bds 20 Pleasant
Spaulding Lorenzo Q. sewing machines, Richmond's block, h 5 Congress
Spence James, pattern maker, h 5 Temple
Spence Thomas, moulder, h cor Wash & Plymouth
Spence Wm. N. moulder, h 14 Shrewsbury
Spencer C. M. bds Lincoln House
Spencer Jared S. farmer at hospital
Spencer John, grain measurer, 26 Elliot
Spencer Lucien, farmer at hospital
Spencer Wm. laborer, h 19 Franklin
Spiers James, paper maker, h Apricot
Spiers John, machinist, h Lodi
Spooner A. J. bookkeeper at J. B. Lawrence's, h Clinton cor Chatham
Spooner H. B. Union Art Gallery, h 2 Quincy
Spooner Moses, printer, 212 Main, h 4 High
Sprague A.B. R. (Lee Sprague & Co.) h 17 Prospect
Sprague Amos, shoemaker, h Main cor Lagrange
Sprague Amos jr. shoemaker, h Main cor Lagrange
Sprague Andrew, machinist, bds 31 Portland
Sprague Daniel, grinder, h 17 Wash. sq.
Sprague John F. stone cutter, bds 24 Green
Sprague Lee & Co. (A. B. R. Sprague) flour and grain, 1 Park, h 1 Hanover
Sprague Philander, carpenter, bds Wall
Sprague Welcome W. painter, h 57 Summer
Spring Charles, currier, h 18 Union
Spring Chas. C. R. R. travelling agt. h 3 Edward
Spring Edwin H. horseshoer, bds 15 Seaver
Spring John G. shoemaker, 205 1-2 Main, bds 15 Seaver
SPRING JOS. W. soap manufacturer, h 15 Seaver
Spring Luther, h 7 Cherry
Spurr Elijah, (Ballard & S.) h 33 Pleasant
Spurr Geo. R. druggist, 201 Main, bds 21 Crown
Spurr Thos. J. bds Oak avenue
Spurr (Zeph.) & Priest, victualling, under Am. house block, h 37 Pleasant
Squires Edw'd H. Connecticut yeast, h 2 Hermon

Squires Whitman O. shoemaker, h Larkin
Stafford John F. woodworker, bds 37 Summer
Stahl John K. engineer at Fox's, h 3 Water
Stamp Edmond L. machinist, h 14 Linc ln
Stamp Wm. S. machinist, h N. Ashland
St Andrew Andrew P. blacksmith, bds "2 Mechanic
St Clair James, blacksmith, h 14 Blackstone
Stauton Geo. laborer, h 7 Burt
Stanton Robert B. barometer maker, h Woodland
Staples Charles, machinist, h 4 School [49 Central
Staples Charles E. manuf'r bitstocks, &c. Exch. h
Staples Samuel E. produce dealer, 283 & 287 Main,
    h 23 Thomas
Stapleton Toby, laborer, h 62 Salem
Stark E. H. boot crimper, h 15 Lincoln
Stark H. J. clicker, bds 36 Front
Stark Niles S. shoemaker, h 15 Lincoln
Stark O. N. clicker, h 15 Lincoln
Starkey John L. gas fitter, bds 3 Carlton
Starkweather Asher, butcher, h Grafton
Start Lorenzo B. clerk Waldo house
Start Rollo N. proprietor Waldo house
Stearns Albert, at rolling mill, bds 3 Lynn
Stearns Albert C. clerk, bds 9 Maple
Stearns Amos E. machinist, bds 41 Summer
Stearns C. C. music teacher, bds 3 Home
Stearns C. H. baker, 86 Pleasant, h 59 Pleasant
Stearns Chas. W. machinist, bds 262 Main
Stearns Geo. E. machinist, h 5 Union
Stearns Geo. F. carriage maker, bds 5 High
Stearns G. O. dentist. Am. house block
Stearns Henry, machinist, bds 3 Everett
Stearns John E. walter Waldo house
Stearns Joseph E. mason, h 26 Portland
Stearns Moses P. machinist, h 363 Southbridge
Stearns Otis, h 83 Salem
Stearns Walter, h 81 Pleasant
Stebbins Edw. S. foreman at Quinsig. iron works
Stebbins Geo. H. wiredrawer, h Cambridge, S. W.
Stebbins Otis, moulder. bds 32 Thomas
Steinberg A. Morris, at L. Lewisson's, bds 8 Maple
Stedman Mrs. Francis, h 3 Salem
Steele J. H. (W. R. & J. H.) bds Lincoln ho.
Steele W. R. N. E. Tea Co. 210 Main, bds Lin. ho.
Stevens Abednego, painter, 244 Main, h Burnside
    court   [ho. bl'k, bds 6 School
Stevens Amasa W. sewing machine manuf'r, Am
Stevens Chas. E. asst. register probate and insol-
    vency, h 21 High
Stevens C. P. (D. & C. P. S.) h 3 Sycamore
Stevens Daniel & C. P. sash, door and blind deal-
    ers, 301 Main, h 3 Sycamore
Stevens Edgar, painter, bds 17 Lamartine
Stevens Edwin, shoemaker, h 5 John
Stevens Joseph, tailor, bds 2 Mechanic
Stevens Olney, at Draper & Clark's, 23 Providence
Stevens Reuben, h 102 Main
Stevens Waldo, driver, bds 19 Orchard
Stevens Warren, bootmaker, bds 41 Mechanic
Stevens Wm. painter, bds 17 Lamartine
Stevens Wm. brakeman B. R. R. bds 17 Orange
Stephenson John T. cutter at Doherty's, bds 2
    Sudbury
Stewart Charles, armorer, h 29 Southbridge
Sthor Henry, wiredrawer, h 8 Central
Stiles Mrs. Abigail, h 27 Pleasant
Stiles Charles, laborer, bds 3 Harrington av.
Stiles Frederic G. carriage painter, 22 School, h 3
    Harrington av.
Stircbler Peter, armorer, h 1 Brown's bl'k, Salem
Stocking Alex. teacher of music, h 43 Chandler
Stockley John, machinist, bds 66 Exchange
Stockwell Albert, clerk, bds 31 Wash. Square

Stockwell Mrs. Cyrus, h 296 Main
Stockwell Dwight, wiredrawer, bds 8 Grafton
Stockwell Emerson M. livery stable, Mechanic, h
    6 Portland
Stockwell Henry, laborer at Ezra Goddard's
Stockwell Leander W. at E. Mellen's bookstore,
    bds 48 Elm
Stockwell Luther, farmer, Southgate
STODDARD E. B. counsellor, 141 Main, h 75 Pleas't
Stoddard J. C. inventor, Cypress, h 116 Pleasant
Stone Amasa S. boxmaker. h 24 Central
Stone Augustus, machinist, bds cor. Union & Thos.
Stono Chas. D. shoe heeler, h 26 Chandler
Stone Chas. W. machinist, h 129 Main
Stone Edward S. boot clicker, bds 1 King
Stone Elisha, bootmaker, h 27 Austin
Stone Geo. W. bootmaker, h 25 Austin
Stone Henry A. machinist, h 73 Austin
Stone Henry D. counsellor. bds Bay State house
Stone James M farmer, h Nelson place
STONE REV. JAMES R. Principal Wor. Academy
Stone John. stitcher, h 28 Shrewsbury
Stone John V. at Earle, Tenney & Co. h 212 Pleas't
Stone Lewis C. machinist at G. & Rice's, h 35 Salem
Stone Lucian B. omnibus proprietor, Main, N. W.
Stone Lucius, machinist, bds 65 Front
Stone Luther, acct. at Miller's, h 15 Oxford
Stone Marshall, roller, h Leesville
Stono Mrs. Mary. h 2 Newbury
Stone Melville C. hostler, bds Academy hill
Stone Oliver, wheelwright, 11 Central, h 13 Salem
Stone Prescott B. machinist, h Webster
Stono Mrs. Sarah, h 36 Thomas
Stone S. V. (S. Thompson & Co.) 247 Main, h Or-
    ange cor Plymouth   [1 King
Stone Timothy S. boot manufacturer, 305 Main, h
Stone Uriah, farmer, Main, N. W.
Stone Wm. U. omnibus driver, Main, N. W.
Stoodley B. H. painter, bds 43 Summer
Story Simeon N. jeweller, 149 Main, h 4 Oxford
Storrs Henry C engineer at hospital, h 63 Summer
Stott David, junk dealer, h rear 9 E. Central
Stott Isaiah, heater, h 8 Grafton
Stott Joseph, rag dealer, 23 E. Central
Stott Thomas, boottreer, h 38 Grove
Stoughton Daniel G. farmer, h Lovell
Stowe A. F. machinist, h 2 King
Stowe Elijah, farmer, h Stowe place
Stowe Henry L. clerk, h 8 Congress
Stowe Mrs. Lovell, h 8 Congress
Stowe Lovell H. clicker, bds Highland court
Stowe Ithamar F. machinist, bds 81 Exchange
Stowe Luther & Co. (E. Muzzy) shoe manuf'rs, 311
    Main, h Highland ct.   [Chatham
Stowe Martin, dry goods, 261 Main, h Crown cor
Stowe Wm. K. clerk. h 8 Congress
Stowe Wm. M. shoefinisher. bds 18 1-2 Portland
Stowell Benj. F. farmer, h Granite
Stowell Mrs. David D. Granite
Stowell (Francis P.) Maynard (J. A.) & Co. (R. G.
    White) provisions &c., city hall, h W. Boylston
Stowell Frederick T. farmer, W. Boylston
Stowell Mrs. Nathaniel, Granite
Stowell Mrs. Sevilla, h 10 Park
Strauss Leopold. (Gross, Strauss & Co.) bds Waldo h
Stratton Chas. H. shoemaker, 205 1-2 Main, bds 4
    Stratton Chas. T. machinist, h Webster   [Central
Stratton Daniel, machinist, h 35 Chandler
Stratton F. A. stairbuilder, 3 School, bds 2 Maple pl.
Stratton F. D. last maker, h 6 Edward
Stratton Robert B. cabinet maker, Woodland
Stratton Sam. restaurant, 75 Main, h Linwood pl.
Stratton S. E. clerk at Taft's hotel

Stratton Mrs. Sarah, h Burt
Streeter Asa, laborer, h 56 Mechanic
Streeter Emory, carter at F. T. Stowell's
Streeter John P. butcher, bds Grafton
Streeter Otis, truckman, h 16 Seaver
STRONG FRANCIS, Green st. coal yard, h 20
Strong John A cabinet maker, h 1 Lynn [Green
Strong R. L. machinist, h 20 School
Strong Simeon S. C. at Webber's, Clinton lane
Strong Solomon, farmer, bds Highland
Strong Wm. G. bookkeeper for F. Strong, bds 20
Stuart John, carriagemaker, h Beacon   [Green
Studley John M. stairbuilder h 4 Prospect
Studley Zenas, stairbuilder, h 5 Prospect
Sturtevant Chas. H. bds 13 Charlton
Sturtevant Mrs. Elisha h 13 Charlton
Sturtevant Harvey, machinist, h 22 Liberty
Sturtevant Lewis, farmer, Harrington
Sturtevant L. W. tailor, 131 Main, h Mulberry cor
     Prospect
Sullivan Mrs. Anne, h cor Beach and Brown
Sullivan Cornelius, at Allen and Wheelock's, h 21
     Franklin
Sullivan Cornelius, moulder, bds 5 Brown's bl'k
Sullivan Cornelius, moulder, h 7 Charles
Sullivan Daniel, laborer, h Eaton place
Sullivan Daniel, laborer, h 6 Wash. sq.
Sullivan Daniel, bootmaker, h 8 Lovell's court
Sullivan David wirecleaner, h 9 Howard
Sullivan Mrs. Elizabeth, 2 Canal
Sullivan Eugene, laborer, h 2 Milk
Sullivan James, grocer, 6 Wash. square
Sullivan James, wheelmaker, h Blossom
Sullivan Mrs. James, h 23 Franklin
Sullivan James E. moulder, bds 3 Lamartine
Sullivan James O. engineer at Bradley's, h 18
Sullivan Jeremiah,laborer, h 12 Vine[Shrewsbury
Sullivan Jeremiah, laborer, h 42 Shrewsbury
Sullivan Jeremiah, tailor, h 17 Blackstone
Sullivan Jeremiah, laborer, h rear 16 Shrewsbury
Sullivan John, ware cleaner, h 83 Front
Sullivan John, fireman, h Goddard's lane
Sullivan John, tailor, h 2 Church
Sullivan John, carpenter, h 26 Shrewsbury
Sullivan John, gas works, h Carbon
Sullivan John, laborer, bds 26 Madison
Sullivan John, beltmaker, bds 4 Bridge
Sullivan John, laborer, h 16 Union
Sullivan John, bootmaker, bds 4 Front
Sullivan John, laborer, h 18 Shrewsbury
Sullivan Martin, bootbottomer, h Smith court
Sullivan Mrs. Margaret, h 29 Shrewsbury
Sullivan Michael, laborer, h 21 Grafton
Sullivan Patrick, at Earle & Jones', h 59 Salem
Sullivan Patrick, laborer, h Blossom
Sullivan Patrick, bootmaker, rear 16 Shrewsbury
Sullivan Patrick, laborer, h E. Central
Sullivan Thomas, laborer, h Cross
Sullivan Thomas, laborer, h 4 E. Central
Sullivan Thomas, laborer, h 5 Foyle
Sullivan Timothy, laborer, h 24 Chandler
Sullivan Timothy, laborer at Dan'l Harrington's
Sullivan Timothy, laborer, h 29 Shrewsbury
Sullivan Wm. laborer, h 26 Madison
Sumner Edwin A. clerk, bds 24 Irving
Sumner Mrs. F. h 53 Summer
Sumner Geo. (Barnard, S. & Co.) bds 1 Everett
Sumner Wm. teacher of music, h Chatham st. pl.
Sutherland John, shoemaker, bds 2 Sudbury
Sutler Wm. wiretemperer, h Belmont
Sutton Charles, fireman at flour mill, Manches-
     ter, bds 95 Summer   [Thomas, h 1 George
SUTTON GEO. T. pump and lead pipe maker, 8

Sutton Jas. flour & oil mill, Manchester, h Main
Sutton Mrs. John, h 10 School   [N. W.
Sutton John F. machinist, h Leicester, N. W.
Sutton Joseph R. bds 95 Summer
Sutton Mrs. Lucy, h 95 Summer
Sutton Thos. h 17 Chestnut
Sutton Walter T. cashier Grafton Bank, bds 10
Swallow Freeman M. painter, h 7 Maple   [School
Swallow Wm. A. at A. S. Brown's, Exchange, h
     Belmont cor Edward
Swan Elliott, Swan's hotel, Wash. sq.
Swan Geo. attorney, 5 Flagg's bl'k. h 18 Harvard
Swan Michael, laborer at Hacker's, h Ward
Swan Miss M. S. clairvoyant. 22 Exchange
Sweeney Mrs. Catherine, h 65 Exchange
Sweeney James, farmer, h 5 Brown
Sweeney Patrick, laborer, h 24 E. Worcester
Sweeney Patrick, moulder, h Columbia
Sweeney Wm. tailor and sewing machines, 41
     Front, h 13 Temple
Sweeny Dennis, hostler, h Exchange
Sweeny Edmund, laborer, h 12 Wash. sq.
Sweeny Hugh, shoemaker, h 12 Pond
Sweet Alfred, machinist, h 20 Millbury
Sweet Peter, shoemaker, h Foyle
Sweetser Chauncy B. clicker, h Mulberry ct.
Sweetser Geo. machinist, h 7 Chandler
Sweetser Geo. W. wire roller, bds 22 Grove
Sweetser J. E. laborer, h Nashua cor Crescent
Sweetser J. A. acct, bds Lincoln cor Harrington
     avenue   [rington avenue, cor Lincoln
Sweetser Rev. Seth, pastor Central ch. h Har-
Sweetser S. S. (Walker & S) h 288 Main
Swoetser Wm. P. clerk, bds Bay St. House
Swett Samuel D. hackman, h Eden   [House
Swett Wm. O. grocery store, 186 Main, bds Lin.
Swift John, wirebundler, h Quinsigamond
Swift John W. clerk for E. F. Rogers, bds 90 So'-
Swift Wm. A. machinist, bds Quinsig.   [bridge
Syme Mrs. James B. h 11 Providence
TABER (WM. B.) & CHOLLAR (J. D.)furniture
     15 1 Main, h 39 Pleasant
Taft Alfred, farmer, h Granite
Taft Andrew, blacksmith, bds Taft's Hotel
Taft Benjamin, 107 Main, bds 1 Providence
Taft Cyrus, carpenter, 1 Fountain
Taft Edwin F. machinist, bds 17 School
Taft Genera, boxmaker, h 10 Arch
Taft Geo. C. manufacturer of copying presses and
     wrenches, Merrifield's, h 6 Chandler
Taft George W. farmer, Granite
Taft Henry G. (8. Taft & Son) h 10 Portland
Taft John E. rubber goods, 214 Main, h 12 Irving
Taft Joseph, Granite
Taft Jotham W. shoe dealer, h 11 Pleasant
Taft Judson, farmer, bds 10 Reservoir
Taft Levi M. farmer, Granite
Taft (Lyman J.) & Lilley (A. J.) fruit store and
     eating house, 237 Main, h 2 Ashland
Taft Moses, (Harding & T.) h 1 Providence
Taft Mrs. Polly, h 53 Shrewsbury
Taft Putman W. carpenter, h 9 Pearl
Taft P. W. wiredrawer, h 16 Grove
Taft Rufus M. machinist, bds 13 Portland
Taft Mrs. Sarah W. h 3 Prescott   [tel
Taft Stephen, mechanic. court mill, bds Taft's ho-
Taft Stephen & Son, (H. G. Taft,) grocers, 31
Taft Stephen, hotel, 90 Main   [Front, h 7 Salem
Taft Timothy F. machinist, h 17 School
Tague John, at rolling mill, h 12 E. Worcester
Tainter Carver, machinist, h 76 Southbridge
Tainter Daniel, woolen machinery, Union, h 5
     Hanover

Tainter Ephraim C. (J. A. Fay & Co.) Junction shop. h 12 Crown
Tainter Harvey S. machinist. h 81 Southbridge
Talbot David C. engineer at Allen & Wheelock's, h 136 Southbridge
Talbot Thomas, boottreer, bds 5 High
Talbot Thos. laborer at W. Harris', h E. Central
Taney Patrick, laborer, h 2 Brown's block
Tanner Mrs. Sarepta, h 9 Washington
Tansey Martin, laborer, h 8 Pond
Tansey Michael, wiredrawer, bds 5 Brown
Tapley Chas. E. photographer, h Dewey
Tapley David G. pattern maker, h 55 Austin
Tarbell John B. clerk. 186 Main, h 9 John
Tarbell Mrs. Sarah B. h 33 Thomas
Tarbox John L. baker, h 20 Union
Tarlin Mrs. Rosanna, h 35 Madison
Tarly Michael, rolling mill, bds rear 53 Salem
Taro Samuel, moulder, h 33 Madison
Tatman Chas. wiredrawer, Greenwood
Tatman Daniel, farmer, Greenwood
Tatman David D. butcher, h 16 Liberty
Tatman John, farmer, Greenwood
Tatman John A. clicker, bds 300 1-2 Main
Tatman Levi, farmer, Greenwood
Tatman Reuben, farmer, Greenwood
Tatman Rufus D. farmer, Greenwood [William
Taylor Clarke W. harness maker, 244 Main, h 9
Taylor Geo. G. machinist, h 28 Summer
Taylor Geo. M. carpenter, h 11 Portland
Taylor Geo. W. express driver, h rear 9 William
Taylor Henry. weaver, h 7 Millbury
Taylor H. F. last maker, bds 2 Wilmot
Taylor Hosea R. machinist, h 2 Wilmot
Taylor James, machinist, bds 5 Washington
Taylor James A. grinder at ct. mill, h 27 Main
Taylor John, machinist. h 4 Lexington
Taylor Joseph, armorer, h Bluff
Taylor Peter, machinist, ct mill, h 20 Orchard
Taylor Ransom C. tripe dealer, h Quinsigamond
Taylor Mrs. Rebecca, bds 12 Providence
Taylor Robert W. acct. at C. Foster & Co.'s, bds
Taylor Sam'l, machinist, h 3 Carroll [18 Pleasant
Taylor Samuel, cigar maker, 27 Chatham
Taylor Samuel, h 15 School
Taylor (Simeon jr.) & Farley (J. A.) melodeon makers and piano forte dealers, 315 Main, h 18 Wellington [Newbury
Taylor Wm. H. Leonard's Ex. messenger, h 14
Taynton Chas. H. moulder, bds 9 Thomas
Teague Edwin C. carriagemaker, bds 30 Thomas
Teague Geo. F. moulder, bds 30 Thomas
Tebbets Mrs. Abby, h 151 Pleasant
Tebbets Mrs. Adaline, tailoress, h 13 Thomas
Tehen Daniel, laborer, h 1 Hibernia
Tehen Mrs. Wm. h 8 Lafayette
Temple Charles, map seller, h 83 Summer
Temple Chas. A. clerk at Barnard, Sumner & Co.'s
Temple Chas. A. S. boottreer, h 18 Liberty
Temple D. G. 39 Exchange [h 6 Mulberry
Temple Jason, dealer in paper stock, Shrewsbury.
Temple Obed R. carpenter, Russell st place
Templeton Anson, hod carrier, h cor Brown and
Templeton John, bootmaker. h 2 Carroll [Beach
Tenney Mrs. Caroline, h 4 Salem
Tenney Chas. A. (Earle, T. & Co.) bds 5 Vine
Tenney Chas. R. patternmaker, h Wall
Tenney Jas. saloon, 1 Wash. sq. h 12 Cherry
Tenney John, bootmanufacturer, 24 Front, h 180
Tenney Joseph A. h 5 Vine [Pleasant
Tenney Mrs. Mary, h 22 Southbridge
Terry Ell, (Holbrook & Terry) bds 18 Pleasant
Terry John, bootfitter, h S. Irving

Tew Chas. F. gas fitter, h 33 Irving
Tevan Dominick, laborer. bds 31 Mechanic
Thatcher Jos B. fish dealer, So'bridge, bds 13 Park
Thayer Adin counsellor, 218 Main, bds 18 Pleas't
Thayer Alden, h Dewey
Thayer (Alex.) Houghton (Hannibal H.) & Co. machinists, Wash. h 51 Thomas
Thayer Amos, farmer, h 25 Orange
Thayer Benj. (Lewis & T.) h 70 Front
Thayer Mrs. Benjamin, h Lincoln
Thayer C. A. porter at Lincoln House
Thayer Charles L. machinist. h 18 Chandler
Thayer Cushman, grocer, 102 Southbridge, h 59
Thayer Davis, farmer, Malden av. [Chandler
Thayer Mrs. Dolly A. h 8 Irving [dler
Thayer Edward I. S. saloon, Mechanic, h 3 Chan-
Thayer Eli, congressman, h at Orend [Pleas't
THAYER ELLIS, brush maker, 10 Foster, h 44
Thayer Horace, farmer, Holden
THAYER LEWIS, real estate agent, Cen. Exch. bds 13 Harvard
Thayer Mrs. Mary A. h 57 Chandler
Thayer Perry, h Lovell
Thayer W. E. music teacher, 207 Main, bds Bay
Thayer Mrs. Wm. D. h 378 Main [State House
Thenius Moritz, blacksmith. h 3 Pond
Thing Everett, clerk, bds 12 Thomas
Thomas Anne, nurse, bds 294 Main
Thomas Enos, machinist, h Main, N. W.
Thomas Henry, wheelmaker at S.G. & C.C. Reed's
Thomas Henry M. bds 2 Sudbury
Thomas James, printer, 3 Towpath
Thomas John, gardener, h Bloomingdale
Thomas Luther, charcoal, bds 27 Mechanic
Thomas Mrs. Seneca. h 8 Pond [Bay St. H.
Thompson Alex. Y. dry goods, 5 Flagg's bl'k, bds
Thompson Alex. wiredrawer at Goddard's
Thompson Arvin, carpenter, h 77 Southbridge
Thompson Charles, shoemaker, h Lamartine
Thompson Charles. h E. Central
Thompson Daniel C. fish dealer, 25 Southbridge, h Cambridge, N. W.
Thompson E. R. bootcrimper, h 8 West
Thompson Edward, harness maker, bds 64 Front
Thompson Edward P. bds 10 Grove
Thompson Edwin, machinist, bds 9 Thomas[Arch
Thompson F. H. nonpariel salve, 263 Main, h 21
Thompson Francis, shoemaker, bds Lamartine
Thompson Geo F. boot packer, h 7 Reservoir
Thompson J. A. wood agent B. R. R. h 63 Austin
Thompson John, farmer, bds Swan's Hotel
Thompson John A. court mill, 5 Prescott
Thompson Mrs. John W. h 7 Liberty
Thompson P. E. wiredrawer, h 16 Grove
Thompson S. B. bootmaker. h 23 Laurel
Thompson S. & Co. (S. V. Stone,) books, periodicals &c 247 Main. h Elm
Thompson Thos. H. (Hill & T.) h 12 Market
Thompson Wm. wiredrawer at Goddard's
Thompson Wm. harness maker, bds 9 Millbury
Thompson Wm. C. h 19 Lincoln
Thomson John, sewing machine manufacturer, 14 Central, h 72 Pleasant
Thorpe David H. pattern maker. h 18 Washington
Thurston (Daniel C.) & Bliss, (Geo. L.) Bay State eating house, h 10 Reservoir
Thurston David C. stoves &c. 231 Main, bds 44 Front
Thurston Mrs. Joseph, h 8 Laurel
Thurston Samuel, boottreer, bds 23 Exchange
Tiffany Pardon D. h 2 Harvard
Timby T. R. (J. M. Merrick & Co.) bds Bay State [House
Timon John, moulder, h 20 Laurel
Timperley Jos. W. machinist, h 21 Lincoln

Tingley Francis, bootmaker, bds 33 Wash. sq.
Tirrell Cyrus J. cabinet maker, h Tirrell, N. W.
Titus Reuben, bds Lincoln House
Tobey John G. Am. telegraph manager, h 3 West
Tobin Michael, laborer, bds 81 Front
TOLMAN ALBERT & CO. (G. W. Russell,) carriages & harnesses, 10 Exchange, h Catherine
Tolman Lucius C. roadmaster, B. R. R. h 5 Elliot
Toner Dennis, tailor, h 13 Foundry
Tonray John, laborer, h 56 Shrewsbury
Tonray Patrick, teamster, h Hill
Tooke Michael, hod carrier, h 15 Hibernia
Toole Austin, city laborer, h 10 E. Central
Toole Austin, laborer, h Hill
Toole Edward, bootfitter, h 10 Charles
Toole Mrs. Elizabeth, h 25 E. Central
Toole Jeremiah, tailor, h 7 Spring
Toole John, laborer, h 2 Hind's ct.
Toole Owen, laborer, h 10 E. Central
Toole Peter, laborer, bds 10 E. Central
Toomay John, bootmaker, bds 37 Mechanic
Toomy Jeremiah, gas works, h Carbon
Toomy Michael, laborer, h rear 58 Mechanic
Toppin Elisha, laborer, h 66 Union
Tornay Jeremiah, laborer, h 11 Spring
Torpay Morris, crimper, h 34 Southbridge
Torpay Patrick, laborer, h Canterbury
Torrey Jos. R. strop manuf'r, h 11 Charlton
Toulmin John (Kean & Co.) h Leicester, N. W.
Tourtellott Samuel, millwright, h 21 Green [Main
Tourtellott J. N. dentist, 1 Harrington cor. bds 319
Tourtellott G. H. flag'n, Prov. R. R. bds 27 Wash.
Tourtelot Mrs. R. h 27 Washington
Tourtelott John A. clerk, h 27 Bowdoin
Tourtelott Lora B. machinist, h 78 Southbridge
Tourtelott Rufus B. fireman B. & W. R. R. bds 78
Southbridge   [285 Main, h 27 Wash.
Tourtelott (Stephen D.) & Peck (C. H.) architects,
Tower C. D. carriage trimmer, bds 3 Carlton
Tower Chas. H. clerk Peo. Ins. Co. bds 31 Pleas't
Tower H. N. carpenter, h 31 Pleasant
Towle John, printer, bds Shelby
Towne Dean, physician, h 13 Market
Towne Enoch H. clerk, cor Mason and Pleasant
Towne Joseph, car repairs, B. R. R. h 72 Front
Towne Joshua, car repairer, h 33 Portland
Towne (Loison D.) & Harrington (Adam,) manuf'rs
mowing machine knives &c., Exchange, h 10
Harvard
Towne Moody, moulder, bds 1 Court hill
Towne Preston D. & Co. (J. H. Dodd,) manuf'rs of
perforated board & metals. Union, h 6 Prospect
Towne Wm. H. farmer, h Boylston
Townly Geo. packer at J. B Lawrence, h 15 Beach
Townsend Frederick W. machinist, h 18 Salem
Townsend V. B. wiredrawer, h 8 Grafton
Tracy Jennie J. teacher Ladies Collegiate Inst.
Tracy Michael, blacksmith, h Columbia court
Tracy Michael, gas works, h Carbon
Tracy Wm. S. shoemaker, h Tracy place
Tracey Thomas, foller, bds 1 Millbury
Train Christopher, wiredrawer, h Garden
Trainer Bernard, laborer, bds Lamartine
Trainer Francis, laborer, h Kendall
Trainer James, gas works, h Carbon
Trainer John, laborer, h rear Bangs block
Trainer Owen, bootmaker, h 16 Pond
Trainer Owen, laborer, bds 5 Charles
Trainer Peter, bootbottomer, h 50 Southbridge
Travers John, bootfinisher, h 10 E. Worcester
Trevett M. T. carpenter, h 54 Chatham
Troy David, bootmaker, 49 Mechanic
Troy Michael, bootmaker, h 1 Carlton

Trusdel Henry, furniture painter, bds 44 Front
Trumbull Chas. P. bds Park cor Green
Trumbull Geo. A. h Park cor Green
Trumbull (Jos.) Waters (Lucius,) & Co. envelope
manuf'rs, Grafton. bds cor Park and Green
Tucker Edwin R. machinist, h 61 Austin
Tucker Ephraim, woodworker, Cypress h. 14 Elliot
Tucker Erastus, pump maker, 23 Pleasant
Tucker Geo. last maker, bds 2 Vine
Tucker Mrs. Larned h 6 School
Tucker Mrs. Jane. nurse, h 31 Summer
Tucker Jasper G. wheelwright at Reed's, h 9 Ver-
Tucker Rev. J. J. h 14 Fruit   [non
Tucker Julius E. at Palladium office, h 29 Crown
Tucker J. M. clerk, bds 29 Crown
Tucker Nath'l G. plumber, 23 Pleas't, bds 9 School
Tucker Oliver W. carriage maker at Breck's, h 1
Tucker Thos. prop'r Waldo House, Waldo [Church
Tufts Frank A. bookkeeper at J. E. Browning &
Co. bds 29 Crown
TUFTS GFO. H. pattern maker, Merrifield's building, Cypress, h 75 Exchange
Tufts James H. at Bay State saloon
Tully John. shoemaker, bds 63 Southbridge
Turner Chas. S. freight ag't Nor. R. R. h 9 Park
Turner Gardner G wiredrawer, h 32 Grove
Turner Stillman, carpenter, h Tirrell
Turner P. J. (Earle, Tenny & Co.) bds Swan's
Turner Samuel, at Grove mill, h Holden
Turner T. N. conductor Nor. R. R.
Turner Wm. B. machinist, bds 15 Gold
Turner Wm. H. clerk Nor. R. R. fr't ho. h 2 Salem
Turner Wm. R. reedmaker, bds N. Ashland
Twiss Asa, machinist, h 21 Grove
Twiss Charles, bds Chester
Twiss Geo. A. shoe trimmer, bds 21 Grove
Twiss Geo. A. shoemaker, bds Chester
Twiss Stephen P. counsellor, 3 Flagg's bl'k, bds
Twiss Thos. shoemaker, h Chester   [Waldo H.
Twiss Vernon R. shoemaker, bds 21 Grove
Twombly Rev. J. H. pastor Park St. church, h 10
Oxford
Tyler Geo. Nash. R. R. bds 19 Washington
Tyler Samuel W. clerk at F. Harrington's
Tyse Joshua, weaver, bds 1 Towpath
Ufford Amasa, machinist, h Jefferson
Ufford Edward W. hackman, h 16 Washington
Underwood Geo. currier, h 5 Bridge
Underwood James H. varnisher, h East
Underwood Thomas B. machinist, h 18 Mulberry
Underwood Wm. machinist, h 2 Hudson
Upham Baylies, h 85 Pleasant
Upham Charles, W. R. R. repairs, bds 8 Union
Upham Chester, fish & oysters, 9 Pleas't, h 30
Mechanic
Upham Freeman, carpenter, h 4 Prospect
Upham Geo. clerk, bds Farmer's hotel
Upham Harvey G. wood measurer, Lin. sq. bds 8
Upham Henry P. machinist, h 16 Grove [George
Upham Joel W. millwright, Merrifield's building,
h 48 Austin   [bds 3 Hanover
Upham L. Wesley, ag't Clark's sewing machine,
Upham Mrs. Susan G. h 8 Union
Upton Chas. A. dry goods. h Harrington avenue
Upton Geo. W. D. machinist, bds 6 School
Usher Reuben tinman at Russell's, bds 27 Mechanic
Utley Francis E. machinist, bds 28 Thomas
Utley John W. oysters, 10 Foster, h 28 Thomas
Uvershutt Stephen, fur cutter at Knights'. bds 8
Vail Jeffry, moulder, bds 21 Temple   [Maple
Vail Robert, stone layer, h 21 Temple
Vail Wm. laborer at Hacker's, h Columbia
Vaill David, laborer, h Gold

VAILL EDW. W. furniture dealer and auctioneer,
1 Flagg's block, h 4 Walnut
Vaill Morris, tailor, h 8 Temple
Valentine Geo. W. machinist, bds 4 Glen
Valentine Gerry, boot pattern maker, 15 Central,
h 59 Summer
Valentine Gilbert, machinist, bds 4 Glen
VALENTINE GILL, surveyor, 285 Main, h 16
Portland
Valentine Henry C. salesman, bds 39 Summer
Valentine Mrs. Nancy T. boarders, h 4 Glen
Valentine Wm. Henry. clerk, bds 59 Summer
VanDeusen Charles H. bookkeeper, bds 1 Ct. hill
Vanness Francis. moulder, h 8 Maple
Vanornum W. H. boottreer, h 18 Myrtle
VanLoon Albert A. potter, h cor Green & Winter
Venese Peter F. moulder, h 8 Maple   [257 Main
Veneze Mons. A. De. prof. French, at French Inst.
Verry Geo. F. counsellor, 4 Central Exch. h Cedar
Vie ze Charles, armorer, h 14 S. Irving
Viall Nathaniel A. shoemaker. Langdon
Vizinet Peter. blacksmith, h Ward
Volkmar Reinhold, armorer, bds 21 Madison
Walley Isaac L. engineer W. R. R. h 22 Green
Wadsworth Henry C. at Allen & Wheelock's, bds
378 Main
Wadswo th Joseph, real estate, h Hudson
Wageley Louis, German teacher, bds 257 Main
Wagner John O armorer, bds 14 Salem
Walmot Daniel, tinsmith, bds Uninn
Waite A.Ward.(L.Harrington &Co.)bds 325 Main
Waite Mrs. Alvin, h 294 Main
Waite Andrew J. carpenter, h Plantation
Waite C E. Nash. R. R. repairer, h 10 Lincoln
Waite Curtis V. clerk, h rear 32 Shrewsbury
Waite Nathaniel. clerk. bds 325 Main
Waite Samuel, car maker, h 10 Goddard
Wakefield Mrs. Almira, h 21 Austin
Wakefield Mrs. Matilda, h rear Ward
Wakefield Timothy, machinist, h 69 Exchange
Wakefield Willard C. pattern maker. h 2 Clinton
WALBRIDGE ALBERT, boy'sclothing, 7 Lincoln
house block, bds 15 Shelby   [15 Shelby
Walbridge Henry, overseer Wheeler's furnace, h
Walbridge Henry D. supt. union club, 229 Main,
h 15 Shelby
Walcott Edward F. butcher, bds 16 Oxford
Walcott Eli. clicker at Childs & Walker's, h 16
Wales Henry, moulder, bds 12 Charlton   [Oxford
Walkden Wm. boottreer, h 31 Summer
Walker A. C. clicker, bds 1 May
Walker Aaron G. (Childs & W.) 1 Bangs bl'k, h 1
Walker Allen, barber, bds 64 Union   [May
Walker Appleton, silver plater & saddlery hard-
ware, 65 Main, h 23 Lincoln
Walker Asa, merchant tailor,217 Main,h 56 Pleas't
Walker Asa A. laborer, h rear 5 Chandler
Walker A. W. wiredrawer, bds 16 Grove
Walker (Benj.) & Sweetser (S. S.) ice dealers, 4
Exchange, h 6 Lexington, cor Prescott
Walker Chas. N. clicker, h 86 Southbridge
Walker Freeman C. bootsider, h 55 Chandler
WALKER GILBERT, wig manuf'r, under Bay
State house, Main, h 10 Liberty
Walker James, moulder, bds 3 Lamartine
Walker J. B. carpenter, bds 16 Central
Walker Jos. & Co. boot & leather dealers, Lin. sq.
Walker Jos. H. (J. Walker & Co.) bds 18 Wellington
Walker Melville, clicker, h 26 Thomas
Walker Melville E. clerk, bds 80 Main
Walker Samuel P. clicker, bds 22 Salem
Walker W. W. A. professor English & Arithmetic,
College Holy Cross

Walks James, carpenter, h 13 Millbury
Wall Caleb A. reporter for Spy, bds Lincoln house
Wall James H. 375 Main
Wall Michael, laborer, h 60 Salem
Wall Richard. laborer, h 6 Charles   [bridge
Wallace Church. city street repairs, h 74 South-
Wallace John. fidd'er, h Cross
Wallace Sumner, silver plater, 37 Exchange, h 35
Exchange
Wallace W. H. bootfitter, h 43 Exchange
Wallis Chapman, at court mill, h 16 Wilmot
Walton Edward A. machinist, bds 13 Orange
Walton Edwin D. painter, h rear 11 Orange
Walton Gilderoy, shoemaker, h 13 Orange
Walton Henry S. bootmaker, bds 13 Orange
Ward Asa W. farmer, h Upland
Ward Chas. A. machinist, bds 8 Salem
Ward Daniel, Register Deeds office, bds 10 State
Ward Edward L. farmer, Heywood
Ward Frank, painter, at Chase & Nichols,
Ward Geo. H. machinist, h Quincy
Ward Geo. L. machinist, h Lovell
Ward Henry D. coachman at Bay State house
Ward Hugh, engineer B. R. R. h 10 Winter
Ward Michael, hostler, bds 18 Central
Ward Patrick, helper. court mill, h 2 Cherry
Ward T. & Co. (W. Fitzgerald,) fancy dry goods
& millinery, 6 Flagg's block, h 5 Fruit
Ward Thomas, farmer, 266 Main
Ward Willard, carpenter, h Allen
Ward Wm. farmer, Gate's lane [Front, h 20 Park
Warden (John,) & Jones (D. W.) beltmakers, 77
Warden Samuel, h Park, east of Common
Warden Samuel jr. carpenter, h Park east of Com'n
Ware A. L. clicker at Stone's, h 60 Front
Ware A. P. & Co. clothing store, 168 & 170 Main,
bds 18 Pleasant
Ware Jos. S. gun maker, 205 Main, bds 3 Carlton
Ware Leonard, pattern maker, h 22 Providence
Warfield Alex. J. (Fawcett & W.) h 7 Congress
Warfield Stephen T. bootcrimper, h 11 Eliot
Warner Mrs. Catharine, h Pink   [Waldo house
WARNER EARL, hose & belt maker, Front, bds
Warner E. D. watchmaker, 45 Salem
Warren Calvin, stair builder, Mechanic,h 35 Wash.
Warren Mrs. Charles, h 2 Warren
Warren Daniel D. bds 12 Liberty
Warren Mrs. Frederick, h 2 Warren
Warren Geo. painter, bds 76 Main
Warren Geo. tanner, Northville, h Grove
Warren Joseph G. carpenter, h 1 Madison
Warren Lewis, moulder, h 4 Lexington
WARREN OTIS, stove manuf'r, S. Wor. h 1 Allen
Warren Patrick, laborer, h 29 Shrewsbury
Warren Sam'l. tanner, &c. h Millbrook
Warren Sam'l P. printer, bds 12 Thomas
Warren Mrs. W. W. dressmaking, 222 Main, over
Warren Willard W. h 175 Pleasant   [City Bank
Washburn Chas. & Son, (Chas. F.) iron & wire
manufacturers, Quinsigamond, h 12 Summer
Washburn Chas F. (Chas. W. & Son,) h Quinsig.
Washburn Emery jr. law student, bds Lincoln h.
Washburn Geo. I. bds 12 Summer
Washburn Henry H. bds cor Vernon & Winthrop
WASHBURN HENRY S. wire manuf'r, Bloom-
ingdale. h cor Vernon & Winthrop
Washburn I. & Co. (P. L. Moen,) wire manuf'rs,
Grove mill, h 14 Summer   [bds 1 Linden
Washburn John D. counsellor, 4 & 5 Brinley hall,
Washburn James, wiretemperer, bds 41 Summer
Washburn John E. agt. at Braman, Perham & Co.
steam & gas pipe makers, 6 Pearl, h 37 Austin
Washburn Thomas S. moulder, h 6 Grafton

Washburn Nathan, railway iron & car wheel manufacturer, Bloomingdale, h 16 Elm
Washburn Wm. A. clerk, bds 67 Main
Wason Mrs. Maria. bds 1 Orange
Waters Buckley, wiredrawer, h Agricultural
Waters James L. cigar maker, bds Taft's hotel
Waters J. L. (Trumbull, W. & Co.) h 10 Charlton
Waters Levi, h 8 Burt
Waters Parley, machinist, bds 44 Pleasant
Waters Samuel, mechanic, h 10 Orange
Waters Stephen, tailor, h 4 Spring
Waters Thomas, at Strong's coal yard, b's Ward
Waterman (Henry,) & Hollander, merchant tailors, 269 Main, h 3 Church
Waterson Mrs h Newton
Watkins Elbridge G. h 2 Winter
Watkins Francis G. carpenter, bds 2 Winter
Watkins Mrs. John F. h 17 Gold cor Assonet
Watson Mrs. Abigail, h 16 Union
Watson John H. machinist, bds 4 Central
Watson Samuel B. farmer, Belmont   [Main
Wayland Rev. H. L. pastor 3d Bap. Church, h 380
Weaver Mrs. Esther, bds 51 Thomas
WEAVER GEO. R. shoemaker & repairer, 24 Front, h 39 Austin
Weaver Madison, bootforms, bds 82 Main
Weaver Thomas R. wireworker. bds 44 Front
Webb Julius, freight agent, Salisbury
Webber Geo. W. shoemaker, bds 27 Central
Webber Luther P. wiretemperer, bds 27 Central
Webber Oliver B. farmer, h Clinton lane
Webber Thomas K. shoemaker, h 27 Central
Webber Sylvester, stone cutter, Clinton lane
Webster Benj. weaver, h Leicester, V. F
Webster John N. machinist, bds 81 Summer
Wedge Benj. blacksmith, h Leicester
Weeks Walter F at T. M. Lamb's, bds 50 Central
Weidner Christian, gunmaker, h 37 Beacon
Weigand Frederick, machinist, h 16 Central
Weir Geo. machinist, h Millbury
Weir James, spinner, Webster
Weir James, machinist, h Millbury
Weixler Herman, at court mill, bds 7 Mechanic
WEIXLER JACOB P. basket manuf'r, 110 Main, h 8. Newbury   [Newbury
Weixler Jacob P. jr. jeweller at Goddard's, h 10
Welch Mrs. Catharine, h 23 1-2 Winter
Welch Charles, laborer, cor Beach & Brown
Welch David, bootmaker, h 8 Temple
Welch Edmund, laborer, h May
Welch James M. vegetable dealer, h 6 Burt
Welch John, at Hacker's, h 19 Franklin
Welch John, grocer, 53 Salem cor Madison, h 96 Southbridge
Welch John T. boottreer, h 25 Winter
Welch Mrs. Mary, h 53 Salem
Welch Mrs. Mary, h 10 Pond
Welch Michael, clerk, bds 53 Salem
Welch Michael, laborer, h 19 Blackstone
Welch Michael, car repairer, Nor. R.R. h Lovell's ct
Welch Michael, laborer, bds 9 Bridge
Welch Michael, laborer, h Millbury av.
Welch Patrick, laborer, h 8 E. Worcester
Welch Mrs. Patrick, h 2 S. Irving
Welch Richard, laborer, h S. Irving
Welch Thomas, marble cutter; h 6 Spring.
Welch Thomas, tailor, h 20 Winter
Welch Thomas J. at N. Washburn's rolling mill, h 112 Southbridge   [Channing
WELLINGTON T. W. coal yard, Manchester, h
Wells Enos B. hackman, h 306 Main
Wells Frank L. machinist, bds 45 Summer
Wells Julia, h 12 Shrewsbury

Wendall Matthew, laborer, Gates' lane
Wentworth Charles W. machinist, h 9 William
Wentworth Royal J. at Nash. ft. depot, h 6 School
WESBY JOS. S. bookbinder, 239 Main, h 7 Home
Wesson Charles, farmer, Westboro
Wesson Edwin, bds 22 High
Wesson Ephraim, h Granite
Wesson Franklin, gun manuf'r, Armsby's building, Central, h 1 Claremont
Wesson Geo. R. hotel, 12 Grafton
Wesson James A. bootfinisher, bds Granite
Wesson Leander, bootmaker, h Stafford
Wesson Rufus, farmer, Harrington
Wesson Rufus jr. shoe manuf'r, 1 Park, h 22 High
Wesson Samuel jr. machinist, h 03 Austin
Wesson Samuel A. clicker, bds Heywood
West John A. furnace builder. 10 Plymouth
West Jonas B. billiards, 229 Main, h 3 Clinton
Westall Robert, machinist, bds cor Beacon & Herbert
Weston A. Judson, printer, bds 32 Portland [mon
Weston Mrs. J. H. boarding house, 8 Maple
Wetherbee E. D. & Co. (H. E. Clapp,) druggists, 33 Wash. sq. bds 28 Green
Wetherbee J. G. Farmer's hotel, 15 Mechanic
Wetherbee Mrs. Oliver, h 3 Shrewsbury [12 John
Wetherell E. F. express messenger, Nash. R. h
Wetherell John W. counsellor, 246 Main, h 2 State
Wetherell Lorin. patent horse hoe, h 3 Webster
WEYER R. manufacturer of gilt mouldings, Sargent's block, junction Main & Southbridge
Whalan Dennis, blacksmith. 91 Summer
Whalen David, mason, h 16 Bridge
Whalen Edward, laborer, h Lovell's court
Whalen John, peddler, h rear 72 Mechanic
Whalen John jr. moulder, h Kendall
Whalen John, laborer, h Kendall
Whalen Patrick, repairs, Nor. R. R. h 30 Oxford
Whalen Patrick, laborer, h 48 Southbridge
Whalen Patrick, moulder. h Kendall
Whalen Patrick, hostler, h Cambridge
Whalen Pierce, carpenter, h Canal
Whalen Pierce, laborer, h 5 Blackstone
Whalen Thomas, laborer, h 10 Bridge
Wharton Jos. wirecleaner, bds Goddard's lane
Wharton Robert, wiredrawer, bds Goddard's lane
Wheaton Elijah, mason, h 210 Pleasant
Wheeler Ambrose C. bread driver, h 195 Pleasant
Wheeler Asa N. machinist, bds 45½ Salem
Wheeler Charles, at Devens & Hoar's, bds 294 Main
Wheeler Charles A. machinist, h 43 Thomas
Wheeler Daniel, h 25 Orchard
Wheeler Elisha, shoemaker, h 7 Washington
Wheeler Erastus W. farmer, h Forest
Wheeler Misses Frances & Nancy, h 71 Summer
Wheeler Geo. W. city treas. office City Hall, h 49 Thomas
Wheeler Geo. W. jr. janitor, bds 49 Thomas
Wheeler Gilman, carpenter, h 9 Winter
Wheeler Mrs. Henry, h 31 Main   [Westminster
Wheeler Henry M. at Life Ins. Co. 98 Main h
Wheeler Joshua S. machinist, h 16 Congress
Wheeler Moses A. clerk, bds 30 Lincoln
Wheeler Mrs. Nelson, h Elm cor Chestnut
WHEELER WM. A. foundry and machine shop, 32 Thomas, h 30 Lincoln
Wheeler Wm. A. moulder, bds 25 Orchard
Wheelock Abner & Co. (R. H. Berkley,) cigars, &c. 243 Main, bds 53 Thomas
Wheelock Albert D. stone mason, h Agricultural
Wheelock Amos M. armorer, h 23 Portland
Wheelock Andrew, varnisher at George G. Hildreth's, h Hudson
Wheelock Charles G. jobber, h 77 Exchange

Wheelock Clarendon. h 10 Myrtle
Wheelock Daniel W. h Grafton
Wheelock Dexter M. bds 19 Washington
Wheelock Eleazer,armorer. h Jackson cor Bencon
Wheelock Estes. stabler, Waldo house, h Waldo
Wheelock Geo. H. clothing. bds 46 Elm [Myrtle
Wheelock Henry M. trunk maker, 245 Main, h 17
Wheelock Jerome, engineer at N. Washburn's, h 8 Plymouth [50 Front
WHEELOCK JOHN, trunk manuf'r, 245 Main, h
Wheelock J. F. moulder, h 33 Summer
Wheelock Joel H. painter, h 24 Central
Wheelock Jubal, farmer, h Grafton
Wheelock Luke. gun maker, h 59 Front
Wheelock Paul N. farmer, Lake farm
Wheelock Rinaldo R. machinist, h 81 Summer
Wheelock Mrs. Susan,h 46 Elm [cor May & Mason
Wheelock Thomas, clothing, 5 Lincoln H. block,h
Wheelock T. P. (Allen & W.) h Wellington
Whipple Albert B. machinist, bds 3 Prospect
Whipple Franklin, Ins. agt. Richmond block, 263 Main, h South end Benefit
Whipple James A. h 20 Orange
Whipple Percival, machinist, h rear Ward [ford
Whitcomb Alonzo, (C. Whitcomb & Co.)h 13 Ox-
Whitcomb Andrew J. (L. & A.J.) bds 26 Thomas
Whitcomb Benj. F. artist, bds North Newton
Whitcomb Calvin M. wiredrawer, h 22 Grove
Whitcomb Carter & Co, (A. W.) manuf'rs of copying presses, &c. Exchange, h 25 Portland
Whitcomb Chas. B. shoemaker, h rear 173 Pleas't
Whitcomb Charles H. machinist,bds 34 Mulberry
Whitcomb David (C. Foster & Co.) h 6 Harvard
Whitcomb F. C. machinist, bds 3 Maple
Whitcomb H. H. machinist, bds 37 Summer
Whitcomb Jeremiah, clicker, h 3 Myrtle
Whitcomb Leonard, wiredrawer, bds 26 Thomas
Whitcomb Lyman, Main, N. W.
Whitcomb Lyman L. & A. J. painters, h 35 Mul-
Whitcomb P H. printer, bds 12 Thomas [berry
White Aaron, machinist, h 53 Thomas
White Amos jr. manufacturer, h Leicester, N. W.
White A. P. bootfinisher, bds 38 Newbury
White Benj. gardener, h 5 Everett
White Chas. boot manuf'r, 305 Main, h 36 Chat-
White Chas. H. clerk, h 18 William [ham
White Dutee S. engineer Nash. R. R. h 27 South-
White Ellery, laborer, h 12 Gold [bridge
White Frank, wrenchmaker, Leicester
White Geo. T. law student, bds 36 Chatham
White Geo. W. eng. Nash. R. R. bds 5 Maple
White Henry, machinist, bds 89 Summer
White James, carpenter, h Eaton place
White John C. & Co. (S. M. Kendall,) paints and colors, 6 Front, h 13 Chatham
White John M. liquor store, 17 Wash. square, bds Swan's hotel
White Jonathan A. farmer, h Burncoat
White Jonathan G. machinist, h 32 Mulberry
White J. P. shoefinisher. h 38 Newbury
White Leonard, acct. h 22 Irving
White Levi, moulder, bds 104 Southbridge
White Luther. machinist, Cypress, h 89 Summer
White Peter, tinman, h School court [Madison
White Rollin G. (Stowell, Maynard & Co.) h 3
White Taft, machinist. h 35 Mulberry
White Talbot C. h 4 Fulton [Shrewsbury
White Miss Tamerson, Matron Orphan's Home, 64
White Thomas, carpenter, h Gold [bds Gold
White Thomas jr. grocer,cor.Portland & Madison,
White Wm. coppersmith, 21 Winter
White Wm. gardener, h Highland
White Wm B. cl'k at Barnard, Sumner & Co.'s

White Wm J. coffee & spice grinding. Exchange, h 69 Summer
Whitehouse James, armorer, h Piedmont
Whiting Amos, music teacher, Mechanics Hall, h Oxford place [Hammond
Whiting Chas. B. asst. cashier Wor. bank, h
Whiting Chas. H. grocer, 31 W. sq. h 20 Lincoln
Whiting David O. engineer, Nashua R. R. bds 1 Clinton [manuf'rs, 31 W. sq. h 17 Laurel
Whiting (Geo F.) & Woodbury (A. W.) vinegar
Whiting Geo. W. carriage maker, h 16 Carroll
Whiting Hersey L. brakeman W.R.R. h 21 Mech.
Whiting Mrs. Homer L. h 6 Laurel [Plymouth
Whiting Wm. C. carriage maker, 1 Mechanic, h 5
Whitmore Joseph, armorer h Bencon cor Herman
Whitney Amos, miller. South Worcester
Whitney Chas. civil engineer, h 61 Southbridge
Whitney Edward, stationer, 218 Main, bds 21
Whitney J. H. law student, bds 8 Maple [Thomas
Whitney J. Lovell, jobber, h King
Whitney Mrs. Elizabeth S. h Houchin avenue
Whitney Mrs. M. h 13 Clinton
Whitney Polly, upholsterer, h 7 Lincoln
Whitney S. A. valentine manuf'r, h Abbott
Whitney Sam'l N. sash maker, h 9 Crown
Whiton Mrs. James M. h 18 Elm
Whittaker Josiah, spinner, b 1 Water
Whittemore Aaron F. butcher, bds 38 Main
Whittemore Mrs. Abigail W. upholsterer, h 17
Whittemore Asa D. h 2 Prospect [Summer
Whittemore Chas. D. machinist, bds 43 Summer
Whittemore Chas. (F.Willard & Co.) h 197 Pleas't
Whittemore Chas. P. shoe manuf'r, Am. H. blk, h
Whittemore David H. bds 6 Quincy [19 Salem
Whittemore E. L. boxmaker, h 9 Maple
Whittemore Frederick H. bds 9 Maple
Whittemore Geo S. h 17 Salem [Junct.h 6 Quincy
WHITTEMORE H. S. agt. Bay St. apple parers,
Whittemore Henry S. jobber, h 84 Chandler
Whittemore Henry W. clerk at Freeland's, bds 38
Whittemore N. B. shoemaker, h 8 Myrtle [Main
Whittemore S. V. machinist, bds 3 Maple
Whittemore Victor. machinist, bds 17 Summer
Whittemore W. A. butcher, bds 38 Main
Whittemore Wm. C. engraver, bds 17 Summer
Whittemore W. W. shoemaker, h 38 Main [bury
Whittier C. M. clerk Nash. R. R. shop, bds Salis-
Wight A.W. (G. F. Bonney & Co.)h 59 So'bridge
Wight C. B. clerk, Grove mill, bds 3 Arch
Wight Hiram C. at Ball & Williams, h 63 Sum'r
Wilcox A. W. harmonium manufacturer,h 8 West
Wilcox Chas. W. overseer at Chenery's, W.Boyls-
Wilcox Rollin, teamster, bds 8 Sutton [ton
Wilcox Wm. needle maker, Merrifield's building, Exchange, h Harrison
Wild John, machinist, h Burt
Wilde Thomas, machinist, h 5 Foyle
Wilder Alex. H. reg. of deeds, Ct. H. h 8 State
Wilder Chas. clerk at Wheeler's, h 2 Kendall
Wilder Chas. E. manuf'r of boot tools, Exchange, h Millbrook [State
Wilder Harvey B. clerk at reg. of deeds', bds 8
Wilder Martin, h 17 Prescott [Southbridge
Wilder Thos. portrait & ornamental painter, h 67
Wilkins Daniel, butcher, bds Hill
Wilkins Elisha, laborer, h Hill
Wilkins I. G. machinist, bds Taft's Hotel
Wilkins John, farmer, Webster
Wilkinson Charles D.C. comedian, bds 15Charlton
Wilkinson Joseph, at Nash. R. R. h Garden
Wilkinson Mrs. Sarah B. h 15 Charlton
Willard Calvin, counsellor, h 3 Portland
Willard Cephas moulder, h 11 Market

st, bds 13 Prescott
bds 21 Central
, h 82 Chandler
. A. Lombard, C. Whit-
lin.) machinists, Union
scott
t. h 66 Exchange
er, h rear 17 Central
inite
. Granite
Southgate
h Shrewsbury

smith, h Endicott
17 William
bds 12 Elliot
ourt mill. h 12 Elliot
r, bds 22 Park
er, College hill
at Pratt & Inman's,bds
ay St. H. [17 Chestnut
'rown [h 22 Exchange
d's express messenger,
iaker, 52 Mechanic
oppersmith, h 81 Main
'e
(Dewey & W.) counsel-
larvard [Winter
o'r Am. telegraph, h 2
Lincoln
:. h 11 Liberty
ir, bds 309 Main
' Exchange, h 19 Exch.
im [Main, h 129 Main
f goods, &c. 127 & 116
's charcoal yard,Garden,

i East cor Belmont
. presser, bds 8 Harvard
her. 222 Main, over City
t W.) h Salisbury [Bank
ds Leicester, V. F.
nsellor, 2 Cen. Ex.h Ce-
ge [dar
dbury
h 10 Union
d
, bds Burncoat
er, Burncoat
13 Thomas
ker, bds 31 Union
oith, h 64 Front
st, h 44 Thomas
1½ Main
.ver, h 25 Orange
ouf r, 3 Pleasant, h 5High
it jail [Providence
ounder at Allen's, bds 22
4 Salem
nist, 3 Lexington
er. h 31 Grove
5 Brown
oir
ith, h head of Reservoir
i 1 High st. court
nter, h 16 Salem
at John Firth's,h Austin
collector, h Adams sq.
ist, h Lodi
t. repairs 8½ Myrtle
r, h rear 32 Chandler
per at Lee Sprague &Co's,
,shland and Bowdoin

Wilson Wm. M. machinist,bds cor Elliot &Carroll
Winch John, at rolling mill, bds E. Central
Windle John, farmer, Fowler
Winn Charles F. wheelmaker, h 12 Portland
Winn Jeremiah, (Fitch & Winn) Cypress, h 2
Winn J. H. wheelmaker, h 11 Hanover [Clinton
Winn Michael, laborer, h Goddard's lane
Winslow John C. bootbottomer, h Palmer
Winslow Samuel, (S. C. & S.) h 2 Congress
WINSLOW SETH C. & SAMUEL, gear makers
& machine jobbers, Cypress, h 27 Laurel
Wetherbee D. F. tailor, h 8 Quincy [mouth
Witherby Cyrus, fireman B. & W. R. R. h 20 Ply-
Witherby C. K. (T. H. Witherby & Co.) h 42
Summer cor Prospect
Witherby Geo. T. acct. bds 1 Portland [1 Portland
Witherby Luke B. bookkeeper,Ball & Williams', h
Witherby Thos. H. & Co. (C. K. W.) iron fences.
School, bds Exchange hotel [land
Withey Anson A. at Tolman & Co's, bds 24 Port-
Witt Albert, Lion saloon, h 257 Main
Witt (E. F.) & Pratt (C. B.) livery stable, Foster,
h 4 Clinton [h Salisbury
Witter Henry M. bookkeeper at Nash. R.R. office,
Wolfe John, striker, bds 5 Shrewsbury
Wolfe Martin, carpenter, h 5 Shrewsbury
Wolfe Richard, laborer, h 64 Front
Wood Amos, carpenter at hospital, h 28 Summer
Wood Aurin. (Wood, Light & Co.) h 44 Chatham
Wood Azor B. clerk at shoe manufactory, Am. H.
Wood A. J. h 4 Quincy [block, h 8 George
Wood A. W. bookkeeper. Curtis' mill, h Tirrell
Wood (Chas.) Light (J. F.) & Co. machinists'
tools, Junction shop, h Lagrange
Wood Charles, machinist, bds Beacon cor Charl-
Wood C. N. h 20 Green [ton
Wood Corbin O. gunsmith, h 37 Washington
Wood Darius A. grocer, 8½ Myrtle, h 28 Portland
Wood D. O. machinist, Main, N. W.
Wood Edward G. baggage master at Junction, h
73 Austin [Chatham st place
Wood Edwin A. bookkeeper at Alzirus Brown's, h
Wood Edwin H. h May
Wood Edwin H. machinist, h 5 Hanover
Wood Elias, bds 77 Summer [as
Wood Geo.H. at Moore's livery stable,bds 3 Thom-
Wood Geo. L. eng. Prov. R.R. h cor Myrtle&Main
Wood Jas. E. prop'r Pleasantville Omnibus line,
h cor Nashua & Byron
Wood James H. carpenter, bds 13 Salem
Wood Joel A. machinist, h 4 Quincy
Wood Joel D machinist, h 8 Liberty
Wood John H. machinist, h 4 Wilmot [Myrtle
Wood John M. musical inst. maker, h Main cor
Wood Jonathan, bookbinder and paper ruler, h 2
School [berry cor Prospect
Wood Justin F. ticket agent, West. depot. h Mul-
Wood Luther N. blacksmith, h 9 Prospect
Wood Melville. watchmaker, Bay St. block, h 26
Wood Pamella,boarders.h 31 Portland [Mulberry
Wood Simeon, h 56 Southbridge
Wood Warren, truckman, bds 8 Edward
Wood Watson L. brickmaker, h Burncoat
Wood W. L. currier, Milton
Wood Wilder, at S. & G. Warren's
Wood Wm. H. clerk, bds 12 Thomas
Wood W. S. h 30 Portland
Woods F. H. wiredrawer, bds Newport
Woods Jason, wiredrawer, h 2 Newport
Woods Jonas W. machinist, h Mill. N W.
Woods Wm. cabinet maker. h 2 Beach
Woodis Erastus W. butcher. bds 25 Mechanic
Woodis John M. wiredrawer, h 20 Thomas

Woodbury A. W. (Whiting & W.) h 7 Carroll
Woodbury Mrs. Brooksey M. h 5 Cottage
Woodbury Calvin P. clicker, h 18 Grove
Woodbury Charles C. clicker, h 26 Oxford [Irving
Woodbury Charles L clerk at J. Q. Hill's, bds 8
Woodbury Leonard, shuttlemaker, h 8 Irving
Woodbury Luther F. confectionery &c. 5 Pleas't,
  h 3 Pearl   [er's Hotel
Woodbury Simon, conductor B. R. R. bds Farm-
Woodcock Alonzo, carpenter, h 1 Fruit
Woodcock Bela, carpenter, h S. Irving
Woodcock Geo. M. blacksmith, h 16 School
Woodcock Geo. S. moulder, h 18 Washington
Woodcock Ira E. carpenter, h 12 Shrewsbury
Woodcock Isaac, veterinary surgeon, h 20 Main
Woodcock Isaac A. blacksmith, bds 20 Main
Woodcock James, carpenter, bds S. Irving
Woodcock Sanford M. at Arcade iron Co. h 8 Fult'n
Woodard A. B. att. at hospital   [h 10 Gold
Woodman David O. card maker at T. K. Earle's,
Woodruff Henry H. butcher, h 1 Bartlett place
Woodward Benj. carpenter. 9 Mech'c, h 79 Sum'r
Woodward Mrs. David, h 28 Green
Woodward (David M.) & Sibley (Cyrus) stone
  cutters, Plymouth, h 1 Assonet
Woodward D. A. at A. Penslee & Co, bds 21 Pleas't
Woodward E. P. at Trumbull, Waters & Co. bds
  Bay State house
Woodward Mrs. Esther, h 77 Exchange
Woodward F. G. manuf'r switch stands, shop
  at Junction, h 37 Salem   [bds 28 Green
Woodward Geo. M.counsellor,2 Central Exchange,
Woodward Henry, treas. Mec. Sav. b'k, h 15 West
Woodward Jos. L. farmer, h Plantation
Woodward J. W. gas fitter, bds 77 Exchange
Woodward Rufus, physician, 2 Elm
Woodward Mrs. R. T. h 90 Southbridge
Woodward Sam'l, (Kinnicutt & Co.) h 20 Pearl
Woodward T. M.sign painter, 82 Main, h 24 Sum'r
Woodworth James C. clerk, bds 8 Vine
Woodworth James S.carpenter & builder,h 8 Vine
Woodworth Mrs.Stephen boarders,h 27 Chatham
WORCESTER ACADEMY, Rev. J. R. Stone,
  principal, Summer
Worcester Edward J. machinist, h 5 Chandler
Worcester Oliver W. painter, bds 8 Grafton
Worcester T. h 2 Newton
Worford Geo. L. bootmaker, 35 Washington Sq.
Workman Wm. physician, 13 Elm
Works Russell, clicker, h 44 Elm
Wren Humphrey, laborer, h 89 Front

Wren Cornelius, B. & W. F. House, bds 80 Front
Wright Andrew, blacksmith. rear 32 Chandler
Wright Andrew J. machinist, bds North Newton
Wright Chas. blacksmith, h 3 Home
Wright Edward, moulder, bds 24 Central
Wright Edward, machinist at Crompton's
Wright Geo. S. clerk, Nash. R. R. office, bds 1
  Congress
Wright Geo W. clicker, bds 20 Pleasant
Wright Jabez L. machinist, h North Newton
Wright Jabez W. painter, bds North Newton
Wright James, moulder, h 10 Prospect
Wright John, machinist, h 46 Chatham
Wright John, machinist, h 39 Green
Wright Samuel, shoemaker, h 37 Mechanic
Wrigley Wm. H. carpenter, h 49 Main
Wunderlich Charles, musical instrument maker,
  h 32 Exchange
Wyman Alfred,flour dealer, Norwich,h 17 Harvard
Wyman Alfred F. Worc. Bank, bds 6 Laurel
Wyman Daniel. machinist, h 6 Laurel
Wyman Horace. machinist, h 25 Green
Yarrington Perry. machinist, bds 19 Washington
Yeaw Joseph C. freight master, Prov. R. R. 17
  Washington
Young Albert, pattern maker. bds 25 Salem
Young Alpheus, engineer at wire works, h God-
Young Asa, weaver, h Leesville   [dard's lane
Young Daniel. machinist, h 2 Newport
Young Rev. Edmund J. prof. rhetoric &c. College
  Holy Cross
Young Edward S. clerk. bds 14 Goddard
Young Horace A. machinist. h 39 Austin
Young John. shoemaker. h Farwell
Young Justus, butcher, 52 Front. h Clark
Young Lovell F. wiredrawer at Goddard's
Young Mrs. J. W. h 3 Everett
Young Loring, miller, h Leicester, V. Falls,
Young (N. D.) Hesior (J.) & Co. (T. Norcross,)
  flour and produce dealers, 16 Front
YOUNG PRIESTLEY, variety store, 209 Main h
Young S. E. butcher, City Hall   [9 Harvard
Young S. P. bds Burncoat
Young Thomas C. wiredrawer, h 25 Austin ;
Young Wm B. trader, h 14 Goddard
Young Wm. H. Nor. R. R. bds 7 Myrtle
Young Wm. H. bootsider, bds 1 Wash. sqr.
Young Wm. H.machinist at Wheeler's, h rear 44
Young Mrs. Zelotes, h 7 Myrtle   [Thomas
Zaeder (Benj.) & Boemer, saloon, 8 Foster
Zeby Maynard, laborer, h Northville

LAUNDRESSES.

Brooks Rhoda, Pine court
Durkins Mrs. h 11 Austin
Jones Mrs. T. H. 13 Austin
White Mrs. Ellery, 12 Gold

DRESS MAKERS,

Barber Mrs. Lucy A. 21 Park
Blodget Mrs. N. P. cor Belmont & Elizabeth
Conant Mrs. J. 49 Main
Gleason Miss L. 266 Main
Metcalf Mrs. L. A. 61 Front
Nelson Miss E 92 Summer
Reed Mrs. A. S. h 26 Salem
Tucker Miss Anne, 31 Summer

TAILORESSES.

Allis Phebe, 1 Walnut
Folsom Mrs. Eliza, 13 Thomas
Tebbetts Mrs. Adaline, 13 Thomas

NURSES.

Ames Mrs. Sarah, 19 Hanover
Angier Mrs. Charlotte M. 25 Shelby,
Brown Mrs. Sarah, h 20 Bowdoin
Crawford Mrs. R. 21 Prescott
Crosby Mrs. Mary, bds 16 Grove
Leach Mrs. Eliza, 8 Edward
Moore Mrs. Abigail, h 8 Prospect
Pierce Mrs. Louisa, 71 Exchange
Tarbell Miss Harriet, 33 Thomas
Thomas Ann, h 294 Main
Tucker Mrs. Jane, h 31 Summer
Watson Mrs. John. h 71 Exchange
Whitney Mrs. Olive, bds 19 William
Woodbury Mrs. C. 53 Thomas

17

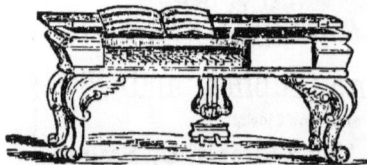

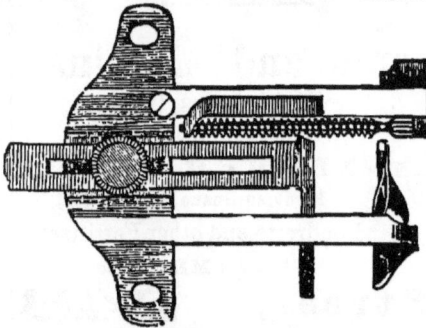

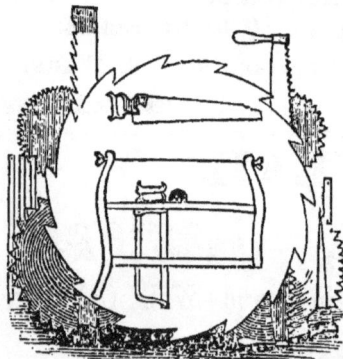

19

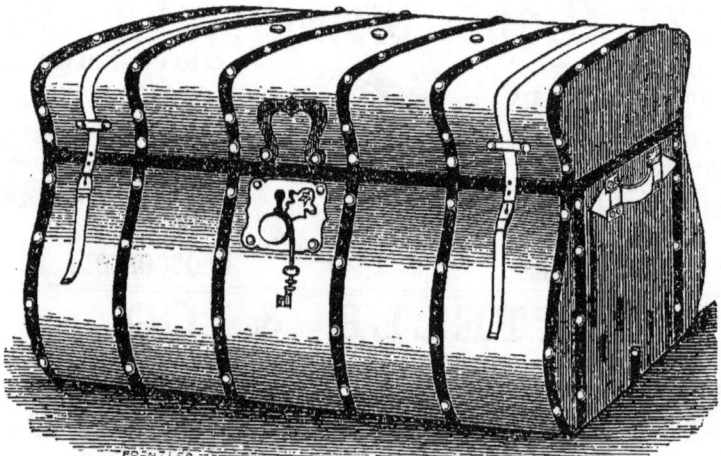

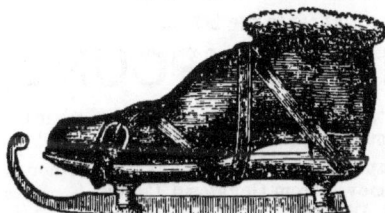

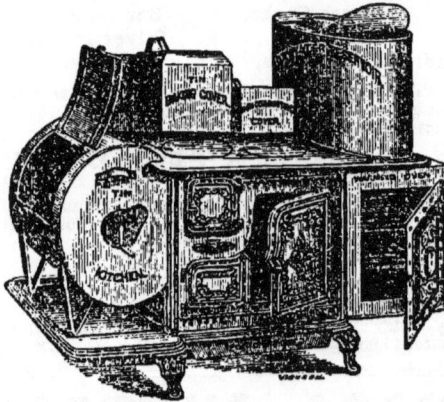

www.ingramcontent.com/pod-product-compliance
Lightning Source LLC
Chambersburg PA
CBHW030616270326
41927CB00007B/1197